D0806084

Educational Audiology
Across the Lifespan

This book is printed on recycled paper. ♻

Educational Audiology Across the Lifespan

Serving All Learners with Hearing Impairment

by

Kristina M. English, Ph.D.
Child Language Intervention Program
University of Pittsburgh
Pittsburgh, Pennsylvania

·P A U L·H·
BROOKES
PUBLISHING C°

Baltimore • London • Toronto • Sydney

Paul H. Brookes Publishing Co.
Post Office Box 10624
Baltimore, Maryland 21285-0624

Copyright © 1995 by Paul H. Brookes Publishing Co., Inc.
All rights reserved.

Typeset by Brushwood Graphics, Inc., Baltimore, Maryland.
Manufactured in the United States of America by
The Maple Press Company, York, Pennsylvania.

Library of Congress Cataloging-in-Publication Data
English, Kristina M., 1951–
    Educational audiology across the lifespan : serving all learners
with hearing impairment / by Kristina M. English.
       p.   cm.
    Includes index.
    ISBN 1-55766-203-7
    1. Deaf—Means of communication.   2. Deaf—Education—United
States.   3. Deaf—Services for—United States.   I. Title.
HV2471.E54   1995
371.91′2—dc20   94-37693
                                                                      CIP

(British Library Cataloguing-in-Publication data are available from the British Library.)

Contents

Foreword

The evolution of educational audiology—the practice of audiology in the school environment—has realized substantial development and growth as a result of the Education for All Handicapped Children Act of 1975, Public Law 94-142. Even before this mandate, however, audiology services were being defined and provided to children in some schools.

To put the present into perspective, take a few moments with me to reflect and look back. For fun, I searched my bookcase to find texts from my college courses related to educational audiology. Perusing sources that I had not looked at for a long time was enlightening and, to some extent, a little surprising. The most notable reference was in a chapter by Jones (1973), "The Audiologist in the Educational Environment," from *The Hearing Impaired Child in a Regular Classroom*. Jones cites what may well be the most distinctive early reference to educational audiology when she discusses the report of the 1965 Joint Committee on Audiology and Education of the Deaf, edited by Ira Ventry. Jones notes that this report recognized the need for the audiologist to be "a full-time participating member of the instructional staff of each educational program for deaf children" (p. 77). Other services this document delineated for the audiologist in the school setting included the following (p. 81):

- complete audiological evaluation of children related to their admission to the educational program
- annual assessment of children's hearing, including an interpretation of the results for the teacher
- selection, orientation, and maintenance of hearing aids for children
- application of knowledge concerning speech reception and speech pathology to the speech problems of deaf children
- in-service training to orient teachers to new procedures and information
- counseling of parents
- selection, evaluation, and application of amplifying systems and/or equipment used in the school
- liaison service between the school and the college or university training program and/or community speech and hearing center
- research

Jones (1973) also notes the Joint Committee report's discussion of academic preparation, the need for the educational audiologist to

> have the experience and information to make meaningful rehabilitative and educational recommendations to educators, parents, and deaf individuals. . . . Audiologists should also be trained in language development, language disorders caused by deafness, history of education of the hearing impaired, educational philosophy, and psychological and social aspects of deafness. (p. 81)

Flexibility to adapt services to various classroom settings, regular school settings, and schools for the deaf was also recommended. Other than overlooking students who were hard of hearing, this document was quite visionary. Interestingly, several of the components outlined here are included in PL 94-142.

Jones insightfully adds that by "adapting and modifying audiological tests and techniques traditionally used in clinical settings," the educational audiologist "can more adequately define and provide for the acoustic needs of the children." She continues by recognizing that "it is only as an integral member of the educational staff, however, that the educational audiologist can maximize audiological services to children" (p. 77).

Similar references to educational audiology in the early 1970s were made by Alpiner, Berg, and O'Neill. The work of Berg deserves the most credit in terms of the recognition and development of educational audiology. In addition to developing a training program for educational audiology through a U.S. Department of Education grant, Berg also contributed early texts, including *The Hard of Hearing Child*, which he co-edited with Fletcher (1970), and *Educational Audiology: Hearing and Speech Management* (1976).

In the mid- to late 1970s, there was a significant increase in the number of audiologists working in the schools. As more audiologists were employed by schools, they quickly realized that the clinical audiology model learned in most graduate schools was not effective in the educational setting. Although much has been written about educational audiology since the 1980s, progress has been slow. The field remains poorly understood, children's hearing aids still do not work consistently, our students are grossly underserved, and we continue to struggle with implementation of the full scope of audiology services in the schools in most states.

This text offers a fresh and contemporary approach to educational audiology. Dr. English considers this field as a lifespan process, one that continues from infancy through adulthood and complements our culture's promotion of lifelong learning. In this way, the effects of hearing impairment are always considered as they apply to "a lifetime of learning experiences." The role of the educational audiologist is presented as part of a holistic model in which the audiologist is part of a larger team of professionals who work with the child or individual to explore and define, in the broadest and most logical sense, what are necessary and appropriate services.

This is the first text devoted to the profession of educational audiology that is molded by the federal mandates of the 1970s, 1980s, and 1990s and that incorporates the definition and refinement of services that have resulted. Advocacy and empowerment are powerful themes throughout the text.

This text will be valuable to all audiologists, educators, and allied professionals who want an understanding of the educational role of audiology. Students in audiology will find this text particularly useful to guide their coursework in educational audiology, especially if they are preparing to work in schools. One of many unique aspects of this text is the inclusion of suggested learning activities with each chapter. These activities offer relevant assignments to guide students' exploration of and involvement with the educational setting.

As Dr. English mentions (see Chapter 1), the terminology "a new creature on the educational scene" was used to describe early educational audiology. Educational audiology is 30 years old now, and educational audiologists are no longer new creatures. This text is a testimony to the work done by the force of approximately 1,000 audiologists practicing in the schools every day. Through Dr. English's description and development of the full scope of our practice, we are reminded that, for most of us, only about 25% of our time is spent in basic audiology functions as taught in our graduate programs. The remaining time is spent on the "critical stuff"—management, coordination, public relations, and advocacy responsibilities.

As Dr. English promotes, our job first and foremost is advocating for the needs of individuals with hearing impairments whom we serve.

Cheryl DeConde Johnson, Ed.D.
Audiology Consultant
Colorado Department of Education
Greeley, Colorado

REFERENCES

Berg, F. (1976). *Educational audiology: Hearing and speech management.* New York: Grune & Stratton.

Berg, F., & Fletcher, S. (Eds.). (1970). *The hard of hearing child.* New York: Grune & Stratton.

Education for All Handicapped Children Act of 1975, PL 94-142. (August 23, 1977). Title 20, U.S.C. 1401 et seq: *U.S. Statutes at Large, 89,* 773–796.

Jones, B. (1973). The audiologist in the educational environment. In W. Northcutt (Ed.), *The hearing impaired child in a regular classroom* (pp. 77–82). Washington, DC: Alexander Graham Bell Association for the Deaf, Inc.

Preface

When I first started working in a school setting as an audiology graduate student, I couldn't help but marvel at my supervisor, Linda Schroeder. Where did she get all those "school skills"? How did she come to understand the intricacies of an IEP, or special education law, or the use of FM systems, or working with teachers? I soon realized that the **experience** of working in schools provided her a type of postgraduate training in educational audiology.

Soon I moved on to an educational audiology position of my own, but spent a lot of time calling Linda and other educational audiologists and consulting with them about the parameters of the job. It was only small comfort to learn that most educational audiologists have also developed their expertise "in the trenches" rather than from training in graduate audiology programs.

As the overall scope of audiology continues to broaden, I hope that more graduate programs will include coursework and practicum in educational audiology so that newly hired professionals will know exactly what is expected of them in their jobs. This text was designed to contribute toward that goal.

When thinking of the persons who helped contribute to this project, dozens of names and faces come immediately to mind. My editor, Carol Hollander, has been a godsend. Her editorial expertise will always be appreciated, but just as important, I will never forget the good humor and support she provided from the first time we talked. For their longtime encouragement on both professional and personal levels, I wish to thank Drs. Rena Lewis and Eleanor Lynch of San Diego State University and Drs. Daryl Smith and Joseph Weeres of Claremont Graduate School. By far the best part of my years in the joint doctoral program of these schools was getting to know and working with these faculty members and friends.

In addition, I would like to thank the following friends and colleagues:

- the faculty of the Department of Communicative Disorders at San Diego State University
- the Executive Board of the Educational Audiology Association
- my old friends at the East County Special Education Local Planning Area, San Diego, California
- my new friends at the Child Language Intervention Program at the University of Pittsburgh—Dr. Howard Goldstein, Dr. Louise Kaczmarek, Nancy Hepting, Ruth Pennington, Holly Polatas, and my "buddy" Karin Shafer
- Larry McLean of Telex Communications, Inc., San Diego, and Katie English of Upper St. Clair High School, Pennsylvania, for their technical assistance

- friends who provided much assistance with chapter reviews—Karen Anderson, John Sexton, Margaret Silva, Shari Mainwall Johnson, and Dr. Mark Whitney

Although there are too many to name here, I would like to thank the learners I have served as an educational audiologist, who quickly taught me, "It's more than just the ears!" They have all contributed to my understanding and growth.

Finally, an expression of tremendous gratitude to my family. Thank you to Lewis, Jason, and Katie and to my extended family for humoring me as I lived in "the land of the distracted" and for providing me with support and encouragement when I needed it. I am blessed with your love and care.

To Lewis

Educational Audiology
Across the Lifespan

1

"A New Creature on the Educational Scene"

PROVIDING AUDIOLOGY SERVICES IN SCHOOL settings for learners with hearing impairment is a relatively new specialty. A handful of audiologists were employed by schools in the 1960s, but, as a discipline, the field of educational audiology was officially recognized and defined in the mid-1970s, with the Education for All Handicapped Children Act of 1975 (Public Law 94-142), which authorized special education services for children between the ages of 6 and 21. Because of the committed work of advocates, researchers, and hundreds of practitioners in the field, educational audiology continues to develop a unified and focused professional identity.

WHY EDUCATIONAL AUDIOLOGY?

Even prior to Public Law (PL) 94-142, Alpiner (1974) speculated "whether there are sufficiently basic differences between the clinical audiologist and the educational audiologist" (p. 52) to warrant a distinction between the fields. When asked if there are differences, educational audiologists answer with a resounding "Yes!" But when asked if they entered their positions in schools with adequate training and experience in educational issues, a majority regretfully say, "No." The difference between educational and clinical audiology has typically been described as the need for additional skills above and beyond the clinical skills acquired in graduate programs. In other words, the educational audiologist must, of course, know how to evaluate hearing levels; recommend and fit amplification devices; provide counsel regarding hearing conservation, room acoustics, and communication strategies; and give instruction in speech reading and listening skills. However, knowing how to evaluate, recommend, counsel, and instruct in a school setting has been found to require a different set of skills than those necessary in a clinical setting. In addition, the ability to take on the roles of advocate, collaborator, consultant, team member, supervisor, and community liaison is also needed in order to serve learners effectively (Bess & McConnell, 1981; Blair, Wilson-Vlotman, & Von Almen, 1989; English, 1991; Wilson-Vlotman, 1986).

The purpose of this book, then, is to provide audiology students and new practitioners with the information needed to best serve learners with hearing impairment in their school environment. This information has been identified from professional and scholarly literature, but is not to be considered "carved in stone." One of the most interesting aspects of working in schools is participating in the ongoing effort to improve the educational process. Trends come and go; philosophies are considered, applied, evaluated, and modified; techniques, procedures, and curricula undergo manipulation or, sometimes, radical overhaul. Audiology students interested in working in schools must realize that part of their work will require maintaining a close watch on the national dialogues regarding school reform. Educators and citizens alike are scrutinizing how schools are preparing students for the changing global economy, for the explosion in knowledge and technology, and for the need to develop lifelong and self-directed learning skills. Elected officials and administrators who make policy decisions regarding the future of education also affect the learning environment for students with hearing impairment (HI); without knowledgeable advocates, the accommodations these learners need can easily be overlooked in the fever for change.

It is an exciting time to work in the schools, and there is increasing interest in the expertise that the educational audiologist brings to the field of education. Together, practitioners in special education and general education are working in a growing effort to teach students with disabilities in regular classrooms. Improvements for which the educational audiologist advocates, such as optimal listening conditions and supportive visual cues, are likely to assist **all** students in the classroom, with or without disabilities. There is now a unique window of opportunity for educational audiologists to positively affect the learning environments of all learners, and practitioners are encouraged to take full advantage of this opportunity.

In the remainder of this chapter, the following topics are introduced:

- Laws that define the responsibilities of audiologists in schools
- Audiological services that learners with HI can expect to receive
- Current status of services received by learners with HI
- Development of guidelines, recommended practices, and philosophies that best describe the roles and responsibilities of the educational audiologist

MANDATED RESPONSIBILITIES

Audiologists who work in school settings should have an understanding of the legislation that has mandated audiology support to students. Before discussing specific statutes and regulations, a brief presentation of the terminology and process of legislation is in order.

When laws are passed by Congress, appropriate federal agencies are assigned to develop **regulations**, which provide directions for enforcing the laws. When laws pertain to education, the federal Department of Education is the agency responsible for developing the regulations (Osborne, 1992). Regulations are first published in the *Federal Register*, which is the daily public record of all proceedings of Congress that is available in most libraries. Regulations are published to promote public response. When the agency has considered public reactions and concerns, a final ruling is published and and becomes part of the *Code of Federal Regulations* (CFR). The CFR is the collection of regulations, which are divided into 50 **titles** representing broad areas of federal regulation. Regulations for education are found in Title 34; a revised CFR for Title 34/Education is published on July 1 every year.

Each title is divided into **chapters**, and chapters are divided into **parts** and **sections**. Therefore, the citation 34 CFR 300.12[b] is read as Title 34 (Education), Chapter 300, Part 12, Section b (Office of the Federal Register, 1985). With this information, audiologists can locate and cite relevant regulations when necessary.

PL 94-142, the Education for All Handicapped Children Act of 1975

As mentioned, providing audiology services in school settings was mandated by the Education for All Handicapped Children Act of 1975 (PL 94-142). When PL 94-142 was passed, the U.S. Department of Education developed regulations to help districts comply with the law. These regulations included definitions for **primary services**, which are those directly related to education, and **related services**, which are those that are required to assist a child to benefit from special education. Audiology was identified as one of several related services. The following, from the *Code of Federal Regulations*, defines audiology services in schools:

> *Audiology* includes:
> (i) Identification of children with hearing loss;
> (ii) Determination of the range, nature, and degree of hearing loss, including referral for medical or other professional attention for the habilitation of hearing;
> (iii) Provision of habilitation activities, such as language habilitation, auditory training, speech reading (lipreading), hearing evaluation, and speech conservation;
> (iv) Creation and administration of programs for prevention of hearing loss;
> (v) Counseling and guidance of pupils, parents, and teachers regarding hearing loss; and
> (vi) Determination of the child's need for group and individual amplification, selecting and fitting an appropriate aid, and evaluating the effectiveness of amplification. (34 CFR 300.12[b])

A second regulation (34 CFR 300.303) expands on item vi: "Each public agency shall insure that the hearing aids worn by deaf and hard of hearing children in school are functioning properly."

PL 99-457, the Education of the Handicapped Act Amendments of 1986

Educational services were expanded later to include children from the ages of birth to 5 in October 1986, when Congress reauthorized PL 94-142 with the Education of the Handicapped Act Amendments of 1986, PL 99-457. This legislation included amendments that mandated special education services for children from ages 3 to 5, as well as funds for early intervention programs for infants and toddlers (birth to age 3) and their families (Roush & McWilliams, 1990).

PL 99-457 identified 10 professional disciplines as providing "qualified personnel" for the delivery of early intervention services (34 CFR 303.12[e]). These professionals are: audiologists, nurses, nutritionists, occupational therapists, physical therapists, physicians, psychologists, social workers, special educators, and speech-language pathologists.

Audiology services were expanded in the *Code of Federal Regulations* for PL 99-457 to include:

> (i) Identification of children with impairments, using at risk criteria and appropriate audiological screening techniques;
> (ii) Determination of the range, nature, and degree of hearing loss and communication functions, by use of audiologic evaluation procedures;

(iii) Referral for medical and other services necessary for the habilitation or rehabilitation of children with auditory impairment;

(iv) Provision of auditory training, aural rehabilitation, speech reading and listening device orientation and training, and other services;

(v) Provision of services for prevention of hearing loss; and

(vi) Determination of the child's need for individual amplification, including selecting, fitting, and dispensing of appropriate listening and vibrotactile devices, and evaluating the effectiveness of those devices. (34 CFR 303.12[d])

These regulations are virtually identical to those defined for PL 94-142, but now include children from birth to age 5.

PL 101-476, the Individuals with Disabilities Education Act of 1990

In 1990, PL 94-142, which had been expanded by PL 99-457 in 1986, was reauthorized and further amended by PL 101-476. At this time, the name of the legislation was also changed to the Individuals with Disabilities Education Act (IDEA). (See p. 29 for further discussion of these laws.)

Interpretation of Mandates at the State Level

The interpretation of these federal regulations into practice is left to each state. Perhaps not surprisingly, this latitude has resulted in great differences in the services available from state to state. DeConde Johnson (1991) conducted a comprehensive study of services for all 50 states and the District of Columbia; some of the differences found among states include the following. 1) Fourteen states had no requirements for licensure or certification for providers of audiological services in schools. 2) Only 13 states had written guidelines for audiological services in schools. 3) Only 4 states had criteria to establish a caseload limit for a full-time audiologist position. 4) Depending on the state in which he or she lives, to qualify for services, a student must demonstrate a minimum pure tone threshold in the better ear ranging from 15 dB to 35 dB. Regardless of the interpretations of the federal mandates made by the states across the country, only a fraction of school children with hearing impairment are receiving services (Casby, 1991).

CURRENT LEVEL OF SERVICES:
STUDENTS WITH HI ARE UNDERIDENTIFIED AND UNDERSERVED

Estimates of the number of learners with hearing impairment (HI) are difficult to obtain with existing data bases (Lundeen, 1991; Shepard, Davis, Gorga, & Stelmachowicz, 1981). The conservative estimated incidence rate is 1.6% of the school-age population, which means that, of the 39.5 million schoolchildren in the U.S., approximately 632,000 have a hearing impairment (Ross, Brackett, & Maxon, 1991). Higher estimates indicate that as many as 1.4 million–8 million students have a hearing impairment and are therefore entitled to educational audiology services (Berg, 1986; Lenich, Bernstein, & Nevitt, 1987).

Even if utilizing the conservative estimate of a 1.6% incidence rate, it is with dismay that we realize that **less than one tenth of students with HI receive services** to which they are entitled. According to Table 1.1, only 56,955 students with hearing impairment from ages 5 to 21 are receiving special education services. (We cannot report on children from birth to age 5 because states are not required to identify the disabilities of infants, toddlers, and preschoolers receiving services [Blake & Shewan, 1992; U.S. Department of Education, 1993].)

Table 1.1. Number of children with disabilities receiving special education services under PL 94-142, school year 1989–1990

State	Speech or language impairments	Hearing impairments	Deaf-blind	Specific learning disabilities	All disabilities[a]
Alabama	21,528	991	21	32,132	89,916
Alaska	2,917	144	1	7,535	12,213
Arizona	10,496	964	0	30,312	52,231
Arkansas	6,951	527	11	22,653	42,283
California	94,355	6,819	198	246,619	410,448
Colorado	8,103	774	78	25,029	50,220
Connecticut	8,985	625	26	31,254	57,788
Delaware	1,769	191	23	6,801	12,208
D.C.	749	50	9	2,800	5,695
Florida	60,858	1,371	58	88,909	206,124
Georgia	19,888	1,137	35	27,074	90,442
Hawaii	2,129	243	6	6,679	11,727
Idaho	3,501	344	0	10,907	18,506
Illinois	55,176	2,901	50	105,062	221,505
Indiana	35,491	1,159	58	40,060	103,219
Iowa	9,199	768	36	23,875	52,641
Kansas	10,531	629	6	16,800	39,628
Kentucky	21,136	802	9	22,606	68,264
Louisiana	17,962	1,219	17	26,307	63,902
Maine	5,715	286	14	11,165	25,208
Maryland	22,751	1,172	52	41,949	80,878
Massachusetts	28,841	1,712	72	49,592	135,431
Michigan	32,743	2,388	0	68,630	148,332
Minnesota	13,575	1,362	25	32,913	71,561
Mississippi	17,472	486	10	27,057	54,492
Missouri	24,649	888	64	46,587	96,294
Montana	3,680	205	3	8,050	14,507
Nebraska	7,651	513	3	12,689	28,795
Nevada	3,335	145	1	9,226	15,496
New Hampshire	2,939	227	7	10,427	17,235
New Jersey	48,449	1,294	172	82,820	160,634
New Mexico	9,259	473	86	15,180	31,544
New York	24,055	3,999	60	163,562	272,928
North Carolina	23,006	1,853	21	49,009	109,519
North Dakota	3,644	172	12	5,420	11,406
Ohio	49,525	2,093	6	74,077	189,787
Oklahoma	15,661	630	30	28,896	59,992
Oregon	12,739	1,429	22	26,746	51,120
Pennsylvania	52,474	2,744	2	82,837	192,843
Rhode Island	3,066	159	7	12,170	18,492
South Carolina	17,968	961	5	28,280	69,072
South Dakota	3,852	254	28	5,788	12,648
Tennessee	22,404	1,196	23	49,871	93,935
Texas	60,234	4,313	53	174,410	306,574
Utah	7,253	537	40	18,940	40,585
Vermont	3,437	204	4	5,752	12,352
Virginia	22,241	1,212	10	50,222	97,107
Washington	12,788	1,660	65	37,016	71,171
West Virginia	10,035	379	19	18,314	40,089
Wisconsin	13,506	213	5	23,785	71,064
Wyoming	2,499	138	1	5,175	9,412
50 states, D.C.	973,170	56,955	1,564	2,049,969	4,219,463

From Blake, A., & Shewan, C. (1992). An update on PL 94-142. *Asha, 34*(1), 52; reprinted by permission.

[a]The figures, representing children 6–21 years served under Chapter 1 of Elementary and Secondary Education Act (State-Operated Programs) and IDEA, Part B, include the four selected categories shown here and mental retardation, serious emotional disturbances, orthopedic impairments, visual impairments, multiple disabilities, and other health impairments.

Other researchers have suggested that when borderline-normal hearing levels, unilateral loss, and fluctuating loss due to otitis media are considered, the number of students with hearing impairment is significantly higher and closer to 8 million, which represents a 20% incidence rate of educationally significant hearing impairment (Berg, 1986). If we take into consideration all levels and manner of hearing loss, we have to acknowledge that **we are serving only 1% of the population with hearing impairment in schools** (American Speech-Language-Hearing Association, 1993; DeConde Johnson, 1991; Flexer, 1990).

Identification procedures are improving, and services to students are becoming more readily available as more audiologists become part of the school environment. Soon after the passage of PL 94-142 in 1975, it was estimated that approximately 700 audiologists were serving students with hearing impairments (Garwood, 1978). Unfortunately, the number of audiologists employed by schools has not increased significantly.

Recently published guidelines (American Speech-Language-Hearing Association, 1993) indicate that school districts should hire one full-time audiologist for every 12,000 students. This guideline would require the services of over 3,200 school audiologists in the U.S. Until that criterion is met, the specialty of educational audiology needs to continue to promote its services and contributions to education and to strive to increase its visibility. (This area is covered in more detail in Chapters 3 and 9.)

HOW BEST TO SERVE LEARNERS WITH HI?

American Speech-Language-Hearing Association Guidelines

Up to this point, we have emphasized that the levels of services available to students with HI are inadequate, but we have not been specific about what those services entail. As mentioned before, states use widely varying interpretations of appropriate services. To address the changing conditions in education, a set of guidelines has been developed by the American Speech-Language-Hearing Association (ASHA) (1993) to provide direction to states and local educational agencies in developing a full spectrum of services. Guidelines are provided for the following areas.

Hearing Conservation   Programs are described to assist audiologists in developing a curriculum regarding the prevention of hearing loss.

Identification Programs   Periodic screening of all children for hearing impairment must be provided, which includes pure tone and acoustic immittance procedures. The identification program must be conducted by trained personnel and supervised by an audiologist.

Assessment   Students with a known hearing impairment or who fail a hearing screening must have a complete audiological assessment in order for educators to make appropriate educational decisions. Assessment information should include conventional audiometric information, speech recognition and speech reading abilities in noise and in quiet, and functional performance with amplification. Other individual areas of functioning that might require assessment may include cognition, vision, social-emotional development, and gross and fine motor skills.

Habilitation and Instructional Services Habilitation concerns often require the educational audiologist to work with other specialists such as teachers, speech-language pathologists, school psychologists and nurses, and/or occupational and physical therapists. Habilitation may involve medical issues, amplification, the development of optimal learning environments, counseling, and transitions between programs or grades.

Instruction to the learner may be provided directly by the audiologist, in the form of speechreading and auditory training integrated with other academic materials, or (more frequently) indirectly through consultation or team teaching.

Follow-Up and Monitoring A viable system of communication among teachers, parents, support staff, and community members is required to ensure that referrals are acted upon and that recommendations are followed and evaluated.

Equipment and Materials Access to technologies and materials is essential in order to serve students with HI in schools. Equipment is needed to test hearing levels and hearing aid/FM systems/cochlear implant performance; to evaluate acoustic properties of a classroom; to repair minor amplification problems; to make earmold impressions and modifications; to provide amplification on an emergency or daily basis; and to assess and remediate auditory, speechreading, and central auditory processing skills (American Speech-Language-Hearing Association, 1993).

These ASHA guidelines were developed to help practitioners improve services at state and local levels. Toward this end, the guidelines can be used as a standard by which to evaluate the status of existing services within a state or region, as well as to provide guidance to state agencies interested in defining the responsibilities for the audiologists in their schools (DeConde Johnson, 1993).

Recommended Practices

The *Code of Federal Regulations* for IDEA identifies **what** the audiologist's responsibilities are. To encourage practitioners to examine **how** to meet these responsibilities, various specialties in education are developing sets of "**recommended practice**," which consist of plans of clearly defined procedures that ensure that the needs of students are being met. Recommended practices have also been called best practices, preferred practices, exemplary, emergent, or most promising practices. Regardless of the name, the purpose of recommended practice is to identify strategies and methodologies that serve as indicators of quality services (Peters & Heron, 1993).

For example, as mentioned earlier, under the CFR for IDEA schools are required to ensure that hearing aids are functioning properly. But exactly how should this be done? In a recent study conducted to identify recommended practices (English, 1991), audiologists overwhelmingly supported a daily check of student amplification (see Figure 1.1). Audiologists indicated that this daily check could be conducted by teachers, classroom aides, speech-language pathologists, school nurses, and health clerks, under the supervision of the audiologist. Audiologists would enlist the commitment of at least one person on the site to conduct the check, and then oversee the training and monitor the daily checks. A majority of audiologists (69%) also supported electroacoustic analysis of amplification on a monthly or semesterly basis. So, in answer to the question "How will a school ensure that amplification is working properly?" audiologists, as a discipline, can answer "With the use of daily listening checks by persons trained and supervised by an audiologist, and by routine electroacoustic evaluation conducted by an audiologist."

In this study, audiologists were also asked to identify mechanisms by which they might contribute to the best overall auditory management of learners with HI. A full consensus supported the expansion of the educational audiologist's role to include consultation, staff development, and supervision of screening programs. Support was not as strong for including clinical responsibilities, such as monitoring middle ear function of students prone to otitis media, as recommended practices.

As part of the process of developing recommended practices, educational audiologists began to identify ways in which traditional clinical approaches were less than effective in schools, and formal and informal communication among practitioners supported efforts to describe problems and seek solutions. One identified problem was the clinically trained audiologist's lack of familiarity with the school as an environment and a social system. The following section discusses one model of the system of "school" and how it affects educational audiologists and other support personnel.

Understanding the System

The title of this chapter, "a new creature on the educational scene" (Ross, 1982, p. 231), was how educational audiology was described in its early days. Initially the

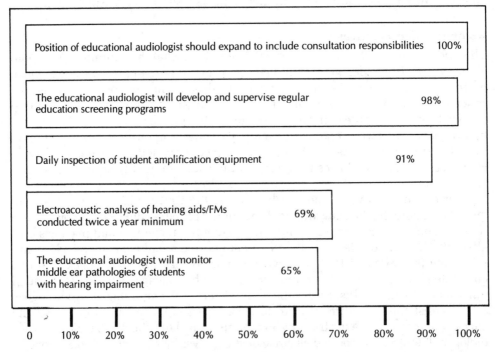

Figure 1.1. Educational audiologists indicate level of support for five professional practices in the school setting. Vertical scale = recommended practice, horizontal scale = percent support.

model employed to manage the effects of hearing impairment was simply to apply existing clinical skills to the school environment. The first designs for service delivery in school settings directly reflected the experiences and training of graduate school in clinical audiology: soundbooths were installed, testing schedules were established, equipment was purchased to analyze hearing aid performance, and recommendations were made to purchase and use large-group amplification.

However, using this model led to only moderate satisfaction with results. The application of a clinical model to a nonclinical environment succeeded only to a limited extent, and practitioners had to question why. Consider these hypothetical situations and see if you can define the problem:

- An audiologist recommends to Malcolm's first-grade teacher that his hearing aids be checked daily. She leaves a stethoscope, battery tester, wax loop, and checklist in a small box with the teacher. Two weeks later, she drops by unannounced and finds the box just as she had left it. Malcolm's right hearing aid is dead, and no one had known it.
- Maria is a middle school student with HI. Her history classroom is next to a woodshop, where even students with normal hearing strain to follow a lecture. The audiologist had not been consulted about Maria's placement, nor is he able to convince the teacher or principal of the need to change it.
- An audiologist provides a high school teacher with a handout on providing visual cues for her new student Lin. In subsequent classroom visits, he observed no differences in teaching behaviors.

The Science and Art of Educational Audiology

After considering situations such as these, practitioners realized that they did not know how to accomplish their goals in an educational setting. Educational audiologists realized that additional skills, beyond the scope of their clinical graduate training, were needed to positively affect the environment of their students with HI. Already mastered through all graduate programs are the abilities to evaluate hearing levels, fit amplification, analyze the acoustical properties of a room, and provide and supervise speechreading and auditory training programs to students—all skills that can be considered part of the "science" of clinical audiology. Missing from most graduate programs are components to develop the skills that comprise the "art" of educational audiology: collaborative consultation, team participation, staff development, student advocacy and service coordination, and an understanding of the organization of school environments. The successful integration of these skills can be considered an "artful science" (Idol, Paolucci-Whitcomb, & Nevin, 1986), a concept borrowed from other professional writings, which describe the ability to participate effectively in interdisciplinary activities.

In a clinical setting, an expected set of behaviors typically occurs: An audiologist is sought for consultation, makes recommendations, and expects compliance. However, in the situations above, this set of behaviors did not occur. The audiologist was not sought out for consultation; furthermore, when recommendations were offered, they were not followed.

Part of the explanation lies in the differences in models for service delivery between education and audiology. For example, an audiologist who expects to be actively sought out for his or her expertise in hearing impairment may wait a long time in a school setting. In this situation, he or she is operating in an "expert model," while other service providers (teachers and administrators) in the setting are operating in a "collaboration model." The differences between these and other models and the important methodological and practical implications of these differences are discussed further in Chapter 3.

Models of the Environment or Setting

First, however, we need to consider the models of the environment, or setting, that different professions—in this case, audiology and education—use. The clinical settings that typically comprise the externship experiences for audiology graduate students belong to organizations that follow a **rational** model. The rational model operates on an "if–then" philosophy that expects that the correct change in an activity will lead to an expected improvement in an outcome (Patterson, Purkey, & Parker, 1986). There is a logical, predictable if–then flow to the succession of events in the clinic: 1) if a patient comes to the clinic, then we will test his or her hearing; 2) if the patient has a hearing impairment, then we will make recommendations; 3) if the patient follows our recommendations, then he or she will experience an improvement in his or her hearing abilities.

Given the experiences acquired in graduate clinical audiology programs, it comes as a shock to realize that this model of expectations often does not apply in school settings. If school settings followed a rational model as described above, we should expect the following: 1) if we recommend that hearing aids be checked every day, then someone will meet that recommendation; 2) if we inform a teacher of the need to stand 10 feet from the student with HI in order to facilitate speechreading, he or she will comply with this new information; 3) if we indicate that high noise levels interfere with optimum listening conditions for students with HI, administrators will consider this when making student placement decisions.

As our examples earlier indicated, these events are not likely to happen. One reason is that schools operate as **nonrational** systems. It is important to note that this does not mean that the school model is irrational, which would mean that behaviors are unpredictable or chaotic. Rather, the school as a nonrational system follows a **complex logic** rather than a **simple logic** (if–then). School systems address continually changing needs of many constituencies (parents, teachers, support personnel, administrators, school boards, and community members) as well as new research, national trends and changes in philosophies, changes in federal and state laws, and competition for funding to accomplish it all.

Consider this example: The teachers and staff of Metro Elementary School come to school in September ready to address these issues: administrators are demanding higher test scores; the parent organization wants computers available to all children; the school board wants to include a biology textbook in the curriculum that discusses creationism and avoids mention of Darwin and evolution; the county decides to eliminate three classroom aide positions to help trim the budget; some teachers are demanding to be part of the school-based management movement; and five students with varied special needs will be attending this school for the first time.

These concerns are not necessarily mutually supportive; in fact, they may actually affect each other negatively. The individuals involved may feel that their group's concerns are the highest priority, but, in reality, they must compete with each other for resources. As the school year progresses, more issues will arise that contribute to a stimulating, rich, but complicated, working environment. Accommodating to and compromising with the needs of all these constituencies and demands requires a flexibility of response not found in a rational system.

Understanding the system of schools, and learning to become an effective player in the system rather than an outsider or someone who is simply overlooked, may be the most important nonclinical skill for audiologists to develop when working in the school environment. For until one achieves an understanding of the system, and uses it effectively, well-informed recommendations for students with HI are likely to be received and implemented with limited success.

A Lifespan Approach

This section has addressed how best to serve learners with HI by describing the development of guidelines and recommended practices, as well as the environment in which educational audiology services are provided. A final recommendation for the educational audiologist looking for ways to best serve the learner with HI is to frame his or her services within a **lifespan approach**: that is, a conscientious consideration of the effects of HI on a lifetime of learning experiences. A lifespan perspective encourages service providers to look beyond the traditional school years to consider the needs of the learner after high school.

To briefly review: audiologists have provided educational support services to students with HI from 6 to 21 years of age since before the passage of the Education for All Handicapped Children Act of 1975 (PL 94-142). With the implementation of PL 99-457 in 1986, audiologists were recognized as qualified service providers for infants and toddlers, expanding the scope of educational audiology practice to include learners from birth to 21 years of age. A theme throughout this text, especially in Chapter 8, is that educational audiologists are strongly encouraged to take the long view in service delivery, looking beyond high school levels to higher education and vocational training. National trends in education point to the growing number of adult learners in college, the acknowledged need for lifelong learning or for retraining during an adult's vocation or career, and the overall social status placed on a college education in our country. As Lipsky and Gartner (1992) wrote, "Students cannot learn all they will need to know for a lifetime in the short years of schooling" (p. 8). It would be very short-sighted to view a child with HI as simply a second-grader struggling with sightreading, or a sixth-grader reluctant to admit he can't follow a classroom video, or a high school student trying to take notes in chemistry class and speechread simultaneously. Rather, this text advances the concept of promoting the development of the skills for **self-advocacy**, in preparation for the day when a student faces a learning difficulty without the safety net of special education programs. It is recommended that educational audiologists see **each** learner with HI as a **lifelong learner with HI**, and develop a lifespan approach to problem solving that not only provides an immediate service, but also supports the long-term goal of self-advocacy for learners with HI (Dancer & Rittenhouse, 1992; Maxon & Brackett, 1992; Sanders, 1993).

SUMMARY

The driving force behind the growth of educational audiology as a specialty is the commitment to serving learners with hearing impairment of all ages, with all degrees of hearing loss, in all educational placements. Flexer (1991) eloquently describes the fundamental philosophy by which educational audiologists seem to operate:

> A child cannot possibly learn information that has been inaccurately received. There- fore, allowing a child to sit in class without receiving a clear and complete speech sig- nal is more than "undesirable"—it is a violation of that child's human rights because that child is being deprived of an opportunity to learn. (p. ii)

The promotion of the human right to learn is the focus of the professional iden- tity of educational audiology. In summary, an audiologist may describe in one word the difference between working in a school setting and in a clinical setting: **ad- vocacy**. In a clinical setting, a client is a self-advocate because he or she seeks out or is referred for services because of an acknowledged difficulty in hearing. In schools, by virtue of age and experience, a child with HI is not empowered to serve as his or her own advocate. Furthermore, because of the invisible nature of the im- pairment, and the general lack of understanding regarding the full impact of HI upon learning, there is always a need for individuals to work **for** the student, to ensure that his or her needs as a learner with HI are not marginalized or overlooked.

Subsequent chapters describe in detail the skills needed to advocate for all learners with HI, and to support students in their development as self-advocates in their lifelong learning endeavors.

Learning the Language

To establish credibility in the field of education, it is imperative to be able to use the language of educators. Review the following concepts from this chapter and discuss with a colleague.

- Students with HI as an underserved population
- The differences between regulations and recommended practices
- Rational and nonrational systems
- Lifespan approach to learning and remediation
- Advocacy

Educational Audiology in Action
Suggested Learning Activities

Project. Interview an educational audiologist.

Obtain a referral from your instructor, or call a local school district for the name of an educational audiologist to contact. If you experience difficulty, contact the Educational Audiology Association (see Resources) for a referral to an audiologist in your area.

Request a ½-hour appointment and find out the following information from the educational audiologist:

- Educational and professional background
- Description of students served
- Description of responsibilities
- Level of job satisfaction
- Areas of job frustration
- Programs developed
- Advice for interested students

If time permits, ask to tour the audiologist's work environment.

Discuss your impressions and observations with a colleague. What were the similarities and differences compared to your experiences with clinical settings?

Resources

American Speech-Language-Hearing Association
School Services Branch
10801 Rockville Pike
Rockville, MD 20852
(301) 897-5700 (voice or text telephone)

The School Services Branch of ASHA is a resource for information on school issues for audiologists and speech-language pathologists. Fact sheets and brochures regarding legislative issues, educational reform, and recommended practices are available upon request.

Educational Audiology Association
c/o Department of Communication Disorders
Utah State University
Logan, UT 83222-1000

This organization was started in 1984, and now has approximately 600 members, mostly practitioners. The EAA publishes quarterly newsletters and a bi-annual monograph devoted to issues for audiologists in schools. Annual meetings are held in conjunction with the American Speech-Language-Hearing Association and the American Academy of Audiology convention. Membership is $20, and $25 for individuals outside of North America.

National Information Center for Children and Youth with Disabilities
Interstate Research Associates
PO Box 1492
Washington, DC 20013
(703) 893-6061
(800) 999-5599

Provides directories, fact sheets, booklets, and other materials on disabilities and special education issues for early childhood through adolescence. Specify interest in area of HI.

National Information Center on Deafness
Gallaudet University
800 Florida Avenue, NE
Washington, DC 20002
(202) 651-5051 (voice)
(202) 651-5052 (text telephone)

Provides fact sheets, booklets, and reading lists on hearing impairment, employment, communication, and disabilities; maintains a collection of publications on the topic of deafness.

References

Alpiner, J. (1974). Educational audiology. *Journal of the Academy of Rehabilitation Audiology, 7,* 50–54.

American Speech-Language-Hearing Association. (1993). Guidelines for audiology services in the schools. *Asha, 35* (Suppl. 10), pp. 24–32.

Berg, F. (1986). Characteristics of the target population. In F. Berg, J. Blair, S. Viehweg, & A. Wilson-Vlotman (pp.1–24), *Educational audiology for the hard of hearing child.* Orlando, FL: Grune & Stratton.

Bess, F., & McConnell, F. (1981). *Audiology, education, and the hearing impaired child.* St. Louis: C.V. Mosby.

Blair, J., Wilson-Vlotman, A., & Von Almen, P. (1989). Educational audiologists: Practices, problems, directions, recommendations. *Educational Audiology Monograph, 1,* 1–14.

Blake, A., & Shewan, C. (1992). An update on PL 94-142. *Asha, 34*(1), 52.

Casby, M. (1991). National data concerning communication disorders and special education. *Language, Speech, and Hearing Services in Schools, 20,* 22–30.

Dancer, J., & Rittenhouse, R. (1992). Lifespan issues in persons with hearing loss: A framework for discussion. *Volta Review, 94,* 5–7.

DeConde Johnson, C. (1991). The "state" of educational audiology: Survey results and goals for the future. *Educational Audiology Monograph, 2,* 74–84.

DeConde Johnson, C. (1993). ASHA's guidelines for audiology services in the schools: What is the potential impact? *Educational Audiology Newsletter, 10*(2), 3–4.

Education for All Handicapped Children Act of 1975, PL 94-142. (August 23, 1977). Title 20, U.S.C. 1401 et seq: *U.S. Statutes at Large, 89, 773–796.*

Education of the Handicapped Act Amendments of 1986, PL 99-457. (October 8, 1986). Title 20, U.S.C. 1400 et seq: *U.S. Statutes at Large, 100,* 1145–1177.

English, K. (1991). Best practices in educational audiology. *Language, Speech, and Hearing Services in Schools, 22,* 283–286.

Flexer, C. (1990). Audiological rehabilitation in the schools. *Asha, 32*(4), 44–45.

Flexer, C. (1991). Preface. *Seminars in Hearing, 12*(4), i–iii.

Garwood, V. (1978). Audiological management of the hearing impaired child in the public schools. In F. Martin (Ed.), *Pediatric audiology* (pp. 448–487). Englewood Cliffs, NJ: Prentice Hall.

Idol, L., Paolucci-Whitcomb, P., & Nevin, A. (1986). *Collaborative consultation.* Rockville, MD: Aspen Publishers, Inc.

Individuals with Disabilities Education Act of 1990 (IDEA), PL 101-476. (October 30, 1990). Title 20, U.S.C. 1400 et seq: *U.S. Statutes at Large, 104,* 1103–1151.

Lenich, J., Bernstein, M., & Nevitt, A. (1987). Educational audiology: A proposal for training and accreditation. *Language, Speech, and Hearing Services in Schools, 18,* 344–356.

Lipsky, D., & Gartner, A. (1992). Achieving full inclusion: Placing the student at the center of educational reform. In W. Stainback & S. Stainback (Eds.), *Controversial issues confronting special education: Divergent perspectives* (pp. 3–12). Newton, MA: Allyn & Bacon.

Lundeen, C. (1991). Prevalence of hearing impairment among children. *Language, Speech, and Hearing Services in Schools, 22,* 269–271.

Maxon, A., & Brackett, D. (1992). *The hearing impaired child: Infancy through high school years.* Boston: Andover Medical Publishers.

Office of The Federal Register. (1985). *The Federal Register: What it is and how to use it.* Washington, DC: U.S. Government Printing Office.

Osborne, A. (1992). Citing legal material in APA journals. *Remedial and Special Education, 13*(5), 56–57.

Patterson, J., Purkey, S., & Parker, J. (1986). *Productive school systems for a nonrational world.* Alexandria, VA: Association for Supervision and Curriculum Development.

Peters, M., & Heron, T. (1993). When the best is not good enough: An examination of best practice. *Journal of Special Education, 26*(4), 371–385.

Ross, M. (1982). *Hard of hearing children in regular schools.* Englewood Cliffs, NJ: Prentice Hall.

Ross, M., Brackett, D., & Maxon, A. (1991). *Assessment and management of mainstreamed hearing impaired children.* Austin, TX: PRO-ED.

Roush, J., & McWilliams, R. (1990). A new challenge for pediatric audiology: Public Law 99-457. *Journal of the American Academy of Audiology, 1,* 196–208.

Sanders, D. (1993). *Management of hearing handicap: Infant to elderly* (3rd ed.). Englewood Cliffs, NJ: Prentice Hall.

Shepard, N., Davis, J., Gorga, M., & Stelmachowicz, P. (1981). Characteristics of hearing impaired children in the public schools: Part 1. Demographic data. *Journal of Speech and Hearing Disorders, 46,* 123–129.

Upfold, L. (1988). Children with hearing aids in the 1980's: Etiologies and severity of impairment. *Ear and Hearing, 9,* 75–80.

U.S. Department of Education. (1993). *Fifteenth annual report to Congress on the implementation of the Individuals with Disabilities Education Act.* Washington, DC: U.S. Government Printing Office.

Wilson-Vlotman, A. (1986). Management and coordination of services to the hard of hearing child. In F. Berg, J. Blair, S. Viehweg, & A. Wilson-Vlotman, *Educational audiology for the hard of hearing child* (pp. 181–203). Orlando, FL: Grune & Stratton.

2

Educational Issues

HEARING IMPAIRMENT IS AMONG THE most common disabilities in children. Berg (1986) estimated that when all levels of hearing impairment are considered—from mild to profound and including permanent and fluctuating and bilateral and unilateral—approximately 20% (8 million of nearly 40 million) of schoolchildren in the U.S. have educationally significant hearing impairment. Stated another way, children with hearing impairment are "likely to be found in every school building in the country" (Shepard, Davis, Gorga, & Stelmachowicz, 1981, p. 123). In this chapter, we discuss the impact of an educationally significant hearing impairment and the legal and philosophical support systems available to address the educational significance.

IMPACT OF HEARING IMPAIRMENT UPON LEARNING

Terminology

Before examining the issues surrounding an educationally significant hearing impairment, it is imperative that consistent terminology be introduced. Among the general population, hearing status is often simplistically understood as either hearing or deaf—an all or nothing concept. However, only a small percentage of children with hearing impairment (6%–8%) have a profound impairment or are deaf. The majority of children with hearing impairment have losses ranging in severity from mild to moderate to severe, and are appropriately considered to be "hard of hearing" (Flexer, Wray, & Ireland, 1989). This point is made because, while obvious to students of audiology, it is less than clear to many professionals in the field of education. One of the most fundamental efforts of educational audiology is the clarification of this distinction so that educational personnel can understand the benefits of amplification, the deleterious effects of noise, and the relationship of degree of loss to language development. To maintain consistency with the literature in audiology, we use the following terms throughout this book. **Hearing impairment** indicates any unspecified level of hearing loss. The term hearing impairment does not describe the level or nature of loss, but only refers to the full possible continuum of impairment. Individuals with hearing impairment can be described in one of two ways. First, an individual may be **hard of hearing**, which means that the individual has a mild to severe hearing impairment. A person who is hard of hearing typically benefits from amplification to perceive both speech and environmental sounds. Second, an individual may be **deaf**, or have a bilateral profound impairment, which is a pure tone average of greater than 90 dB in the better ear. A person who is deaf may benefit from amplification to perceive environmental sounds; however, speech sounds are generally beyond amplification (see Figure 2.1).

In addition, we use **"people first" language**, which requires that the individual is identified first, followed by the particular disability. Examples of people-first language include "children with hearing impairment" and "learners who are hard of hearing." This terminology was formally established with the enactment of the Americans with Disabilities Act of 1990 (ADA) (PL 101-336) and the Individuals with Disabilities Education Act (IDEA) (PL 101-476, 1990), the reauthorization of PL 94-142, in response to objections by persons with disabilities who did not wish to be "lumped" into categories and identified first by their disability (for example, to be referred to as "the mentally retarded" or "the disabled"). The only exception to people-first language in this book is the occasional reference to persons who identify with the Deaf culture. The use of "the Deaf" as a cultural community is considered appropriate by its members (Luetke-Stahlman & Luckner, 1991; Padden & Humphries, 1988).

Learning Problems in Individuals with HI

Regardless of the degree of hearing impairment, the educational impact of the impairment can be significant. Unless immersed in a fully signing environment, children learn language through the auditory pathways; if the input is distorted or inconsistent, the language learner can experience a variety of difficulties such as vocabulary deficits, delayed syntax development, and inappropriate use of morphological markers and figurative speech (Cooper & Rosenstein, 1966; Davis & Blasdell, 1975; Davis, Elfenbein, Schum, & Bentler, 1986; Dobie & Berlin, 1979; Grant, 1987; Groht, 1958; Kluwin & Kelly, 1993; Levitt & McGarr, 1988; Ling, 1976; Matkin, 1988; Quigley & Power, 1972; Quigley & Thomure, 1968; Ross, 1982; Schmidt, 1968; Wilcox & Tobin, 1974; Young & McConnell, 1957).

Consider the example of a 3-year-old girl with a bilateral moderate sensorineural hearing impairment with the audiogram presented in Figure 2.2. Because the speech energy for the high-frequency, low-intensity phoneme /s/ is perceived at approximately 4000 Hz, 20 dB, this child, without amplification, is not able to receive this auditory input. This particular phoneme is also subtle to speechread. Therefore, she will not readily learn the many functions that the phoneme /s/ plays in the English language, such as forming plurals (cats), possessives (cat's), and in person-verb agreement (I eat/she eats).

These difficulties can result from missing just 1 of the 46 phonemes in the English language (Shames & Wiig, 1982). It is no surprise, then, that we find children with even a mild or unilateral hearing impairment who experience vocabulary deficits and inconsistent use of language rules (Oyler, Oyler, & Matkin, 1988).

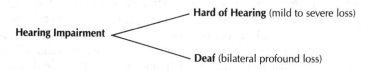

Figure 2.1. The two types of hearing impairment.

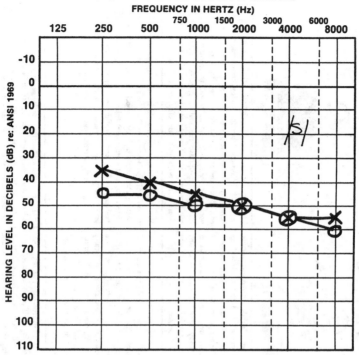

Figure 2.2. Sample pure tone audiogram.

The deficits in a child's language development can have a direct effect upon cognitive development (learning). Students with HI have often been found to repeat grades (Kodman, 1963), have depressed math skills (Jensema, 1975), and have reading levels that plateau at the fourth- or fifth-grade level (Boothroyd, 1982; McClure, 1966). One study measured the reading skills of 1,250 students with HI in Iowa and noted a leveling off of reading skills at a fourth-grade reading level by the age of 16 (Davis, Shepard, Stelmachowicz, & Gorga, 1981).

Deficits in language and communication skills may also affect the development of social skills. Antia and Kreimeyer (1992) described how children with hearing impairment have difficulties in their communicative processes with their families and friends. A child with hearing impairment may not have "the same opportunities as their hearing peers to engage in reciprocal interactions with adults and peers. Consequently, they do not necessarily acquire the social competence skills learned through these interactions" (p. 160).

Anderson and Matkin (1991) have developed a comprehensive table that describes the effects of hearing impairment upon academic performance and pyschosocial development. In this chart (Figure 2.3), each aspect of a child's development is considered relative to the degree of hearing impairment. It is generally appropriate to say that learning difficulties increase as the severity of the hearing impairment increases.

Degree of Hearing Loss Based on modified pure tone average (500-4000 HZ)	Possible Effect of Hearing Loss on the Understanding of Language & Speech	Possible Psychosocial Impact of Hearing Loss	Potential Educational Needs and Programs
NORMAL HEARING -10 - +15 dB HL	Children have better hearing sensitivity than the accepted normal range for adults. A child with hearing sensitivity in the -10 to +15 dB range will detect the complete speech signal even at soft conversation levels. However, good hearing does not guarantee good ability to discriminate speech in the presence of background noise.		
MINIMAL (BORDERLINE) 16-25 dB HL	May have difficulty hearing faint or distant speech. At 15 dB student can miss up to 10% of speech signal when teacher is at a distance greater than 3 feet or if the classroom is noisy, especially in grades K through 3 when verbal instruction predominates.	May be unaware of subtle conversational cues which could cause child to be viewed as inappropriate or awkward. May miss portions of fast-paced peer interactions which could begin to have an impact on socialization and self concept. May have immature behavior. Child may be more fatigued than classmates due to listening effort needed.	May benefit from mild gain/low MPO hearing aid or personal FM system dependent on loss configuration. Would benefit from soundfield amplification if classroom is noisy and/or reverberant. Favorable seating. May need attention to vocabulary or speech, especially with recurrent otitis media history. Appropriate medical management necessary for conductive losses. Teacher requires inservice on impact of hearing loss on language development and learning.
MILD 26-40 dB HL	At 30 dB can miss 25-40% of speech signal. The degree of difficulty experienced in school will depend upon the noise level in classroom, distance from teacher and configuration of hearing loss. Without amplification the child with 35-40 dB loss may miss at least 50% of class discussions, especially when voices are faint or speaker is not in line of vision. Will miss consonants, especially when a high frequency hearing loss is present.	Barriers beginning to build with negative impact on self esteem as child is accused of "hearing when he or she wants to," "daydreaming," or "not paying attention." Child begins to lose ability for selective hearing, and has increasing difficulty suppressing background noise which makes the learning environment stressful. Child is more fatigued than classmates due to listening effort needed.	Will benefit from a hearing aid and use of a personal FM or soundfield FM system in the classroom. Needs favorable seating and lighting. Refer to special education for language evaluation and educational follow-up. Needs auditory skill building. May need attention to vocabulary development, articulation or speechreading and/or special support in reading and self esteem. Teacher inservice required.
MODERATE 41-55 dB HL	Understands conversational speech at a distance of 3-5 feet (face-to-face) only if structure and vocabulary controlled. Without amplification the amount of speech signal missed can be 50% to 75% with 40 dB loss and 80% to 100% with 50 dB loss. Is likely to have delayed or defective syntax, limited vocabulary, imperfect speech production and an atonal voice quality.	Often with this degree of hearing loss, communication is significantly affected, and socialization with peers with normal hearing becomes increasingly difficult. With full time use of hearing aids/FM systems child may be judged as a less competent learner. There is an increasing impact on self-esteem.	Refer to special education for language evaluation and for educational follow-up. Amplification is essential (hearing aids and FM system). Special education support may be needed, especially for primary children. Attention to oral language development, reading and written language. Speechreading and speech therapy usually needed. Teacher inservice required.

22

Degree of Hearing Loss	Possible Effect of Hearing Loss on the Understanding of Language and Speech	Possible Psychosocial Impact of Hearing Loss	Potential Educational Needs and Programs
MODERATE TO SEVERE 56-70 dB HL	Without amplification, conversation must be very loud to be understood. A 55 dB loss can cause child to miss up to 100% of speech information. Will have marked difficulty in school situations requiring verbal communication in both one-to-one and group situations. Delayed language, syntax, reduced speech intelligibility and atonal voice quality likely.	Full time use of hearing aids/FM systems may result in child being judged by both peers and adults as a less competent learner, resulting in poorer self concept, social maturity and sense of rejection. Inservice to address these attitudes may be helpful.	Full time use of amplification is essential. Will need resource teacher or special class depending on magnitude of language delay. May require special help in all language skills, vocabulary, grammar, pragmatics as well as reading and writing. Inservice of mainstream teachers required.
SEVERE 71-90 dB HL	Without amplification may hear loud voices about one foot from ear. When amplified optimally, children with hearing ability of 90 dB or better should be able to identify environmental sounds and detect all the sounds of speech. If loss is of prelingual onset, oral language and speech may not develop spontaneously or will be severely delayed. If hearing loss is of recent onset speech is likely to deteriorate with quality becoming atonal.	Child may prefer other children with hearing impairments as friends and playmates. This may further isolate the child from the mainstream, however, these peer relationships may foster improved self concept and a sense of cultural identity.	May need full-time special aural/oral program for deaf children with emphasis on all auditory language skills, speechreading, concept development and speech. As loss approaches 80-90 dB, may benefit from a Total Communication approach, especially in the early language learning years. Individual hearing aid/personal FM system essential. Participation in regular classes as much as beneficial to student. Inservice of mainstream teachers essential.
PROFOUND 91 dB HL or more	Aware of vibrations more than tonal pattern. Many rely on vision rather than hearing as primary avenue for communication and learning. Detection of speech sounds dependent upon loss configuration and use of amplification. Speech and language will not develop spontaneously and is likely to deteriorate rapidly if hearing loss is of recent onset.	Depending on auditory/oral competence, peer use of sign language, parental attitude, etc., child may or may not increasingly prefer association with the deaf culture.	May need special program for deaf children with emphasis on all language skills and academic areas. Program needs specialized supervision and comprehensive support services. Early use of amplification likely to help if part of an intensive training program. May be cochlear implant or vibrotactile aid candidate. Continual appraisal of needs in regard to communication and learning mode. Part-time in regular classes as much as beneficial to student.
UNILATERAL One normal hearing ear and one ear with at least a permanent mild hearing loss	May have difficulty hearing faint or distant speech. Usually has difficulty localizing sounds and voices. Unilateral listener will have greater difficulty understanding speech when environment is noisy and/or reverberant. Difficulty detecting or understanding soft speech from side of bad ear, especially in a group discussion.	Child may be accused of selective hearing due to discrepancies in speech understanding in quiet versus noise. Child will be more fatigued in classroom setting due to greater effort needed to listen. May appear inattentive or frustrated. Behavior problems sometimes evident.	May benefit from personal FM or soundfield FM system in classroom. CROS hearing aid may be of benefit in quiet settings. Needs favorable seating and lighting. Student is at risk for educational difficulties. Educational monitoring warranted with support services provided as soon as difficulties appear. Teacher inservice is beneficial.

Figure 2.3. Relationship of degree of long-term hearing loss to psychological impact and educational needs. (From Anderson, K., & Matkin, N. [1991]. Relationship of degree of loss to psychosocial and educational needs. *Educational Audiology Newsletter, 8*[2], 11–12, reprinted by permission.)

We have introduced the learning difficulties a child might experience as a result of a hearing impairment. The following section describes the educational environment that has developed, by law and by philosophy, to educate children with disabilities.

LEGAL FRAMEWORK OF THE EDUCATIONAL ENVIRONMENT

Federal Legislation

After two decades of committed struggle, parents and advocates of children with disabilities cheered the passage of PL 94-142 in November 1975. The law was called the Education for All Handicapped Children Act of 1975, and although it would be reauthorized and amended later (described below), PL 94-142 contained four critical components that have remained constant:

1. The guarantee of a free appropriate public education (FAPE)
2. In the least restrictive environment (LRE)
3. The use of a mechanism to oversee these guarantees, which is the individualized education program (IEP)
4. The right to due process

These components, with citations from the *Code of Federal Regulations* (CFR), are described in the following sections.

Free Appropriate Public Education (FAPE) "The term *free appropriate public education* means special education and related services which are provided at public supervision and direction, and without charge" (34 CFR 300.4[a]). Each child with a disability is entitled to a free public-school education, as is any child without a disability. In addition, services needed to support the education of a child with a disability are paid for by public funds rather than by parents. The term "appropriate" is intentionally left undefined, with the understanding that each child's educational program will be planned based on the individual's requirements.

Least Restrictive Environment (LRE)

> Each public agency shall insure 1) that to the maximum extent appropriate, handicapped children, including children in public or private institutions or other care facilities, are educated with children who are not handicapped, and 2) that special classes, separate schooling, or other removal of handicapped children from the regular education environment occurs only when the nature or severity of the handicap is such that education in regular classes with the use of supplementary aids and services cannot be achieved satisfactorily. (34 CFR 300.550[b])

The concept of LRE is often considered to be synonymous with "mainstreaming," or educating children with disabilities in a local public school among children without disabilities. However, PL 94-142 does not mandate mainstreaming per se, but simply consideration of the least restrictive environment for the most appropriate education. Therefore, LRE is essentially open to interpretation and consequently remains imprecise (McConnell, 1984; Taylor, 1988).

To help schools make educational placement decisions, the *Code of Federal Regulations* requires the following: "Each public agency shall insure that a continuum of alternative placements is available to meet the needs of handicapped children for special education and related services" (34 CFR 300.551[a]). The conventional LRE continuum model is typically represented as linear, moving from most to least restrictive environments (Figure 2.4).

Interpreters of this regulation repeatedly caution that it is not appropriate to generalize about LRE for children with disabilities. The determination of what consititutes the LRE for each child **must** be made on an individual basis (Huffman, 1991; Vergason & Anderegg, 1992). The educational audiologist must be knowledgeable with the placement options provided by the district (American Speech-Language-Hearing Association, 1993).

Individualized Education Program (IEP)   The IEP is a document that serves as a contract between families and professionals. In every IEP for each child, the following components must be included: 1) a statement of the child's present levels of educational performance, which typically includes test reports to provide updated information on the child's progress; 2) a statement of annual goals, describing what will be accomplished in 1 year and including short-term instructional objectives in measurable steps; 3) a statement of the specific special education and related services to be provided to the child, and the extent to which the child will be able to participate in regular education programs; 4) the projected dates of initiation of services and the anticipated duration of the services; and 5) appropriate objective criteria and evaluation procedures and schedules for determining, on at least an annual basis, whether the short-term instructional objectives have been achieved (34 CFR 300.346).

These last three components of an IEP are typically written on a cover page or back page, as shown in the sample IEP form in Figure 2.5.

Right to Due Process   The final component, the right to due process, refers to a set of procedures designed to safeguard fairness and accountability in an individual's educational placement. These procedures include the following rights for parents or guardians and their children: 1) the right to examine all records held on a child, 2) the right to full confidentiality, 3) the right to obtain independent evaluations, 4) the right to obtain written notices of proposed changes in programs, 5) the right to receive an impartial hearing to appeal a decision regarding an educational program (Domico, 1989). (See Appendix A for a detailed explanation regarding a parent's rights related to special education services.)

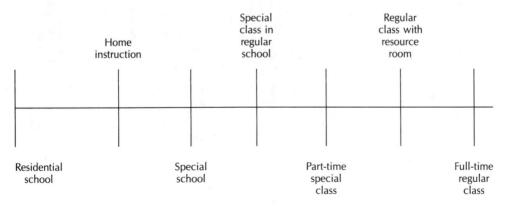

Figure 2.4.   Least restrictive environment (LRE) continuum.

EAST COUNTY SPECIAL EDUCATION
LOCAL PLAN AREA

INDIVIDUALIZED EDUCATION PLAN

STUDENT NAME _____ D.O.B. _____ S.S.# _____ DATE _____

PRIMARY LANGUAGE: HOME _____ STUDENT _____

| Language Assessment Survey Date _____ | Scores: English _____ | Spanish _____ | ☐ Limited English Proficient | ☐ Fluent English Proficient | ☐ English Only |

STUDENT STRENGTHS AND INTERESTS

PRESENT LEVELS OF FUNCTIONING

PRE-ACADEMIC/ACADEMIC/FUNCTIONAL SKILLS (Include readiness skills, reading, reading comprehension, written language and mathematics) _____

_____
_____
_____
_____
_____
_____

COMMUNICATION DEVELOPMENT _____

PERCEPTUAL SKILLS (Include visual and auditory skills) _____

GROSS AND FINE MOTOR SKILLS _____

SOCIAL/EMOTIONAL _____

COGNITIVE ABILITIES _____

PREFERRED LEARNING MODALITY/STYLE _____

PRE-VOCATIONAL/VOCATIONAL SKILLS _____

ADAPTIVE BEHAVIOR (Include daily living, self-help and attendance) _____

HEALTH (Include medical information) _____

SUMMARY

AREAS OF NEED _____

JUSTIFICATION FOR SPECIAL EDUCATION SERVICES _____

REQUIRES LINGUISTICALLY APPROPRIATE GOALS (for speakers of other languages) YES _____ NO _____

PRIORITY AREA(S) FOR GOAL DEVELOPMENT _____

TRANSITION SERVICES _____

COMMENTS _____

26

STUDENT INFORMATION

page _____ of _____

Student Name _____ first _____ middle _____ last _____ D.O.B. _____ Age _____ Sex _____

Student ID # _____ S.S. # _____

Attending District _____ District of Residence _____ Home School _____

Name of Parent _____ Attending School _____ Grade _____ Teacher/Counselor _____

Address _____ Phone (H) _____ Apt. # _____ (W) _____ City _____ Zip _____

Name of Parent _____

Address _____ Phone (H) _____ Apt. # _____ (W) _____ City _____ Zip _____

Guardian/Surrogate _____

Address _____ Phone (H) _____ Apt. # _____ (W) _____ City _____ Zip _____

Student's Home Language _____ [ ] LEP

PURPOSE OF MEETING
[ ] Initial I.E.P.
[ ] Annual Review
[ ] 3 Year Review
[ ] Transition
[ ] Other

RESIDENCY
[ ] Parent/or Legal Guardian
[ ] LCI #
[ ] Foster #
[ ] Hospital
[ ] Residential School
[ ] Juvenile Court
[ ] Other

OTHER SERVICES
[ ] SIP   [ ] Ch. 1
[ ] ROP   [ ] Migrant
[ ] GATE   [ ] Bilingual
[ ] Other

DISABILITY [ ] Severe [ ] Non-Severe

ETHNICITY
[ ] Native American
[ ] Chinese
[ ] Japanese
[ ] Korean
[ ] Vietnamese
[ ] Asian Indian
[ ] Laotian
[ ] Cambodian
[ ] Other Asian
[ ] Hawaiian
[ ] Guamanian
[ ] Samoan
[ ] Tahitian
[ ] Other Pacific Isl.
[ ] Filipino
[ ] Hispanic
[ ] Black
[ ] White

PRIMARY DISABILITY CATEGORY
[ ] Mental Retardation
[ ] Hard of Hearing
[ ] Deaf
[ ] Speech/Lang. Impaired
[ ] Vision Impaired
[ ] Seriously Emot. Dist.
[ ] Orthopedic Impaired
[ ] Other Health Impaired
[ ] Specific Learning Disability
[ ] Deaf/Blind
[ ] Multiple Handicapped
[ ] Autistic
[ ] Traumatic Brain Injury
[ ] Non-Categorical (Infant Only)

PRIMARY PLACEMENT
[ ] Designated Instruction
[ ] Resource Specialist
[ ] Special Day Class (Non SH)
[ ] Special Day Class (SH)
[ ] Special Day Class (Isolated)
[ ] Non Public School
[ ] Day [ ] RTC [ ] Out of State

Percent of Integration _____ %
Integration Activities

AGENCY SERVICES
[ ] Ca. Child Services
[ ] Rehabilitation
[ ] Mental Health
[ ] Regional Center
[ ] Social Services
[ ] Other

PHYSICAL EDUCATION
[ ] Regular
[ ] Modified
[ ] Specially Designed
[ ] Adapted
Comments

TRANSPORTATION
[ ] None
[ ] Regular
[ ] Pick Up Point
[ ] Curb to Curb
[ ] Shuttle
[ ] Other

OTHER PROGRAM INFORMATION
Extended School Year _____
Competencies/Credits (H.S. only) _____
Low Incidence Equipment & Material _____
Vocational Education _____
Receiving all IEP Services [ ] Yes [ ] No _____
I.E.P. Services Will Begin _____
Duration of Services _____
Preschool [ ] RIS [ ] Not RIS _____

EXIT REASONS
Exit Date _____
[ ] Return to Reg. Ed.
[ ] Grad. with Reg. Prof.
[ ] Grad. with Dif. Prof.
[ ] Reached Maximum Age
[ ] Dropped Out
[ ] Trans. within SELPA
[ ] Trans. to other SELPA
[ ] Parent/Student Request
[ ] Other

DESIGNATED INSTRUCTION AND SERVICES
Service | Frequency | Duration

The following were participants in the development of the Individualized Education Program

Parent/Surrogate/Guardian _____ Date _____ Parent/Surrogate/Guardian _____ Date _____

Student _____ Date _____ Speech and Language Specialist _____ Date _____

Administrator Designee _____ Date _____ Other _____ Date _____

Special Education Teacher _____ Date _____ Other _____ Date _____

Regular Education Teacher _____ Date _____ Other _____ Date _____

Psychologist _____ Date _____ Other _____ Date _____

Person who reviewed Due Process Rights with parent _____
Members who disagree with the committee's decision should submit their concerns in writing.

CONSENT FOR PLACEMENT
[ ] I (we) agree to the IEP as described above   [ ] I (we) agree to all parts of the IEP except _____

Parent/Surrogate/Guardian Signature _____ Date _____

Parent/Surrogate/Guardian Signature _____ Date _____

(continued)

Figure 2.5. An example of an Individualized Education Program (IEP) form. (Developed by East County Forms Committee, East County SELPA, San Diego, CA; reprinted by permission.)

Figure 2.5. *(continued)*

INDIVIDUALIZED EDUCATION PLAN

Goals and Objectives

Student's Name _____

D.O.B. _____

Date _____

Area of Need _____	
Current Performance Information (Baseline) _____	

Annual Goal: _____

Short Term Objectives:	Periodic Review Date/Comments/Initials
Person(s) Responsible	
Person(s) Responsible	
Person(s) Responsible	
Final Goal Review _____	

Area of Need _____	
Current Performance Information (Baseline) _____	

Annual Goal: _____

Short Term Objectives:	Periodic Review Date/Comments/Initials
Person(s) Responsible	
Person(s) Responsible	
Person(s) Responsible	
Final Goal Review _____	

Reauthorizations of PL 94-142

In 1986, Public Law 94-142 was reauthorized; that is, it was renewed and funding was continued. It was also amended to include the provision of services for infants and toddlers (Part H). As such, PL 94-142 became PL 99-457, the Education of the Handicapped Act Amendments of 1986 (EHA). In 1990 these laws were reauthorized and amended as the Individuals with Disabilities Education Act (IDEA) (PL 101-476). As mentioned, this law used the preferred term "disability" rather than "handicap" and substituted the term "children with disabilities" for "handicapped children" (people-first language).

PHILOSOPHICAL FRAMEWORKS OF THE EDUCATIONAL ENVIRONMENT: INTERPRETING LEGISLATION

Normalization and Special Education

PL 94-142 made funding available for a proliferation of special programs, materials, and curricula development to support the education of children with disabilities. Consequently, two distinct educational systems began to evolve: "special ed" for children with disabilities, and "regular ed" for children without disabilities.

At approximately the same time, professionals in the human services were reconsidering the decisions that affected persons with disabilities (Wolfensberger, 1972). Service providers asked themselves whether, in reality, the broad field of human services considered its clientele to be deviant, less than human, and therefore not entitled to basic human rights. The concept of **normalization** was introduced, which values the effort of an individual to live as close to "the normal" of his or her culture as possible. For example, the normalization principle, as it is sometimes called, demands that an individual with disabilities be taught not only how to walk, but to walk with as normal a gait as possible; not only to dress independently, but to dress appropriately with his or her age and general fashions, in order to minimize a "perception of deviance" (Wolfensberger, 1972, p. 33).

Another example is the institutional living arrangements for persons with mental retardation, typical of an earlier era. Instead of placing drains in the floors of large rooms for easy cleaning, or keeping lights on 24 hours a day (both formerly common practices), the normalization principle requires us to think how persons **without** disabilities live:

> Life space should be zoned so as to encourage rather than discourage individuals from interaction in small groups at least part of the time, in contrast to space which implies interaction in large groups only, or which discourages almost all interaction. . . . Residential and educational human service buildings have stairs and not merely ramps, and residential facilities generally should provide residents with access to the controls that adjust room and water temperature; turn lights on and off; open and close windows, blinds and curtains, and flush toilets. To do otherwise deprives residents of culturally normal opportunities, restricts their range of learning opportunities, and fosters nonnormative dependency. (Wolfensberger, 1972, p. 33)

Wolfensberger went on to consider the full range of human services provided to persons with disabilities. Regarding education, he noted that services had long been provided in a segregated fashion: children with special needs were placed in

isolated classrooms, with a small teacher–student ratio, and with "special" equipment and learning materials. He suggested that, rather than promoting this state
of segregated learning environment, which was not demonstrating any measure
of success, we consider that "by the very nature of things, integrated education
has certain normalizing features which can make it better than segregated education" (p. 50).

The Regular Education Initiative

In 1986, Madeleine Will, then Assistant Secretary, Office of Special Education and
Rehabilitative Services, U.S. Department of Education, and a parent of a child with
Down syndrome, wrote an article that challenged special educators to the core. "At
the heart of the special approach is the presumption that students with learning
problems cannot be effectively taught in regular education programs even with a
variety of support" (Will, 1986, p. 412). This presumption had informed a full set of
policies that isolated a student with disabilities in special classes or pull-out programs. The article called for reform, for reorganization that supported a collaboration by both special and regular education to meet the needs of individual students
in the regular classroom.

Will's article stimulated practitioners in special education to question whether
the complex system of services for students with disabilities was truly meeting the
intent of the law. The system of special education that evolved from PL 94-142 was
determined by some (e.g., Wang, Reynolds, & Walberg, 1988) as providing a "separate but equal" education, a concept found to be unconstitutional by the Supreme
Court in 1954. In Brown v. Board of Education, the provision of segregated learning
environments based on race was ruled to be a violation of students' civil rights.
Educators uneasily began to ask themselves, "With the best of intentions—are we
doing the same thing? Do we use a 'separate but equal' educational program? Do
special education programs violate the principle of normalization?" (Schattman &
Benay, 1992).

Empirical evidence regarding the effectiveness of special education programs
did not strongly support the dual system of education (Anderson-Inman, 1987;
Leinhardt & Palley, 1982; Semmel, Gottlieb, & Robinson, 1979). A student with disabilities typically was placed in one of three settings: full time in a "special day"
class; part time in a special class and part time mainstreamed into a regular education class; or a majority of the time in a regular classroom with some "pull-out"
programming for individual or small-group instruction. Students often did not
demonstrate increased achievement in segregated special classes; moving between
classes for mainstream or pull-out instruction disrupted the learning process and
seemed to contribute to a student's perception of not fully belonging to the classroom (Brandl, 1983; Lipsky & Gartner, 1992; Tindal, 1985).

From Will's 1986 article evolved a proposal called the general education initiative (GEI) (Wang et al., 1988). The GEI proposed a merger of the different professions serving regular and special education in order to develop a partnership
focused on accommodating the diverse needs of students in the regular classroom.
Rather than use labels, all children would be considered different in their learning
abilities and capable of learning in most normative environments. By 1988, the GEI
had become the regular education initiative (REI), and the proposal to collaborate

with regular educators was considered to be the first major change in special education policy since PL 94-142 (Jenkins, Pious, & Jewell, 1990; McKinney & Hocutt, 1988).

While acknowledging problems with the current system, critics of the REI ad-
vocated a more cautious approach to change rather than adopting a full-scale overhaul of the current dual system. It is important to note that "The REI debate has
largely taken place among researchers and scholars who are affiliated in special
education departments at universities and colleges. Regular educators, for the most
part, have had an extremely limited role in these discussions" (Davis, 1989, p. 441).
In fact, one study found that both regular and special educators in the field were
generally satisfied with the current special education service delivery system
(Semmel, Abernathy, Butera, & Lesar, 1991).

In spite of an apparent lack of consensus among educators regarding the REI,
support is growing for the concept of **inclusion**, which holds that children with
disabilities should be placed first in a regular classroom, with a program "strength-
ened and supported by an infusion of specially trained personnel and other appropriate supportive practices according to the individual needs of the child" (Council
for Exceptional Children, 1993). This view does not match current practice, which
more often places a child with disabilities first in a "special ed" setting, and then
gradually mainstreams him or her, first to nonacademic activities such as lunch or
art, then to academic activities. Supporters of inclusion feel that current practice is
restrictive and should be considered only after a fully inclusive approach has been
tried and found to be ineffective (Lipsky & Gartner, 1992; Wang, Peverly, & Randolph, 1984). In other words, supporters of inclusion feel that the starting point for
considering the full continuum of alternative placements should be the regular
classroom, rather than at the other end (see Figure 2.6). A recent decision by the
Supreme Court supports this position (*Oberti v. Clementon School District, 1993*).

The concept of inclusion is not without its dissenters. For example, The National Joint Committee on Learning Disabilities (1993) published a statement that
reaffirmed the appropriateness of a continuum of services in order to provide an
individualized program for each student with a disability, and stressed that the inclusive placement can be a violation of students' rights to an appropriate education.
Fuchs and Fuchs (1994) have also commented on this issue. Other researchers and
educators have also supported this position (e.g., Kaufmann, Gerber, & Semmel,
1988; Learning Disabilities Association, 1993; Lieberman, 1992).

Research has been conducted that supports the effectiveness of inclusive classroom placements (e.g., Gent & Mulhauser, 1988; Wang et al., 1984). Advocates for
inclusion have stated that even without empirical evidence, inclusion is the moral
or right thing to do; or, more simply, a conviction that "it is better to be with your
peers than apart from them" (Zettel & Ballard, 1982, p. 17). The best placement for
students with disabilities is just one of many areas in which educational audiologists can conduct needed field research.

National Educational Reform

A renewed national interest in the public educational system has accompanied the
changes in special education discussed above. Sparked by the publication of a report called *A Nation At Risk* (National Commission on Excellence in Education,
1983), intense discussion has focused on the inadequacy of the present educational

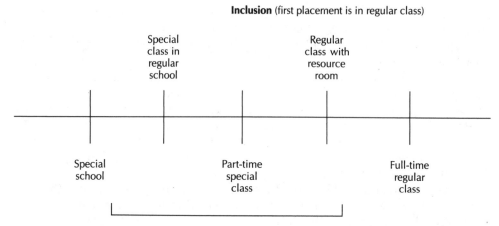

Figure 2.6.   Inclusion or mainstreaming: Where to first place a child with disabilities?

system, and on the poor preparation of students to compete in the global economy. Goals have been set to address these concerns (Peters-Johnson, 1993; U.S. Department of Education, 1994) and are included in Table 2.1.

These goals, however, may be perceived as representing a conflict between the values of excellence and equity. At the same time that special educators are calling for access to the regular education curriculum, with accommodations for students with disabilities, regular education teachers are being asked to make educational excellence their goal. Many teachers feel that the two interests are at odds; that accommodating the needs of a student with disabilities conflicts with the expectations for high performance for the class.

Other waves of school reform have attempted to address educational concerns by attempting to define "effective schools"; by changing the organization of schools to site-based management, whereby teachers, rather than school boards, make curricular and related decisions; by requiring greater teacher competencies; and by considering the parents' choice of schools through a voucher system (Audette & Algozzine, 1992; Ysseldyke, Algozzine, & Thurlow, 1992). Reform efforts such as these keep educators and related support staff continually challenged to rethink the ways in which the educational process should be conducted.

IMPACT OF EDUCATIONAL REFORMS ON LEARNERS WITH HI

The "Communication Debate"

How do issues such as those discussed in the previous section affect students with hearing impairment? Before we consider this question, first it is important to know that these current issues in regular and special education interact with a long-term controversy—in fact, one of the oldest debates in the field of education. The controversy concerns the best way to teach a child with hearing impairment. The "communication debate" regarding the method of education of children with hearing impairment is briefly examined.

Table 2.1. Goals 2000, Educate America Act

1. All children will start school ready to learn.
2. The high school graduation rate will be 90%.
3. Students will demonstrate competencies in core subjects in 4th, 8th, and 12th grades.
4. The United States will be first in the world in the fields of science and math.
5. Every adult will be literate and able to compete in the marketplace.
6. Every school will be safe, disciplined, and free of drugs.

These points summarize key aspects of *Goals 2000, Educate America Act* (U.S. Department of Education, 1994).

The communication debate focuses primarily on children who are deaf and considers the modality of language instruction. Two camps have been identified: promoters of either the **oral/aural approach** or the **manual approach**. Other sources provide in-depth coverage on this topic (see Recommended Readings at the end of this chapter); for our purposes, it is sufficient to highlight the main arguments of each approach.

Oral/Aural Approach   This method advocates an emphasis on speech communication, and optimal use of amplified residual hearing, while discouraging virtually any use of manual communication. This approach was espoused by Alexander Graham Bell (1847–1922) who, in addition to his other accomplishments, was a skilled speech teacher. Supporters of the oral/aural approach feel that "with spoken language, opportunities for higher education are less restricted, a more extensive range of careers is open, and there is greater employment security. Those who can talk also face fewer limitations in the personal and social aspects of their lives" (Ling, 1990, p. 9).

Manual Approach   The manual approach takes the position that the struggle to learn speech skills by an individual with a profound hearing impairment may be futile at worst, and at best be a time-consuming exercise that interferes with or impedes other learning. Supporters of manual communication feel it is more culturally appropriate for deaf children to develop language through a manual system. Several manual systems have been developed; a few are presented here.

American Sign Language (ASL)   ASL is recognized as a legitimate language and has a rich lexicon and a fully developed linguistic structure. It has been in existence for over 200 years and has the unique characteristic of being learned from deaf peers rather than from hearing family members (Hoffmeister, 1990). Because fewer than 10% of deaf children are born of deaf parents, ASL is typically learned from deaf friends rather than from hearing parents. In spite of this limited access to ASL, supporters feel that it should be *the* language of instruction for all children who are deaf.

Signed Exact English (SEE)   While ASL has evolved as a natural language, SEE is a sign system created in the 1960s to address concerns regarding low reading and writing skills. SEE uses manual markers (e.g., for plurality and tense) that correspond directly to the structures of the English language (Gustason, 1990).

Pidgin Sign   Pidgin sign is a "contact language . . . a result of something that occurs when two groups of people need or desire to communicate" (Luetke-Stahlman & Luckner, 1991, p. 10). Like other pidgin languages, pidgin sign combines elements of different languages, in this case a manual and a spoken language. In an exchange, a hearing person communicating with pidgin sign is likely to omit articles such as "the" or "a/an" or the "ing" ending of verbs as in ASL. The word order, however, is almost identical to spoken English.

Total Communication (TC)   TC incorporates the use of many systems of communication: sign language, speech and speechreading, amplified residual hearing, gestures, facial expressions, and body language. TC was introduced in the late 1960s and is sometimes called simultaneous communication. When using TC, a speaker's rate is often slower than that in typical conversation (Hyde & Powers, 1991). The attempt to "speak and sign simultaneously appears to be psychologically and physically overwhelming. Under such difficult conditions, one or both parts of the signal will deteriorate" (Johnson, Liddell, & Erting, 1989, p. 5).

Cued Speech   Also developed in the 1960s, cued speech is not a language, but rather is a visual support to facilitate speechreading. Hand shapes made close to the face represent phonemes, which helps the speechreader discriminate between similar phonemes. For example, the phonemes /k/ and /g/ require distinct handshapes, and thus provide the speechreader with a visual cue to the voiced or non-voiced component of the phonemes (Kipila & Williams-Scott, 1990).

Use of Communication Systems in the U.S.

How are all these different systems actually used across the U.S.? Luetke-Stahlman and Luckner (1991) report that 67% of elementary and secondary students are instructed in some sort of sign, although only 1% are instructed in ASL; 33% are instructed in an oral/aural approach; and 1% receive instruction with cued speech.

It should be noted that forms of sign are also used frequently with students who are hard of hearing and with students with autism and mental retardation as an alternative or supplemental method of communication and instruction (Karlan, 1990).

In spite of the very low usage of ASL in the classroom, the Commission on the Education of the Deaf (1988) supported a bilingual/bicultural approach to instruction for children who are deaf. This approach advocates that ASL or, at the least, a pidgin sign language be taught as the child's first language, and written English taught as a second language (Stewart & Akamatsu, 1988).

The Least Restrictive Environment for a Child with HI

Now that we have considered the range of approaches to **how** an individual with HI is taught, we are ready to consider the aspects of the environment, or **where** the individual receives instruction. The effects of legislation and educational reforms have significantly reshaped the educational environment. We now consider the components discussed previously as they affect the education of a child with HI.

As mentioned in the previous section, least restrictive environment (LRE) for all students is currently interpreted by supporters of inclusion to be the regular education classroom, with appropriate support services as needed. For a child with a hearing impairment, this interpretation may not be appropriate. A child with mild-to-moderately severe HI may succeed in such an environment, if full support is provided to address the variety of language and listening needs that can impede learning. Because so much learning is language-based, it is impossible to generalize on the appropriate environment for individuals who are hard of hearing.

The appropriate environment becomes a more complicated issue for the child who is deaf. The Commission on the Education of the Deaf (1988) held that placement of a deaf child in a regular classroom, even with an interpreter, may be more restrictive than placement in a fully signing environment with deaf peers. Because of communication difficulties, a deaf child may experience unique academic, social, and emotional complications in the regular classroom. In that respect, the regular classroom is **not** the LRE for a deaf child: "Placing a deaf child in the regular classroom without the language needed to function as a participant seriously impedes, if not precludes, the child from receiving any worthwhile education in the class" (p. 33). Data from a recent study support this view by demonstrating significant academic gains among deaf students in the fully signing environment of a residential school, but little academic gain among deaf students in mainstream settings (Braden, Maller, & Paquin, 1993).

The U.S. Department of Education in 1992 issued "policy guidance" to states and school districts (*Federal Register*, October 30, 1992, 57(211), pp. 49274–49276) regarding the LRE for children with severe-to-profound hearing impairment. Noting that "the communicative nature of the disability is inherently isolating" (p. 49274), the Department of Education advised that the LRE provisions of the Individuals with Disabilities Education Act (IDEA) (PL 101-476) may be incorrectly interpreted for children who are deaf. The following factors are of paramount importance when determining the LRE for a child who is deaf:

1. Communication needs and the child's and family's preferred mode of communication
2. Linguistic needs
3. Severity of hearing impairment and potential for using residual hearing
4. Academic level
5. Social, emotional, and cultural needs of the child, including opportunities for peer interactions and communications

The policy guidance furthermore stressed that a range of alternative placements, including special schools or centers, must be made available:

> Any setting which does not meet the communication and related needs of a child who is deaf, and therefore does not allow for the provision of FAPE, cannot be considered the LRE for that child. The provision of FAPE is paramount, and the individual placement determination about LRE is to be considered within the context of FAPE. (p. 49275)

The federal Department of Education is reminding educators that, regardless of current trends and philosophies, IDEA is specific about what constitutes LRE. The concept of "appropriate" involves more than following a particular trend in one direction or another. No interpretation of LRE is meant to override the provision of an appropriate education (Domico, 1989).

THE EDUCATIONAL AUDIOLOGIST AND EDUCATIONAL REFORM

What is the role of the educational audiologist in educational reform? We have looked at the changes that have occurred in special education so far in its short history; we can be sure there will be more changes. Some educational trends may be appropriate to the needs of learners with hearing impairment; some may include components that can actually be detrimental to optimal learning for learners with HI. It is the responsibility of the educational audiologist to be informed about educational reforms and to challenge those who do not support the learning environment of students who are deaf and hard of hearing.

As an advocate for learners with HI, the educational audiologist has a responsibility to take a leadership role in the development of educational reforms (Davila, 1991). Consider some of the factors that Blair and Berg (1982) identified as compromising the learning environment:

1. Underdeveloped listening skills
2. Excessive noise levels and reverberation
3. Inappropriate lighting levels and visual distractions
4. Vocabulary and curriculum beyond a child's abilities
5. Psychosocial difficulties resulting from communication breakdowns

These factors of the learning environment are areas in which educational audiologists have unique expertise, and these factors can affect the learning conditions for all students, not just those with hearing impairment.

Blair (1986) wrote, "The educational audiologist has the responsibility for managing the total spectrum of services for the hearing impaired youngster" (p. 33). It is imperative that an additional component be included in the spectrum of services: monitoring and proactive participation in the philosophical and programmatic changes occurring in both special and regular education.

Learning the Language

Review the following concepts from this chapter and discuss with a colleague.

- People-first language
- FAPE
- LRE
- Mainstreaming
- Full inclusion
- IEP
- Due process
- Normalization
- REI
- Oral/aural versus manual approaches
- Bicultural/bilingual approach

Educational Audiology in Action
Suggested Learning Activities

Project 1. Visit a speech-language pathologist in a school setting who serves at least one student with hearing impairment. While maintaining student confidentiality, find out:

- Does the child demonstrate speech and language deficits? What kinds?
- What are the educational ramifications of these deficits? That is, how do these deficits affect reading, writing, and math development?
- What are the child's IEP goals?
- What is the child's educational placement?
- Does the SLP serve the child in class or in a pull-out program? If in class, what training did he or she receive to work effectively in this setting?

Project 2. Interview a teacher who has expertise in the education of children with hearing impairment. Inquire about the following:

- Find out the approach that the teacher uses in language instruction (i.e., TC, oral/aural, cued speech).
- What are the teacher's opinions regarding the approaches **not** used in the classroom?
- Are the teacher's practices the same as when he or she completed his or her training? If not, what practices have changed and how?
- Find out if there is an organization for educators with a specialty in hearing impairment in your state. If so, ask for membership information and contact the organization to determine the types of concerns it addresses.

Project 3. Interview a regular education teacher to find out:

- What has been his or her experience in teaching children with disabilities in regular class settings?
- How did the teacher regard the experience? Did the teacher feel that he or she received adequate support? Did the student do well in this environment?
- What are the teacher's feelings about the regular education initiative?

Resources

For information regarding issues in special education, contact:

> Council for Exceptional Children
> 1920 Association Drive
> Reston, VA 22091-1589
> (703) 264-9410

A student membership to CEC includes subscriptions to *Exceptional Children* and *TEACHING Exceptional Children* and reduced fees to national and state-level conferences. Membership in the CEC provides educational audiologists with valuable information regarding issues in regular and special education that directly and indirectly affect learners with HI. CEC has a special interest group relevant to educational audiologists (the Division for Children with Communicative Disorders), which publishes a monograph twice a year.

For information regarding the oral/aural communication approach in education, contact:

> Alexander Graham Bell Association for the Deaf, Inc.
> 3417 Volta Place NW
> Washington, DC 20007-2778
> (202) 337-5220 (Voice/TDD)

Members of the A.G. Bell Association receive seven issues of *Volta Review* each year.

For information regarding cued speech, contact:

> National Cued Speech Association
> 1615-B Oberlin Road
> P.O. Box 31345
> Raleigh, NC 27622
> (919) 828-1218 (Voice/TDD)

For information regarding the bilingual/bicultural approach to the education of children who are deaf, contact:

> National Information Center on Deafness
> Gallaudet University
> 800 Florida Avenue, NE
> Washington, DC 20002
> (202) 651-5051 (voice)
> (202) 651-5052 (text telephone)

Recommended Readings

Biklen, D. (1992). *Schooling without labels: Parents, educators, and inclusive education*. Philadelphia: Temple University Press.

The author describes the social movement of inclusion and integration and provides the perspectives of several families to illustrate how the full integration of their children with disabilities into their own family lives can serve as a model for education.

Bornstein, H. (Ed.). (1990). *Manual communication: Implications for education*. Washington, DC: Gallaudet University Press.

Contributing authors provide comprehensive histories and descriptions of the various sign systems and languages used in the United States. ASL, SEE, cued speech, and other systems are included. All chapters attempt to address the concerns regarding the low reading and writing levels observed among many students with hearing impairment.

Leutke-Stahlman, B., & Luckner, J. (1990). *Effectively educating students with hearing impairments*. New York: Longman.

This text is designed for both students and practitioners and provides information on all aspects of education for learners with hearing impairment. The authors advocate a bilingual/bicultural approach to education. Theory and technical support are provided in such areas as speech and language development, communication skills, writing, math, and behavior management. The student of educational audiology will want to have a working familiarity with the content of this text in order to understand the concerns of educators of learners with HI.

Winefield, R. (1987). *Never the twain shall meet: Bell, Gallaudet and the communications debate*. Washington, DC: Gallaudet University Press.

The author provides an objective review of the issues between the oral/aural approach and the manual approach by presenting an historical account of the beginnings of the communication debate and its long-term ramifications. A discussion of the family backgrounds and influences upon Alexander Graham Bell and Edward Minor Gallaudet gives the reader insight into the emotional aspects of this controversy.

References

American Speech-Language-Hearing Association. (1993). Guidelines for audiology services in the schools. *Asha, 35*(Suppl. 10), 24–32.

Americans with Disabilities Act of 1990 (ADA), PL 101-336. (July 26, 1990). Title 42, U.S.C. 12101 et seq: *U.S. Statutes at Large, 104,* 327–378.

Anderson, K., & Matkin, N. (1991). Relationship of degree of loss to psychosocial and educational needs. *Educational Audiology Newsletter, 8*(2), 11–12.

Anderson-Inman, L. (1987). Consistency of performance across classrooms: Instructional materials versus settings as influencing variables. *Journal of Special Education, 21,* 9–29.

Antia, S., & Kreimeyer, K. (1992). Social competence intervention for young children with hearing impairments. In S. Odom, S. McConnell, & M. McElroy (Eds.), *Social competence of young children with disabilities: Issues and strategies for intervention* (pp. 135–164). Baltimore: Paul H. Brookes Publishing Co.

Audette, B., & Algozzine, B. (1992). FAPE for all students: Total quality and the transformation of American public schools. *Remedial and Special Education, 13*(6), 8–18.

Berg, F. (1986). Characteristics of the target population. In F. Berg, J. Blair, J. Viehweg, & A. Wilson-Vlotman, *Educational audiology for the hard of hearing child* (pp. 1–24). Orlando, FL: Grune & Stratton.

Biklen, D. (1992). *Schooling without labels: Parents, educators, and inclusive education.* Philadelphia: Temple University Press.

Blair, J., & Berg, F. (1982). Problems and needs of hard of hearing students and a model for the delivery of services to the schools. *Asha, 24,* 541–546.

Blair, J. (1986). Services needed. In F. Berg, J. Blair, J. Viehweg, & A. Wilson-Vlotman, *Educational audiology for the hard of hearing child* (pp. 25–35). Orlando, FL: Grune & Stratton.

Boothroyd, A. (1982). *Hearing impairments in young children.* Englewood Cliffs, NJ: Prentice Hall.

Braden, J., Maller, S., & Paquin, M. (1993). The effects of residential v. day placement in the performance IQ of children with hearing impairment. *Journal of Special Education, 26*(4), 423–433.

Brandl, J. (1983). The effectiveness of special education: A survey. *Policy Study Review, 2,* 65–70.

Brown v. Board of Education, 347 US 483 (1954).

Commission on Education of the Deaf. (1988). *Toward equality: Education of the deaf.* Washington, DC: U.S. Government Printing Office.

Cooper, R., & Rosenstein, J. (1966). Language acquisition of deaf children. *Volta Review, 68,* 58–67.

Council for Exceptional Children (1993). CEC policy on inclusive schools and community settings. *TEACHING/Exceptional Children, 25,* 4(Suppl.).

Davila, R. (1991). America 2000: A challenging opportunity for special educators. *Teaching Exceptional Children, 24*(1), 5.

Davis, J., & Blasdell, R. (1975). Perceptual strategies employed by normal and hearing impaired children in the comprehension of sentences containing relative clauses. *Journal of Speech and Hearing Research, 18,* 281–295.

Davis, J., Elfenbein, J., Schum, R., & Bentler, R. (1986). Effects of mild and moderate hearing impairments on language, educational and psychosocial behavior of children. *Journal of Speech and Hearing Disorders, 51,* 53–62.

Davis, J., Shepard, N., Stelmachowicz, P., & Gorga, M. (1981). Characteristics of hearing impaired children in the public schools: Part I. Psycho-educational data. *Journal of Speech and Hearing Disorders, 46,* 130–137.

Davis, W. (1989). The Regular Education Initiative debate: Its promises and problems. *Exceptional Children, 55,* 440–446.

Dobie, R., & Berlin, C. (1979). Influence of otitis media on hearing and development. *Annals of Otology, Rhinology, and Laryngology, 88,* Suppl. 60, 48–53.

Domico, W. (1989). The 1986 Education of the Handicapped Act and judicial decisions relating to the child who is hearing impaired. *Asha, 31*(9), 91–95.

Education for All Handicapped Children Act of 1975, PL 94-142. (August 23, 1977). Title 20, U.S.C. 1401 et seq: *U.S. Statutes at Large, 89,* 773–796.

Education of the Handicapped Act Amendments of 1986, PL 99-457. (October 8, 1986). Title 20, U.S.C. 1400 et seq: *U.S. Statutes at Large, 100,* 1145–1177.

Federal Register, October 30, 1992, *57*(211), pp. 49274–49276.

Flexer, C., Wray, D., & Ireland, J. (1989). Preferential seating is NOT enough: Issues in classroom management of hearing-impaired students. *Language, Speech, and Hearing Services in School, 20,* 11–21.

Fuchs, D., & Fuchs, L. (1984). Inclusive schools movement and the radicalization of special education reform. *Exceptional Children, 60*(9), 294–309.

Gent, P., & Mulhauser, M. (1988). Public integration of students with handicaps: Where it's been, where it's going, and how it's getting there. *Journal of The Association for Persons with Severe Handicaps, 13,* 188–196.

Grant, J. (1987). *The hearing impaired child: Birth to six.* Boston: College-Hill Press.

Groht, M. (1958). *Natural language for deaf children.* Washington, DC: Alexander Graham Bell Association.

Gustason, G. (1990). Signing exact English. In H. Bornstein (Ed.), *Manual communication: Implications for education* (pp. 108–127). Washington, DC: Gallaudet University.

Hoffmeister, R. (1990). ASL and its implications for education. In H. Bornstein (Ed.), *Manual communication: Implications for education* (pp. 81–107). Washington, DC: Gallaudet University.

Huffman, N. (1991). Least restrictive environment. *Asha, 33*(6), 43–45.

Hyde, M., & Powers, D. (1991). Teachers use simultaneous communication: Effects on the signed and spoken components. *American Annals of the Deaf, 136,* 381–387.

Individuals with Disabilities Education Act of 1990 (IDEA), PL 101-476. (October 30, 1990). Title 20, U.S.C. 1400 et seq: *U.S. Statutes at Large, 104,* 1103–1151.

Jenkins, J., Pious, C., & Jewell, M. (1990). Special education and the Regular Education Initiative: Basic assumptions. *Exceptional Children, 56,* 479–491.

Jensema, C. (1975). *The relationship between academic achievement and the demographic characteristics of hearing impaired children and youth.* Washington, DC: Office of Demographic Studies, Gallaudet College, Series R, No. 2.

Johnson, R., Liddell, S., & Erting, C. (1989). *Unlocking the curriculum: Principles for achieving access in deaf education.* Washington, DC: Gallaudet University.

Karlan, G. (1990). Manual communication with those who can hear. In H. Bornstein (Ed.), *Manual communication: Implications for education* (pp. 151–185). Washington, DC: Gallaudet University.

Kaufmann, J., Gerber, M., & Semmel, M. (1988). Arguable assumptions underlying the Regular Education Initiative. *Journal of Learning Disabilities, 21,* 6–11.

Kipila, E., & Williams-Scott, B. (1990). Cued speech. In H. Bornstein (Ed.), *Manual communication: Implications for education* (pp. 139–150). Washington, DC: Gallaudet University.

Kluwin, T., & Kelly, A. (1993). Implementing a successful writing program in public schools for students who are deaf. *Exceptional Children, 59,* 41–53.

Kodman, F. (1963). Education status of hard of hearing children in the classroom. *Journal of Speech and Hearing Disorders, 28,* 297–299.

Learning Disabilities Association. (1993). *Position paper on full inclusion of all students with learning disabilities in the regular education classroom.* Pittsburgh: Author.

Leinhardt, G., & Palley, A. (1982). Restrictive educational settings: Exile or haven? *Review of Educational Research, 52,* 557–578.

Levitt, H., & McGarr, N. (1988). Speech and language development in hearing impaired children. In F. Bess (Ed.), *Hearing impairment in children* (pp. 375–388). Parkton, MD: York Press.

Lieberman, L. (1992). Preserving special education . . . for those who need it. In W. Stainback & S. Stainback (Eds.), *Controversial issues confronting special education: Divergent perspectives* (pp. 13–25). Newton, MA: Allyn & Bacon.

Ling, D. (1976). *Speech and the hearing impaired child.* Washington, DC: Alexander Graham Bell Association.

Ling, D. (1990). Advances underlying spoken language development: A century of building on Bell. *Volta Review, 92*(4), 8–20.

Lipsky, D., & Gartner, A. (1992). Achieving full inclusion: Placing the student at the center of educational reform. In W. Stainback & S. Stainback (Eds.), *Controversial issues confronting special education: Divergent perspectives* (pp. 3–12). Newton, MA: Allyn & Bacon.

Luetke-Stahlman, P., & Luckner, J. (1991). *Effectively educating students with hearing impairments.* New York: Longman.

Matkin, N. (1988). The role of hearing in speech development. In J. Kavanaugh (Ed.), *Otitis media and child development* (pp. 311). Parkton, MD: York Press.

McClure, W. (1966). Current problems and trends in the education of the deaf. *Deaf American, 31,* 8–14.

McConnell, F. (1984). Legislative issues in the habilitation of the hearing impaired. In J. Jerger (Ed.), *Pediatric audiology* (pp. 203–224). San Diego: College-Hill Press.

McKinney, J., & Hocutt, A. (1988). The need for policy analysis in evaluating the regular education initiative. *Journal of Learning Disorders, 21*(1), 12–18.

National Commission on Excellence in Education. (1983). *A nation at risk: An imperative for educational reform.* Washington, DC: U.S. Department of Education.

National Joint Committee on Learning Disabilities. (1993). Reaction to "full inclusion": A reaffirmation of the right of students with learning disabilities to a continuum of services. *Asha, 35*(11), 63.

Oberti v. Board of Education of the Borough of Clementon School District, 995 F. 2d. 1204 (3rd Cir, 1993).

Oyler, R., Oyler, A., & Matkin, N. (1988). Unilateral hearing loss: Demographics and educational impact. *Language, Speech, and Hearing Services in Schools, 19*(2), 201–209.

Padden, C., & Humphries, T. (1988). *Deaf in America: Voices in a culture.* Cambridge, MA: Harvard University Press.

Peters-Johnson, C. (1993). Riley announces "Goals 2000: Educate America Act." *Language, Speech, and Hearing Services in Schools, 24*(4), 249.

Quigley, S., & Power, D. (1972). *The development of syntactic structures in the language of deaf children.* Urbana, IL: Institute for Research on Exceptional Children, University of Illinois.

Quigley, S., & Thomure, F. (1968). *Some effects of hearing impairment upon school performance.* Springfield, IL: Division of Special Education Services, Department of Education.

Ross, M. (1982). *Hard of hearing children in regular schools.* Englewood Cliffs, NJ: Prentice Hall.

Schattman, R., & Benay, J. (1992). Inclusive practices transform special education in the 1990s. *The School Administrator, 49*(2), 8–12.

Schildroth, A., & Hotto, S. (1993). Annual survey of hearing-impaired children and youth: 1991-92 school year. *American Annals of the Deaf, 138,* 163–168.

Schmidt, P. (1968). Language acquisition for the deaf. *Volta Review, 68,* 85–105; 123.

Semmel, M., Abernathy, T., Butera, G., & Lesar, S. (1991). Teacher perceptions of the Regular Education Initiative. *Exceptional Children, 58,* 9–24.

Semmel, M., Gottlieb, J., & Robinson, H. (1979). Mainstreaming: Perspectives on educating handicapped children in the public schools. In D. Berliner (Ed.), *Review of research in education* (pp. 223–279). Washington, DC: American Educational Research Association.

Shames, E., & Wiig, E. (1982). *Human communication disorders.* Columbus, OH: Charles E. Merrill.

Shepard, N., Davis, J., Gorga, M., & Stelmachowicz, P. (1981). Characteristics of hearing-impaired children in the public schools: Part 1. Demographic data. *Journal of Speech and Hearing Disorders, 46,* 123–129.

Stewart, D., & Akamatsu, T. (1988). The coming of age of American Sign Language. *Anthropology and Education Quarterly, 19,* 225–252.

Taylor, S. (1988). Caught in the continuum: A critical analysis of the principle of the least restrictive environment. *Journal of The Association for Persons with Severe Handicaps, 13*, 41–53.

Tindal, G. (1985). Investigating the effectiveness of special education: An analysis of methodology. *Journal of Learning Disabilities, 18*(2), 102–112.

U.S. Department of Education. (1994). *Goals 2000: Educate America Act.* Washington, DC: Author.

Vergason, G., & Anderegg, M. (1992). Preserving the LRE. In W. Stainback & S. Stainback (Eds.), *Controversial issues confronting special education: Divergent perspectives* (pp. 45–54). Newton, MA: Allyn & Bacon.

Vernon, M., & Andrews, J. (1990). *The psychology of deafness: Understanding deaf and hard of hearing people.* New York: Longman.

Wang, M., Peverly, S., & Randolph, R. (1984). An investigation of the implementation and effects of a full-time mainstreaming program. *Remedial and Special Education, 5*(6), 21–32.

Wang, M., Reynolds, M., & Walberg, H. (1988). Integrating the children in the second system. *Phi Delta Kappa, 70*, 248–251.

Wilcox, J., & Tobin, H. (1974). Linguistic performance of hard of hearing and normal hearing children. *Journal of Speech and Hearing Research, 17*, 286–293.

Will, M. (1986). Educating children with learning problems: A shared responsibility. *Exceptional Children, 52*, 411–415.

Wolfensberger, W. (1972). *The principle of normalization in human services.* Toronto, Ontario, Canada: National Institute on Mental Retardation.

Young, D., & McConnell, F. (1957). Retardation of vocabulary development in hard of hearing children. *Exceptional Children, 23*, 368–370.

Ysseldyke, J., Algozzine, B., & Thurlow, M. (1992). *Critical issues in special education and remedial education* (2nd ed.). Boston: Houghton Mifflin.

Zettel, J., & Ballard, J. (1982). The Education for All Handicapped Children Act of 1975 (PL 94-142): Its history, origins, and concepts. In J. Ballard, B. Ramirez, & F. Weintraub (Eds.), *Special education in America: Its legal and governmental foundations* (pp. 10–22). Reston, VA: Council for Exceptional Children.

3

Educational Audiology

Beyond the Clinical Role

AUDIOLOGISTS IN SCHOOL SETTINGS FIND that in order to best serve students with HI, they must expand their scope of practice to include new responsibilities, beyond traditional diagnostics and aural rehabilitation. As a school professional, the audiologist not only provides audiological services, but also participates in the total educational process, along with students and other staff. Full participation in the educational process requires that the audiologist understand the demands of the many roles that he or she assumes when working in schools. This chapter describes some of these roles and responsibilities.

An educational audiologist may need to be:

- An educator
- A community liaison
- A public relations expert
- A service coordinator
- A supervisor

This is not to be considered an exhaustive list, but these positions are representative of the experiences of practitioners in the field.

THE AUDIOLOGIST AS EDUCATOR

It may be a surprise to an audiologist new to the educational workplace to learn just how much of his or her time is devoted to educational activities. The most obvious example of the audiologist as educator is as the provider of aural (re)habilitation (i.e., conventional speechreading and auditory training instruction). However, the audiologist also initiates ongoing efforts throughout the year to inform teachers, parents, and community members of technologies and strategies that can greatly support the academic success of a student with HI. The following section describes several ways in which the audiologist assumes the responsibilities of an educator to each of the constituencies mentioned above.

Teaching Students

As an educator of students, audiologists may provide direct and indirect educational services to students with HI. Direct services are those that are provided

45

through personal contact; indirect services are those provided by others who have received training from the audiologist.

Direct Services   Providing direct educational services for students is similar to providing aural rehabilitation services in clinical settings. Direct educational services may involve teaching listening skills and speechreading. Direct services can also involve providing informational or content counseling in which the audiologist provides age-appropriate information to students that is specific to their hearing impairment, such as how to interpret their audiograms, or how to operate their hearing aids. (See Chapter 7 for a description of the differences between informational counseling and social/emotional counseling.) These direct services may be provided in a pull-out program or in a classroom.

Indirect Services   Monitoring student progress by consulting with the student's classroom teachers is an example of a service provided **indirectly** to the student. Monitoring requires frequent contact with teachers and other service providers via telephone calls, brief monthly checklists or questionnaires, visits, or by other procedures that encourage open communication among professionals regarding student performance and success. A district or state may develop a continuum of monitoring services (e.g., Yoshinaga-Itano & Ruberry, 1992). If a student is performing at grade level, he or she may be placed on a "watch list," which indicates that minimal contact with a classroom teacher is needed, perhaps once a semester. Students who experience difficulties in class may require more support services from professionals; as difficulties arise, regular consultations with the student's teacher may be a more appropriate way to monitor his or her progress. Consultation involves a greater time commitment from professionals to share information. Through consultation, the educational audiologist can learn teachers' concerns, provide insight into the learning difficulties concomitant with hearing impairment, and develop strategies that can assist the teacher and the student in addressing their concerns.

By definition, consultation is a one-to-one approach to solving problems. If the same concerns are shared by a number of teachers, however, it may be more efficient to share information with a group through a workshop or in-service. The next section provides some direction in the development of in-service training to colleagues in the schools.

Teaching Teachers and Staff

Advertising Your Services   Often, school professionals do not know the extent of expertise that the educational audiologist can share with them. In order to make this expertise known, the educational audiologist must seek to promote and advertise the benefits of his or her skills or knowledge. An effective strategy is to request time (perhaps 15 minutes) to address a school staff meeting. Begin your address with some remarks regarding the importance of supporting the academic success of students with all degrees of hearing impairment, and then offer to provide more indepth information as needed. Ask staff members to: 1) examine a list or menu of topics relevant to learners with HI (see Figure 3.1), and 2) indicate the topics on which they would like more information. After collecting and reviewing the responses from colleagues, the educational audiologist knows what topics to develop for a workshop, and which staff members to invite. This process is a form

---

Menu of In-Service Topics

How can we help students with special needs and students at risk? Possible topics:

____ Effects of hearing impairment on learning
____ How hearing aids work
____ Monitoring hearing aid use and troubleshooting problems
____ Classroom acoustics
____ Classroom amplification systems (FM, sound field)
____ Teaching strategies for students with HI
____ Speechreading
____ Developing listening skills
____ Other _____

Your name _____Position _____
Phone number at school _____Best time to call _____
Fax _____E-mail _____

Figure 3.1. Menu of topics for in-service training of school staff about audiological services.

of "needs assessment" to help others identify and prioritize particular interests and to ensure that those who attend your workshop are genuinely motivated to learn something new to help their students and for their professional growth (Evans, 1986).

When an educational audiologist shares information with colleagues in a workshop or in-service, he or she does more than simply transmit information from one professional to another. The exchanges, interactions, and relationships that occur during the in-service should also give the participants a sense of the audiologist's commitment to provide support throughout the school year (Ross, 1991; Ross, Brackett, & Maxon, 1991).

Developing In-Service Training Conducting an in-service or workshop for colleagues in the workplace means teaching adults, a process that differs considerably from teaching children. A large body of research on adult learning indicates that adults learn differently from children, and use different strategies and operate from different motivations than children (Hillkirk, Tome, & Wendress, 1989; Knowles, 1984; Moore, 1988; Zemke & Zemke, 1988). Adults prefer learning experiences to be problem-centered, meaningful, and applicable to an immediate concern. Learning experiences are more effective for adult learners when a group-project format is used rather than a classroom or lecture format. (See Chapter 8 for more information about adult learners.)

The following suggestions have proved effective in developing an in-service or workshop for adults:

- Use a collaborative approach. Remind the participants that they share a common interest in the current topic, as identified by the earlier needs assessment. Throughout the in-service, consider activities that promote participation and collegial problem-solving.
- Foster a climate of respect and social support. Arrange chairs in a circle or other casual format that promotes interaction, rather than in formal classroom-style rows.
- Integrate new information with past experiences and knowledge, and provide frequent summarizations.

- Use materials that help learners to organize and to relate new information to what they already know.
- Conclude with an exercise or activity that requires participants to **reflect** upon what he or she has learned in the in-service. For example, ask for written responses to questions such as, "Based on this new information, what should I do to support the needs of my student(s) with HI?"

Figure 3.2 is an example of materials that were developed for an in-service for professional colleagues. In this example, the purpose of the in-service is to explain the value and use of visual cues in the classroom. Note that the suggestions are of a practical, "how-to" nature and are based on sound aural rehabilitation procedures without devoting too much time to theory. Assessing one's own speechreading skills with others or with a television and watching one's speech in a mirror are activities that reinforce speechreading concepts. Discussion of the use of other visual cues and teaching strategies can often generate solutions by teachers to individual student concerns observed in a particular classroom setting.

In the sample in-service handout presented in Figure 3.2, related information was included in addition to information about optimizing the use of visual cues. Related teaching strategies were an appropriate supplement to the original topic because these can contribute to the student's success and provide teachers with pertinent information about teaching learners with HI. It is important to keep the handout brief and directly related to the points covered in the in-service session, because handouts often are not referred to again. Handouts should be supplemented with learning exercises, hands-on demonstrations, and other experiential activities.

Keep in mind that teachers face ever-increasing challenges to accommodate children's individual abilities. These challenges alone are a source of stress and are compounded if information is provided that conflicts with other expectations. For example, a few years ago, much research focused on examining strategies that seemed to be most effective in teaching. This was called the "effective schools movement," and data indicated that effective instruction occurred when maximum classroom time was spent actively engaged in learning tasks, presented by direct instruction at a brisk pace (Heron & Harris, 1987). However, a suggested accommodation to the needs of a learner with HI has been to **slow the pace** of instruction and to take time to routinely rephrase and summarize instruction (Bunch, 1987; Luetke-Stahlman & Luckner, 1991). Teachers may justifiably react negatively to such contradictory suggestions, with responses ranging from confusion to resentment to resistance. It is important for the educational audiologist to find out from teachers what professional expectations are placed on them (by superiors, peers, or self) in order to develop an understanding of any negative responses to suggestions made by the audiologist.

Teaching Parents and Community Members

Parents often indicate a need for information on topics relevant to their child's hearing impairment. Parent programs can provide introductory information for those new to the system of special education, such as the purpose and process of the IEP

Strategies to Optimize Visual Information:
Suggestions for the Classroom Teacher

Students with HI require as much visual cueing as possible. **Comprehension increases significantly** when the student can watch the teacher's face in order to lipread—or, more accurately, to **speechread**.

Some suggestions to facilitate speechreading:

- Face the student as often as possible.
- Allow the student to change seating to better see the teacher's face.
- By using an overhead projector rather than a chalkboard, the teacher is able to face the student during instruction.
- When the room needs to be darkened for slides or films, make sure there is enough light on the teacher's face so that the student with HI can follow commentary or questions. A flashlight is very helpful in this circumstance.
- Lighting should illuminate the speaker's face. It is very difficult to speechread a person standing with his or her back to the window, especially if there is glare.
- Speak at a normal pace and volume. Do not exaggerate your mouth movements. Speak in phrases. If there is a misunderstanding, **rephrase rather than repeat** your instructions.
- DO NOT EXPECT A STUDENT TO SPEECHREAD YOU BEYOND 8–10 FEET.

Try this!
As a check on intelligibility, talk to yourself in the mirror and observe:

- Do you move your lips excessively?
- Do you move them at all?
- Do you talk out of the side of your mouth?
- Do you use natural facial expressions?

DID YOU KNOW that only one third of English sounds are visible? That some people are naturally better speechreaders than others? To better appreciate the difficulty of speechreading, try watching a news program on television, without any sound, and see how much you understand.

Other Visual Cues and Teaching Strategies:

- When talking about something or someone in the room, glance, point, or walk over and touch the object or person.
- As often as possible, write page numbers, homework assignments, PA announcements, and key vocabulary on the chalkboard.
- If you want to get the attention of the student with HI, it may be more effective to gently touch his or her shoulder or arm than to call his or her name.
- Do not assume the student with HI understood everything you have explained, even if he or she nods. Ask the student to repeat the instruction in his or her own words to make sure your instruction was received accurately.
- Pre-tutoring helps the student develop familiarity with new material before it is presented in class. Have the student read ahead as a homework assignment and ask parents to work on new vocabulary and concepts. Peers in class can also help with pre-tutoring tasks.
- Fatigue should not be interpreted as a lack of interest. Persons with HI must often expend considerable energy just to process auditory information.
- When using charts, maps, and handouts, pause to allow the student to look at the material, and then resume speaking. Remember, the student cannot look at written materials and speechread at the same time.
- Provide outlines of discussion topics and filmstrips before the learning experience. Look for films that are open captioned.
- Establish a procedure for class discussions that enables the student to follow class speakers. Ask students to raise their hands, or identify themselves in some way so that the student can find them and speechread them as well as the teacher.

IMPORTANT BENEFIT: These strategies help **all** students in the class, not just those with hearing impairment.

Figure 3.2. Sample in-service material.

and the roles of families and professionals in that process. Topics can also include more specific issues, as determined by the interests of the parents, such as:

- Implications of the Americans with Disabilities Act of 1990 (PL 101-336)
- New information regarding the Education of The Handicapped Act Amendments of 1990 (IDEA) (PL 101-476), such as the policy guidance issued by the U.S. Department of Education regarding LRE and children who are deaf
- Technological advances in hearing aids, FM systems, and sound field amplification
- Availability of closed-captioned television programming and caption decoder options in televisions, text telephones, and other assistive devices
- New policy or policy changes in a district or state
- Impact of educational reform on learners with HI
- Impact of relevant Supreme Court decisions
- Deaf culture issues

Information-sharing programs for parents may be menu-driven, as suggested earlier for teachers and staff, or may be specifically developed from a topic of interest identified by parents. In developing programs, it is necessary to consider when the program should be held, with respect to working parents; transportation issues; and the availability of childcare at the site, by a care provider with sign language proficiency, if appropriate.

The development of programs to teach the community at large is highly dependent on the community itself. There are usually opportunities to become part of the agenda and speak at town council meetings, PTA meetings, and on local radio and television morning shows, among others. Community programs typically address issues that have a general appeal. An excellent topic for community programs is that of hearing conservation and noise trauma because the audiologist can provide information as well as offer proactive measures to protect hearing health. Opportunities to share information among community members serve not only to teach the target audience, but also to generate positive public relations regarding the audiological services provided in the school program. While learning about prevention of noise-induced hearing loss, the audience also learns more about the roles and responsibilities of the educational audiologist.

In summary, the educational audiologist as educator has many opportunities to share information with a wide variety of audiences.

THE AUDIOLOGIST AS COMMUNITY LIAISON

Edwards (1991) has suggested a paradigm shift, or a different way of doing things, in educational audiology services by considering **the whole child**, not just his or her hearing, in terms of auditory management. An extension of that paradigm shift is to include not just the school professionals, but also **the professionals in the community** who contribute services to each learner with HI. A network of communication must be established to ensure that all professionals work together for the benefit of each child, rather than at cross-purposes or with incorrect assumptions. Following are descriptions and responsibilities of some of the service providers in the community who typically may contribute to the well-being of the student. Some school districts have established an admirable communication system among community service providers. For school districts that have not, the educational audiologist will want to investigate procedures to establish collaboration among professionals.

Hearing Aid Dispensers and the Educational Audiologist

Each learner with a hearing aid has a hearing aid dispenser in the community. This person may be in private practice or work within a children's hospital, a physician's office, or at a university site. It is imperative (with parental permission) that the educational audiologist establish contact with the dispenser immediately, first for the purposes of introduction, and later to facilitate the resolution of hearing aid problems as they occur. Copies of test results (aided and unaided) should be provided by the dispenser for the student's school records.

Regular contact with hearing aid dispensers increases the likelihood of well-coordinated services. For example, educational audiologists are interested in optimizing FM fittings with the use of direct audio input to personal hearing aids (Thibodeau & McCaffrey, 1992). However, the dispenser needs to know that an FM system is being used in the school in order to include that capability when ordering new hearing aids for the student.

If a student is new to the area and does not have a local hearing aid dispenser, the student's school, or the audiologist representing the school, typically cannot refer a parent to a specific dispenser. The recommended practice is to develop a list of all qualified dispensers in the area and to suggest that the parent talk to other parents for referrals.

Other Health Care Providers and the Educational Audiologist

Other health care providers in the community who might serve a student with HI can include clinical audiologists, speech-language pathologists, physicians, occupational therapists, and physical therapists. It is important to maintain open communication with all professionals involved with the student, including those outside the school system, in order to coordinate services effectively. Communication may entail telephone contacts, site visits, and sharing of reports among professionals. When professionals in different agencies share information regarding health concerns and educational goals, the student is more likely to benefit from instructions and interventions, which are integrated and mutually supportive.

Social Service Providers and the Educational Audiologist

Families may need help in establishing contact with the social services available in their area. One of the most important supports for families with a child with HI is information about obtaining financial assistance to purchase hearing aids. Each state has its own policy and procedures that families must follow in order to apply and qualify for financial assistance. The educational audiologist should contact the social worker who works with the district or school to obtain telephone numbers and other pertinent information for families. The social worker can also provide assistance in other family and child concerns, such as unemployment, substance abuse, food stamps, and additional aid programs, to name a few.

The Deaf Community and the Educational Audiologist

There have been, regrettably, negative feelings expressed by the Deaf community toward the profession of audiology (Scheetz, 1993). Acrimony has been expressed toward the profession, which is perceived as trying to "fix" deafness with amplification and countless hours of speechreading and speech therapy. As a culture, Deaf persons maintain that they do not need fixing, and that the emphasis on oral communication diminishes the value of natural manual communication (Benderly, 1980; Dolnick, 1993; Humphries, 1993; Jacobs, 1989; Lane, 1992; Padden & Humphries, 1988; Schein, 1989).

To bridge the gap between audiologists and the Deaf community, the educational audiologist has two responsibilities. First, the educational audiologist should develop and maintain at least an intermediate proficiency in sign language. Second, the educational audiologist should develop "cross-cultural competence" by learning and respecting the perceptions and values expressed by the Deaf community.

Both objectives can be met by taking classes that teach both sign language and Deaf culture. American Sign Language (ASL) is difficult for many hearing persons to learn, and mastery of ASL may not be a realistic goal for some audiologists. However, sincere attempts should be made to develop at least some degree of fluency in a pidgin sign. With at least intermediate signing skills, and an appreciation and respect for issues that concern the Deaf community, educational audiologists can serve with credibility as a liaison with children, parents, teachers, Deaf adult mentors, and others.

Providers of Technical Assistance and the Educational Audiologist

In many ways, the educational audiologist serves as a resource for or clearinghouse of information indirectly related to the educational needs of a learner with HI. For example, the educational audiologist may help a student and his or her family obtain appropriate technical assistance. Parents and students may not be aware of the availability of text telephones (TTs, also called TDDs), or telephone relay systems, or amplified telephones. They also may not know whom to contact or that such services are available free of charge. Providers of other types of assistance, such as local support groups, dogs for the deaf, and alerting or assistive listening devices, usually exist but may not be well advertised.

The educational audiologist should collect information on available technical support and personnel and perhaps develop a brochure of this information, to be disseminated to students, parents, other professionals, and community groups.

Service Organizations and the Educational Audiologist

Members of local chapters of organizations such as the Lions, Kiwanis, and Rotary clubs often express interest in being involved in school programs. Connections between schools and service organizations can be established by sharing information on topics such as hearing conservation, educational innovations, and amplification technologies used in schools. In return, the clubs may offer to sponsor activities, projects, or equipment purchases through financial support.

In general, the role of community liaison is rarely well defined in the job descriptions for school personnel. The audiologist may need to create the role of community liaison first by determining specific concerns of students in the district and then gradually developing contacts across the community to meet those concerns.

THE AUDIOLOGIST AS PUBLIC RELATIONS EXPERT

Educational audiologists have indicated some frustration in their ability to effect positive change, due in part to their perception of low visibility with administrators and educators in their district (English, 1991). The complex array of services provided by educational audiologists often are not known or understood, or perhaps they are mistakenly seen as supplemental, rather than essential, to a student's educational program.

To increase the visibility of the services they provide, educational audiologists must develop expertise in marketing and public relations. Ross (1982) recognized that the specialty of educational audiology "has to sell itself and its professional contributions" (p. 231). Related support personnel, including speech-language pathologists, school social workers, and counselors, have also recognized the need to promote the benefits of their services (Block, 1993; Cada & Maruyama, 1991; Gibelman, 1993; Holcomb & Niffengger, 1992; Sharpe, 1993; Thompson, 1992).

Developing a Marketing Plan

Marketing may at first seem a little alien to educational audiologists, but marketing really is simply an organized plan to communicate persuasively to policymakers and others that the educational audiologist's professional contributions are **indispensible** to students' educational success. The more clearly these benefits are understood, the greater the likelihood that there will be administrative support for educational audiology.

The goals for marketing educational audiology are twofold: to increase the visibility of educational audiology services, and to educate specific target audiences about what those services are. To achieve these goals, marketing experts recommend adopting a four-point strategy: develop an **organized** plan of action, implement the plan with **consistent** efforts, **integrate** the plan into the educational audiology program, and draw upon **skills** we already use, planning, education, and advocacy.

An **organized** plan means developing, at the beginning of the school year, a coordinated, supervised, and carefully thought-out plan of action. In a group of two or more audiologists, someone must assume the responsibility of chair of the marketing or public relations team and oversee the efforts of other team members. Tasks must be assigned and deadlines must be established. A **consistent and integrated** plan means that there is a commitment to the concept that from this day forward, public relations becomes a permanent part of the job description of the educational audiologist.

To promote educational audiology, the following steps are recommended:

1. Develop a marketing plan.
    a. Identify your goals.
    b. Identify at least one target audience.
    c. Design some promotional strategies.
2. Implement plan.
3. Evaluate plan.

Identifying goals and identifying at least one target audience (steps 1a and 1b) can be accomplished by conducting the following exercise. A simple chart, as seen in Figure 3.3, can help a marketing or public relations (PR) team consider and define goals and target audiences. Let's consider a hypothetical situation calling for marketing to see how this procedure works.

The educational audiology PR team from Metro School District is concerned about the apparent low visibility of their educational audiology program. The team develops the set of questions (seen in Figure 3.3) that reflect their concerns. For example, they've asked themselves, "Do key people know the names, responsibilities, or phone numbers of the educational audiologists serving their students?" In addition to these basic issues, they've asked if these people appreciate the impact of hearing impairment on the learning process, the effects of noise, and the benefits of FM and sound field amplification. These questions become the **goals** of their marketing efforts.

Next, three persons who influence the education of students with HI were identified: Principal A, Special Education Director B, and Superintendent C. These are the **target audience** of the marketing plan. The target audience may also include school board members, influential parents, and others who make or have an impact upon fiscal and policy decisions that affect the quality of education for learners with HI.

Each question is asked for each identified target audience. Any question answered with a "no" helps in identifying not only the target audiences, but also the subsequent goals of the marketing plan. In our example, Principal A and Special Education Director B seem to have some basic information about the service educational audiology provides, but they could benefit from information regarding HI, noise, and amplification. Superintendent C, however, appears far removed from the goals of this program and needs to be advised in a variety of ways regarding the contributions of educational audiology.

With the goals and target audiences now defined, the next step is to design strategies to consistently promote the positive benefits of educational audiology

Goals	Target audience 1: Principal A	Target audience 2: Special Education Director B	Target audience 3: Superintendent C
1. Does this person know the educational audiologists serving his or her students?	Yes	Yes	No
2. Is this person knowledgeable about the responsibilities of educational audiologists?	Yes	Yes	No
3. Does this person know how to contact the educational audiologist?	Yes	Yes	No
4. Does this person understand impact of HI on learning?	No	No	No
5. Does this person understand concerns of signal-to-noise ratio?	No	No	No
6. Does this person understand benefits of FM and sound field amplification?	No	No	No

Figure 3.3. Define goals and target audiences as the first part of a marketing plan.

(step 1c). A planning chart, such as that in Table 3.1, summarizes the goals and target audiences and leads the PR team to consider promotional strategies for each target audience. These promotional strategies include the use of both print and electronic media, as well as personal contacts. The choice of strategies depends on the creativity, resources, and energy of the PR team.

Marketing Tips

When presenting information for school administrators, prepare and distribute a handout with research data that support your work, for example, the list of issues and services for students with HI shown in Table 3.2.

Look for data that can be presented visually, in graphic form (Figure 3.4) or in a "quick read" format (Figure 3.5).

Personalize strategies with letters from students, or photographs, or invitations to visit the classroom. And, finally, after you conduct an in-service, send a report to a target audience (particularly administrators) describing the topic and the number of participants, and an estimate of how many students will benefit from the in-service training.

The PR team must stay alert to every positive outcome observed from educational audiology services and let others know about it.

Table 3.1. Marketing plan with promotional strategies

Goal	Targets	Promotional strategies
1. Will know names of all educational audiologists	Superintendent C	Media: Send letter of introduction with pictures of students Personal contact: Request to be placed on agenda of a staff meeting in order to present a description of services
2. Will know the responsibilities of educational audiologists	Superintendent C	Media: Distribute "quick read" type of data sheet Personal contact: Invite attendance at an in-service, include a copy of handouts
3. Will know how to contact educational audiologists	Superintendent C	Media: Write a letter Personal contact: Invite to office to inspect new testing equipment, include phone numbers (in letter and on included business cards) for response to invitation
4. Will understand the impact of HI on learning	Principal A Special Education Director B Superintendent C	Media: Write an article on OME[a] for district newsletter Personal contact: Forward a copy of article with personal note
5. Will understand concerns of signal-to-noise ratios	Principal A Special Education Director B Superintendent C	Media: Submit an article to local newspaper re: installation of sound field equipment Personal contact: Send copy of article, include invitation to pizza party in class for a demonstration of equipment
6. Will understand benefits of FM and sound field amplification	Principal A Special Education Director B Superintendent C	Media: Distribution of "fast facts" data sheet Personal contact: Send a set of thank you notes from students for new equipment, with photos

[a]OME, otitis media with effusion.

Table 3.2.   Issues and services for students with hearing impairment

Issue	What the educational audiologist can do		Data
Hearing aids amplify all sounds, classroom noise as well as teacher instruction.	1.	Evaluate class for acoustic modifications.	Berg (1987)
	2.	Fit students with FM equipment.	Finitzo (1988)
Hearing aids and FMs often are not functioning properly.	1.	In-service classroom personnel to conduct daily HA and FM checks.	Zink (1972)
			English (1991)
	2.	Conduct routine electroacoustic analysis.	Bess and McConnell (1981)
	3.	Develop recordkeeping system to monitor condition of devices.	Maxon, Brackett, and van den Berg (1991)
Students with hearing impairment often need training in listening skills.	1.	Assess listening skills or train others to conduct assessment.	Edwards (1991)
			Berg (1986)
	2.	Provide remediation or train others to incorporate listening into other activities.	Erber (1982)
			Flexer, Wray, and Ireland (1989)
Students with HI often feel isolated.	1.	Develop a support group with adults with HI as mentors.	Clark (1994)
			Leavitt (1987)
	2.	Provide counseling regarding psychosocial impact of hearing impairment.	
Regular education teachers often have students with HI placed in their class without any information or technical support.	1.	Serve as technical assistant regarding HA/FM management; provide in-services and other technical supports.	Luckner (1991)
			Chorost (1988)
			Myles and Simpson (1989)
	2.	Serve as liaison for educator of HI.	

Identifying goals and a target audience and designing promotional strategies are the three components of **developing** a marketing plan. After the PR team agrees on particular strategies, the plan is ready for **implementation**. Each person on the PR team will have tasks and deadlines, under the supervision of the PR chair, in implementing the plan.

The final step in a successful PR effort is **evaluation** of the marketing plan. The PR team must regularly (at least once a year) consider the results of its efforts. Did the "no's" on the initial planning sheet become "yes's," were efforts consistent, are modifications needed, did new target audiences emerge? Did the team process work well, or does work need to be redistributed? The evaluation process should lead the PR team to refinements of the marketing plan for the following year.

Broadening the Scope of a Marketing Plan

The procedures described above are intended for the **micro environment**, or your "backyard." The micro environment target audience includes individuals in your school, district, and community and your local professional colleagues. The marketing team should also consider the **macro environment**, which, in this context, consists of fellow educational audiologists at the state and national level. Effective projects should be shared with audiologists beyond the local arena. Information shared at conferences, such as a presentation by Rogers (1992) called Project S.M.I.L.E., 'Sound' Management in the Listening Environment, provides resources to other educational audiologists across the country.

The promotion of a professional specialty depends on efforts by its practitioners. Only educational audiologists can protect and promote the status and future of

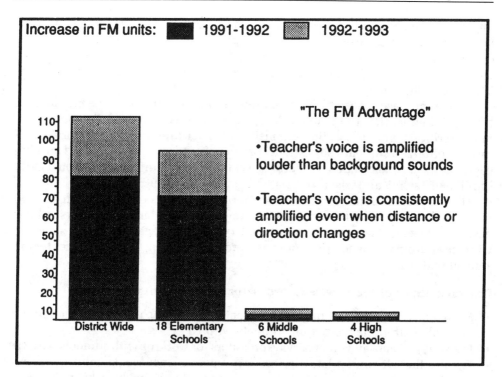

Figure 3.4. Promotional data presented as a graph.

their field. In an era of shrinking educational budgets, it is essential to establish and maintain a high level of visibility and positive public opinion about educational audiology services in order to advance the concerns of students with HI.

THE AUDIOLOGIST AS SERVICE COORDINATOR

Wilson-Vlotman (1986) posed a thought-provoking question: Exactly who is managing the needs of students with HI in schools? Too often, the answer is "no one" (Blair, 1986). When mainstream and inclusion placements are made, the needs of the learner with HI are often overlooked. For example, educators of the hearing

---

Metro School District

Did you know:

- Our school district serves 113 students with hearing impairment, ranging from mild to severe?
- Hearing aids for these students are monitored daily and have an overall functioning rate of 92%, compared to a national average of 50%?
- Some students with hearing impairment have been teaching sign language to Mrs. Bean's third graders?
- Our district's hearing conservation program, "Hearing Matters," won a regional award?
- The most popular color for FM earmolds is neon orange?

Figure 3.5. Fast facts about educational audiology services in Metro school district: Promotional data presented in a "quick read" format.

impaired are usually expected to address only academic concerns, and speech-language pathologists may not have the background necessary to identify the needs of students with HI. Therefore, "Educational audiologists have a role to play [in service coordination] for which no one has currently taken responsibility" (Wilson-Vlotman, 1986, p. 184).

The term "case manager" has been used in the past but it can be problematic because it implies that a student is a "case" that requires "managing." A more accurate description emphasizes the responsibility of **coordinating the services** necessary to optimize a student's educational program (Sanders, 1993). To avoid misconceptions, the term **service coordinator** is used throughout this book (National Early Childhood Technical Assistance System [NEC*TAS], 1989).

The important point is not really the term as much as the realization that too many students with HI have no school professional designated to oversee their needs. To ensure that students receive adequate coordinated services, someone **with the appropriate expertise** should assume the following responsibilities for the student with HI.

Responsibilities of the Service Coordinator for a Student with HI

- Maintains complete and updated information regarding the placement options available within the district for students with HI
- Prepares teachers and other service providers for working with students with HI
- Ensures that all appropriate services (e.g., speech-language pathology, occupational therapy) are coordinated and implemented in a timely fashion
- Maintains contact with teachers and provides technical support as necessary
- Monitors the student's placement and progress
- Supports transitions to other grades, schools, and programs
- Evaluates each student's placement and makes recommendations for changes as needed

The educational audiologist is the professional who is most often fully qualified to fulfill these responsibilities for the student with HI. Some practitioners feel that this is an administrative role that they are not hired or paid to assume (English, 1991). Often, an administrator such as a special education director has the responsibility to oversee service coordination. However, if no one in a district is assuming this role, the educational audiologist is qualified to assume the responsibility to coordinate services for students with HI.

THE AUDIOLOGIST AS SUPERVISOR

Depending on the particular job description or other circumstances, the educational audiologist may be expected to supervise staff and programs, as described below.

Supervising Hearing Screening and Hearing Conservation Programs

The educational audiologist is qualified to develop and supervise programs to screen for hearing impairment and to conserve hearing health. The most efficient use of the audiologist's time and expertise in executing a **hearing screening pro-**

gram is through the training of support personnel or technicians in the requirements of testing, in the protocol of using pass/fail criteria, in providing referrals, and in follow-up procedures. In this way, the program and the implementers are under the supervision of the educational audiologist.

Hearing conservation programs vary widely across school districts. If the school district will support such a program, a group of teachers, aides, volunteers, student teachers, and others can be trained to present a program developed by the audiologist. (See Chapter 7 for an extended discussion of the components of both types of programs.)

Supervising Graduate Students

If the educational audiologist works near a university with an audiology program, he or she may be asked or volunteer to supervise graduate audiology students in their off-campus practica. There is growing interest in providing school placements for graduate students in order to better prepare them for the full array of employment settings (DeConde Johnson, 1993). If an opportunity to supervise does arise, the educational audiologist is likely not to have had much previous training in or experience with supervisory responsibilities. As with the majority of persons who supervise, it is a role into which one "evolves" (Dowling, 1993; Shapiro & Moses, 1989). The American Speech-Language-Hearing Association (1985) recommended that individuals who assume a supervisory role develop appropriate competencies by attending courses, workshops, and convention presentations and by becoming familiar with the literature developed on the subject.

Several models for supervision have been developed (Anderson, 1988; Cogan, 1973). Models of supervision that stress interpersonal relationships seem the most applicable to the school setting, given the high value placed on these relationships among professionals in schools. The use of a particular model should not be inflexible; **reflection** on the supervisory process is strongly recommended in order for the supervision to meet the specific needs of each supervisee (Schön, 1987; Sergiovanni, 1985).

Open communication with the university is essential while supervising graduate students. A lack of understanding can occur regarding the expectations of the off-campus experience, especially if the student is seen by the supervisor as more of a helper than as a professional-in-training (Brasseur, 1989). Good supervision requires that a balance is achieved across the needs of the graduate student, the needs of the school program, and the concerns of the supervisor to provide quality services and opportunities for independent practice for students who may not be prepared to work independently. Anderson (1988) described a continuum of the supervisory relationship, beginning with evaluation and feedback, in which the supervisor is directive and dominant and the supervisee is a passive recipient. Through experience and direction in problem-solving and planning, the supervisee should progress to a stage of self-supervision. At this stage, the supervisee demonstrates self-evaluation skills and effective problem-solving skills, and the two participants in the supervision process develop a relationship of collegiality.

Following are a few strategies that develop shared responsibility in the supervisory process: 1) question students as to their expectations regarding the supervisory process and the school setting experience; 2) encourage, consider, and analyze students' suggestions that differ from your established protocols; and 3) present your own approach for consideration and, as far as possible, try both approaches. Tried-and-true approaches may be the only solution to some issues, but an innovative new approach may be applicable to other problems.

Supervising Equipment Use

The care, maintenance, and overall quality control of testing and amplification equipment generally is the responsibility of the individuals who use the equipment. The educational audiologist can expect to assume the following responsibilities in equipment use and maintenance:

- Coordinate and oversee the annual calibration and servicing of FM systems, portable and desk-model audiometers and impedance equipment, hearing aid analyzers, and sound field equipment.
- Develop and maintain an accurate recordkeeping system to monitor the nature of equipment problems and the turnaround time for repairs.
- Establish a tracking system to oversee the assignment of equipment to students and/or classrooms. A database including equipment serial numbers is useful in quickly locating equipment distributed throughout a district.

There are software programs designed to help the educational audiologist to perform these responsibilities with accuracy and efficiency (Mendel, Wynne, English, & Schmidt, in press). One of the challenges of professional growth in this field is developing an expertise in these and future computer applications.

CONCLUSION

Not all educational audiologists assume all of the roles and responsibilities described in this chapter. In fact, Allard and Golden (1991) indicated that many audiologists have limited involvement in the expanded roles that are described in this chapter. However, it is important to know how to capitalize on your training and expertise as audiologists in school settings. The challenge for practitioners is to persistently encourage school districts to reconsider and gradually expand the scope of practice as defined by the current job description of an educational audiologist. Such changes may only occur in small steps. In earlier discussion, it was stated that only educational audiologists can effectively increase the visibility of their profession. It is also true that only educational audiologists can persuade administrators and colleagues to broaden current limited definitions of educational audiology services.

Learning the Language

Review the following concepts from this chapter and discuss with a colleague.

- Direct versus indirect services to students
- Learning preferences among adults
- Needs assessment
- Community liaison
- Cross-cultural competencies with Deaf community
- Marketing and public relations
- Broadening the scope of a marketing plan
- Service coordination
- Supervision and reflection

Educational Audiology in Action
Suggested Learning Activities

Project 1. Ask a practicing educational audiologist if you may observe direct services provided to students with HI such as instruction in speech reading and auditory training. Was the instruction delivered in a resource room, a classroom, or another site? Was the student with HI the only one receiving instruction, or were other students included in a small group instruction? How were the other students included? Are all direct services delivered in one way, or in a variety of ways?

Project 2. Attend and analyze an in-service or workshop. Consider the principles described in this chapter regarding the learning preferences of adults. Were these principles incorporated into the in-service? What would you change to accommodate to the needs of an audience of adult learners?

Project 3. Practice some marketing skills with your graduate department. Design a marketing plan that will advertise and "sell" a feature of the department or of a student project that you feel would benefit the community or a target audience. Assign tasks to the marketing team, and evalute the effectiveness of the plan. What would need to be revised if you were to implement the plan again?

References

Allard, J., & Golden, D. (1991). Educational audiology: A comparison of service delivery systems utilized by Missouri schools. *Language, Speech, and Hearing Services in Schools, 22*, 5–11.

American Speech-Language-Hearing Association. (1985). Clincial supervision in speech-language pathology and audiology. *Asha, 27*(6), 57–60.

Anderson, J. (1988). *The supervisory process in speech-language pathology and audiology.* Boston: College-Hill Press.

Benderly, B. (1980). *Dancing without music: Deafness in America.* Washington, DC: Gallaudet University Press.

Berg, F. (1986). Characteristics of the target population. In F. Berg, J. Blair, S. Viehweg, & A. Wilson-Vlotman, *Educational audiology for the hard of hearing child* (pp. 1–24). Orlando, FL: Grune & Stratton.

Berg, F. (1987). *Facilitating classroom listening: A handbook for teachers of normal and hard of hearing students.* Austin, TX: PRO-ED.

Bess, F., & McConnell, F. (1981). *Audiology, education, and the hearing impaired child.* St. Louis, MO: C.V. Mosby.

Blair, J. (1986). Services needed. In F. Berg, J. Blair, S. Viehweg, & A. Wilson-Vlotman, *Educational audiology services for the hard of hearing child* (pp. 25–36). Orlando, FL: Grune & Stratton.

Block, F. (1993). Success in the schools. *Asha, 35*(7), 36–37; 54.

Brasseur, J. (1989). The supervisory process: A continuum perspective. *Language, Speech, and Hearing Services in Schools, 20*, 274–295.

Bunch, G. (1987). *The curriculum and the hearing impaired child.* Boston: College-Hill Press.

Cada, E., & Maruyama, E. (1991). Marketing. In W. Dunn (Ed.), *Pediatric occupational therapy: Facilitating effective service provision* (pp. 285–294). Thorofare, NJ: Slack, Inc.

Chorost, S. (1988). The hearing impaired child in the mainstream: A survey of the attitudes of regular classroom teachers. *Volta Review, 90*, 7–12.

Clark, J. (1994). Audiologists' counseling purvue. In J. Clark & F. Martin (Eds.), *Effective counseling in audiology: Perspectives and practice* (pp. 1–17). Englewood Cliffs, NJ: Prentice Hall.

Cogan, M. (1973). *Clinical supervision.* Boston: Houghton Mifflin.

DeConde Johnson, C. (1993). EAA proposes minimum competencies for educational audiology. *Educational Audiology Association Newsletter, 10*(4), 8–10.

Dolnick, E. (1993). Deafness as culture. *Atlantic Monthly, 272*(3), 37–53.

Dowling, S. (1993). Supervisory training, objective setting, and grade-contingent performance. *Language, Speech, and Hearing Services in Schools, 24*, 92–99.

Edwards, C. (1991). The transition from auditory training to holistic auditory management. *Educational Audiology Monograph, 2*, 1–17.

English, K. (1991). Best practices in educational audiology. *Language, Speech, and Hearing Services in Schools, 22*, 283–286.

Erber, N. (1982). *Auditory training.* Washington, DC: Alexander Graham Bell Association.

Evans, M. (1986). Organizational behavior: The central role of motivation. *Journal of Management, 12*, 203–222.

Flexer, C., Wray, D., & Ireland, J. (1989). Preferential seating is NOT enough: Issues in classroom management of hearing impaired students. *Language, Speech, and Hearing Services in Schools, 20*, 11–21.

Finitzo, T. (1988). Classroom acoustics. In R. Roeser & M. Downs (Eds.), *Auditory disorders in school children* (2nd ed.) (pp. 221–233). New York: Thieme Medical Publishers.

Gibelman, M. (1993). School workers, counselors, and psychologists in collaboration: A shared agenda. *Social Work in Schools, 15,* 45–53.

Heron, T., & Harris, K. (1987). *The educational consultant.* Austin, TX: PRO-ED.

Hillkirk, K., Tome, J., & Wendress, W. (1989). Integrating reflection into staff development programs. *Journal of Staff Development, 10*(2), 54–58.

Holcomb, F., & Niffengger, P. (1992). Elementary school counselors: A plan for marketing their services under the education reform. *Elementary School Guidance and Counseling, 27*(1), 56–63.

Humphries, T. (1993). Deaf culture and cultures. In K. Christianson & G. Delgado (Eds.), *Multicultural issues in deafness* (pp. 3–16). New York: Longman.

Jacobs, L. (1989). *A deaf adult speaks out* (3rd ed.). Washington, DC: Gallaudet University Press.

Knowles, M. (1984). *The adult learner: A neglected species* (3rd ed.). Houston: Gulf Publishing.

Lane, H. (1992). *The mask of benevolence: Disabling the Deaf community.* New York: Knopf.

Leavitt, R. (1987). Promoting the use of rehabilitative technology. *Asha, 24*(1), 28–31.

Luckner, J. (1991). Mainstreaming hearing impaired students: Perceptions of regular educators. *Language, Speech, and Hearing Services in Schools, 22,* 302–307.

Luetke-Stahlman, B., & Luckner, J. (1991). *Effectively educating students with hearing impairment.* New York: Longman.

Maxon, A., Brackett, D., & van den Berg, S. (1991). Classroom amplification use: A national longterm study. *Language, Speech, and Hearing Services in Schools, 22,* 242–253.

Mendel, L., Wynne, M., English, K., & Schmidt, A. (in press). Computer applications in educational audiology. *Language, Speech, and Hearing Services in Schools.*

Moore, J. (1988). Guidelines concerning adult learning. *Journal of Staff Development, 9*(3), 2–5.

Myles, B., & Simpson, R. (1989). Regular educators' modification preferences for mainstreaming mildly handicapped children. *Journal of Special Education, 22,* 479–491.

National Early Childhood Technical Assistance System (NEC*TAS). (1989). *Guidelines and recommended practices for the individualized family service plan.* Chapel Hill, NC: Frank Porter Graham Child Development Center, University of North Carolina.

Padden, C., & Humphries, T. (1988). *Deaf in America: Voices from a culture.* Cambridge, MA: Harvard University Press.

Rogers, S. (1992, November). *Project S.M.I.L.E.—"Sound" management in the listening environment.* Poster session presented at the American Speech-Language Association annual convention, San Antonio, TX.

Ross, M. (1982). *Hard of hearing children in regular schools.* Englewood Cliffs, NJ: Prentice Hall.

Ross, M., Brackett, D., & Maxon, A. (1991). *Assessment and management of mainstreamed hearing impaired children.* Austin, TX: PRO-ED.

Sanders, D. (1993). *Management of hearing handicap: Infants to elderly.* Englewood Cliffs, NJ: Prentice Hall.

Scheetz, N. (1993). *Orientation to deafness.* Newton, MA: Allyn & Bacon.

Schein, J. (1989). *At home among strangers: Exploring the Deaf community in the United States.* Washington, DC: Gallaudet University Press.

Schön, D. (1987). *Educating the reflective practitioner: Toward a new design for teaching and learning in the professions.* San Francisco: Jossey-Bass.

Sergiovanni, J. (1985). Landscapes, mindscapes, and reflective practices in supervision. *Journal of Curriculum and Supervision, 1*(1), 5–17.

Shapiro, D., & Moses, N. (1989). Creative problem solving in public school supervision. *Language, Speech, and Hearing Services in Schools, 20,* 320–332.

Sharpe, D. (1993). Image control. *Vocational Educational Journal, 68*(1), 24–25, 55.

Thibodeau, L., & McCaffrey, H. (1992). The complexities of using direct-input hearing aids with FM systems. *Volta Review, 95,* 189–193.

Thompson, R. (1992). *School counseling renewal: Strategies for the twenty-first century.* Muncie, IN: Accelerated Development Inc.

Wilson-Vlotman, A. (1986). Management and coordination of services to the hard of hearing child. In F. Berg, J. Blair, S. Viehweg, & A. Wilson-Vlotman, (Eds.), *Educational audiology for the hard of hearing child* (pp. 181–203). Orlando, FL: Grune & Stratton.

Yoshinago-Itano, C., & Ruberry, J. (1992). The Colorado Individual Performance Profile for hearing impaired students: A data-driven approach to decision-making. *Volta Review, 94,* 159–187.

Zemke, R., & Zemke, S. (1988, July). Thirty things we know for sure about adult learning. *Training,* 57–61.

Zink, C. (1972). Hearing aids children wear: A longitudinal study of performance. *Volta Review, 74,* 41–51.

4

When a Learner with Hearing Impairment Has Additional Disabilities

Implications for Learning

APPROXIMATELY 30% OF STUDENTS WITH hearing impairment have additional disabilities that may contribute to learning difficulties. The data in Table 4.1 show the distribution of these disabilities (Schildroth & Hotto, 1993).

Providing services to students with HI who have additional disabilities is therefore an important component to the scope of practice for educational audiologists. This chapter first presents current information regarding individuals who have disabilities other than HI. In addition, possible effects of other disabilities for an individual with HI are offered.

> The effects of another disability with hearing impairment may be more than additive. That is, hearing impairment with an additional disability can result in a synergistic interaction that can result in more severe learning difficulties than might originally be expected (Mencher & Gerber, 1983).

Responsibilities of the educational audiologist with regard to individuals with these additional disabilities are also presented. The reader should note that this chapter does not address individuals with physical disabilities, such as spina bifida or cerebral palsy, which do not so directly affect learning, apart from requiring modifications to the classroom and school environment.

STUDENTS WITH LEARNING DISABILITIES

As much as 20% of school-age children (ages 5–18 years) have been identified as having a learning disability (Smith & Robinson, 1986). The National Joint Committee on Learning Disabilities (1991b) defined learning disabilities as:

> A general term that refers to a heterogeneous group of disorders manifested by significant difficulties in the acquisition and use of listening, speaking, reading, writing, rea-

Table 4.1.   Percent of students with HI with an additional educationally significant disability

Impairment	Students with
Hearing impairment with learning disability	9%
Hearing impairment with mental retardation	8%
Hearing impairment with vision impairment: not correctable with lenses	4%
Hearing impairment with emotional disability	4%
Hearing impairment with one additional disability	22%
Hearing impairment with two or more additional disabilities	8%

Adapted from Schildroth & Hotto (1993).

soning, or mathematical abilities. These disorders are presumed to be due to central nervous system dysfunction. Problems in self-regulatory behaviors, social perception, and social interaction may exist with learning disabilities but do not by themselves constitute a learning disability. Although learning disabilities may occur concomitantly with other handicapping conditions (for example, sensory impairment, mental retardation, serious emotional disturbance), or with extrinsic factors (such as cultural differences, insufficient or inappropriate instruction), they are not the result of those conditions or influences. (p. 10)

An individual has a learning disability when a significant discrepancy between achievement and potential is observed. A student with a learning disability has at least average intelligence, but may demonstrate inconsistent performance, poor organizational skills, poor attention abilities, and/or problems with memory and sequencing and the acquisition of verbal and nonverbal language skills (Lewis & Doorlag, 1991). Students with learning disabilities often have difficulty processing language quickly, and so they may find themselves responding inappropriately (Donahue, Pearl, & Bryan, 1980).

An individual may present a learning disability in a variety of specific learning problems. For example:

- A child with dyslexia may have difficulty interpreting written words and numbers. A child may experience problems when learning to read, write, spell, and perform math tasks (Zurif & Carson, 1970).
- A child with a visual perceptual problem may have difficulty judging spatial depth, spatial relationships, shapes, and sizes. This type of learning disability is especially important to diagnose in a student who is deaf and who is expected to receive instruction by sign language (Prickett & Prickett, 1992; Ratner, 1988).
- A child with a motor disability may have difficulty controlling his or her fine and/or gross movements. A child with a motor disability may experience difficulty in writing neatly on lines, or in keeping letters from overlapping. A child with a motor disability may appear to be clumsy, and his or her work is often messy.
- A child with an auditory perceptual problem may have difficulty acquiring speech and language skills.

Advocates for students with learning disabilities have been concerned about concomitant social difficulties. The negative social interactions among students with learning disabilities have in the past been attributed to a history of family dysfunction or personality problems (Patterson, 1986; Toro, Weissberg, Guare, &

Liebenstein, 1990); however, more recent research (Spafford & Grosser, 1993) indicates that unsatisfactory social interactions can be attributed to communication deficits and difficulties in language processing.

Two specific types of learning disabilities can call for the involvement of the educational audiologist. The first, **central auditory processing disorder** (CAPD), most typically involves students with normal hearing, but intervention requires the expertise of the educational audiologist. The second learning disability that is of special interest to the audiologist is **attention-deficit/hyperactivity disorder** (AD/HD). Amplification has been used as part of interventions for individuals with each disorder.

Central Auditory Processing Disorder

CAPD has been defined as:

> Deficits in the information processing of audible signals not attributable to impaired peripheral hearing sensitivity or intellectual impairment. Specifically, CAPD refers to limitations in the on-going transmission, analysis, organization, transformation, elaboration, storage, retrieval and use of information contained in auditory signals. (Trace, 1993a, p. 7)

An individual with CAPD is often described as inattentive, distractible, disruptive, and as having difficulty in remembering classroom routine and in following directions. This example describes behavior typical of a child with CAPD and notes the possible interpretations:

> "Okay, class, before you open your science book to page 95 for the next lesson, get out your homework from yesterday, and put it in the right-hand corner of your desk for me to review; then we'll be ready to start."
> Ron takes out his social studies book and stares into space.
> Why didn't Ron follow the teacher's directions? Not listening? Distracted? Not paying attention? Poor conduct? Hearing loss? Any of these explanations is possible. Or maybe Ron hears the sound, but has a problem understanding what is said to him—particularly when the language used is complex, spoken rapidly, or is lengthy, and when there's a lot to look at and lots of noise around him. (American Speech-Language-Hearing Association, 1990, p. 53)

Figure 4.1 illustrates the many possible considerations for children who are inattentive or distractible.

Research suggests that students with CAPD may possibly have neural timing problems (Chermak & Musiek, 1992; Sanders, 1993; Trace, 1993a). For example, some students have been found to have difficulty integrating temporal information within a 100-millisecond time frame, which makes it difficult to process speech with its high rate of temporal acoustical change. A student with CAPD may confuse short vowel sounds, or have difficulty in processing stops (/b, t, d/) and cluster consonants. This difficulty can result in problems with discriminating fine differences in consonants, such as the initial sounds in "Kate/gate," or the vowel sounds in "ten" and "tin."

Assessments of central auditory abilities evaluate how well an individual can "recognize speech, attend to stimuli, inhibit irrelevant stimuli, and recall auditory information" (Maxon & Smaldino, 1991, p. 376). The assessment procedure itself may be a therapeutic process for the student because it can help him or her understand the source of his or her difficulties and target skills that will address them

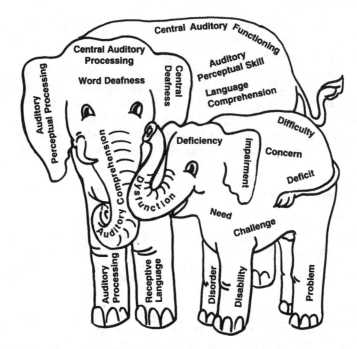

Figure 4.1. Your view depends on which part of the elephant you touch. (From American Speech-Language-Hearing Association [1990]. *What are central auditory processing problems in children? Asha, 32*[8], 53–54; reprinted by permission.)

proactively. Assessments may include staggered sentences, filtered speech, or dichotic listening tasks to determine specific listening difficulties. Interviews with parents and students may help to determine listening difficulties at home as well as at school.

It should be kept in mind that such students with CAPD have **normal** hearing levels. Nevertheless, teachers typically report behaviors in learners with CAPD that are similar to those of students with hearing impairment (Smoski, Brunt, & Tannahill, 1992). One of the consistent characteristics noted in learners with CAPD is the inability to understand speech in noise, or figure-ground discrimination. Learning difficulties in the following areas are associated with CAPD:

- Association
- Attention span
- Auditory closure
- Auditory memory
- Comprehension
- Identification of sounds
- Localization
- Memory (short term and/or long term)
- Speech and language problems

Not surprisingly, then, the adaptations or interventions found to be most effective for learners with CAPD are very similar to those effective for students with HI.

Audiologists have been experimenting with using sound field amplification and FM systems to improve the signal–noise ratio for students with CAPD. Another experimental procedure attempts to desensitize students to noise and provides practice to improve speech discrimination in increasing noise levels (Trace, 1993b). These are areas of intervention in which the educational audiologist will want to be closely involved in order to monitor environmental conditions and to measure changes in student behaviors.

If the student is able to assume some self-advocacy responsibilities, he or she can be taught effective coping strategies in order to be an active problem solver in modifying the environment to meet his or her needs. Slight modifications may be sufficient for an individual, such as reducing the distance between speaker and student to improve signal–noise ratios. Other strategies include: "chunking" (the use of associated words or topics to improve memory); using memo pads to write reminders to oneself and calendars to keep track of assignments; and recording lectures.

To help the student with CAPD, teachers may be asked to increase their redundancy in instruction, to provide additional sensory input (e.g., visual or tactile), to provide pre-tutoring, to allow the student to wear ear muffs to reduce noise when doing independent seat work, or to create a work center with carrels or dividers to reduce visual distractions for the student. Using a buddy system may also help to keep a student with CAPD on task.

Attention-Deficit/Hyperactivity Disorder

Technically, AD/HD is not itself a learning disability. Rather, it is classified as a disruptive behavior disorder (American Psychiatric Association, 1994) with concomitant learning difficulties. Children with AD/HD were authorized for special education and related services in 1991 with IDEA (PL 101-476).

Attention-deficit/hyperactivity disorder has been identified as occurring in from 3%–5% (McBurnett, Lahey, & Pfiffner, 1993) to 20% of school-age children (Shaywitz & Shaywitz, 1992). A student with AD/HD usually has difficulty with work completion and with off-task behaviors and has decreased accuracy in his or her work because of an inability to regulate attention and to control the impulse to move around. In listening tasks, the addition of too much detail or direction disrupts the listening comprehension of an individual with AD/HD. Background noise can be very distracting to a student with AD/HD (Reid, Maag, & Vasa, 1993; Waldron, 1992).

Attentional deficit may be more accurately described as an **attentional bias**: Students, in fact, are typically paying attention, but to inappropriate stimuli. A learner with AD/HD selectively attends to the novel details around him or her, and so becomes distracted from the pertinent signal (Zentall, 1993).

AD/HD is described in the *Diagnostic and Statistical Manual of Mental Disorders* (4th edition). (The DSM-IV, as it is often termed, is the clinical manual developed by the American Psychiatric Association [1994].) A diagnosis of AD/HD considers three related symptoms: inattention, impulsivity, and hyperactivity. Some examples of criterion behaviors in each symptom category are:

- Inattention
    Is easily distracted by extraneous stimuli
    Has difficulty following through on instructions or finishing work
    Seems not to be listening
    Often loses things necessary for schoolwork (pencils, homework)

- Impulsivity
  Has difficulty waiting for a turn in group situations
  Often blurts out answers before questions are completely asked
  Often interrupts others' activities or conversations
  Often seems to "act without thinking"
- Hyperactivity
  Often fidgets with hands or feet, or seems in "perpetual motion" even while
  sitting down
  Has difficulty remaining seated
  Often talks excessively

Research suggests that children with AD/HD may also have difficulties with auditory input. The ability to quickly reorient one's attention to changing auditory stimuli has been found to be impaired among some subjects (Pearson & Lane, 1991).

The use of medication is often prescribed for hyperactivity. Drugs such as Ritalin usually provide immediate and positive effects in parents' and teachers' perceptions of the student's academic performance and social behaviors (Swanson et al., 1993), with varying outcomes depending on the dose and expected behaviors (Aman & Rojahn, 1992; Forness, 1992; Kelly, 1993). Drug therapy is only part of an intervention plan, which also includes behavior management strategies.

Some helpful strategies used in classrooms with students with AD/HD include:

- Limit amount of visual and auditory distractions. Use carrels or desk dividers for seatwork, and earmuffs to block out unwanted sounds.
- When group work is necessary, keep the groups small and separated from other distractions.
- Control for external noise sources and internal reverberation.
- Stand next to the student when giving instructions or presenting a lesson.
- Mild gain amplification with FM systems may provide a favorable signal–noise ratio for students with AD/HD.

By using these and other strategies, 90% of students with learning disabilities have been taught in the regular classroom environment (Hocutt, McKinney, & Montague, 1993; National Joint Committee on Learning Disabilities, 1991a).

Students with HI and Learning Disabilities

Limited information is available regarding learners with HI who also have learning disabilities (Alpin, 1991; Powers, Elliot, & Funderburg, 1987). As mentioned earlier, as many as 20% of school-age children may have learning disabilities. However, only 10% of school-age children with a hearing impairment have been diagnosed as having a learning disability (Elliot & Powers, 1988; Mauk & Mauk, 1992). Why the difference in percentage? It is highly likely that students who have hearing impairment **and** learning disabilities are not easily identifiable. In fact, Powers et al. (1987) stated that such students are "among the most misdiagnosed and underserved" of the school-age population (p. 100). It may be difficult for educators to recognize the overlay of a learning disability in addition to the expected learning difficulties associated with hearing impairment (Alpin, 1991; Bunch & Melnyk, 1989; LaSasso, 1985; Laughton, 1989; Mencher & Gerber, 1983). Students with hearing impairments and learning disabilities have demonstrated problems with determining what topic is being discussed and have indicated an "expectation of failure" due to a high degree of misunderstandings and confusion (Bullard & Schirmer, 1991; Donahue et al., 1980).

Responsibilities of the Educational Audiologist for Students with HI and Learning Disabilities

The educational audiologist must be alert to the concerns regarding the underidentification of learning disabilities in students with HI.

> If a student is experiencing difficulties beyond the expectations for a person with impairment, a referral for an evaluation for learning difficulties is in order.

LD specialists (teachers with specialized training and certification in learning disabilities) may need information regarding the differences between those learning difficulties attributable to HI and those attributable to other factors. LD specialists may also appreciate suggestions for formal and informal assessments that measure abstract reasoning and memory skills without the use of language-dependent instruments (Roth, 1991).

It should be clear that the educational audiologist has a responsibility to stay current with the research addressing hearing and learning. For example, the use of amplification for students with normal hearing, although receiving much attention, may not always be appropriate and so always needs to be monitored by the audiologist. As another example, consider a set of research articles published in the 1970s and 1980s that focused on an auditory perceptual asymmetry called the "right ear advantage" (REA) (e.g., Leong, 1976; Obrzut, Hynd, Obrzut, & Lietgeb, 1980; Zurif & Carson, 1970). The REA refers to the observation that in dichotic listening tasks, most children are better able to perceive linguistic stimuli presented to the right ear, a finding consistent with a left hemisphere dominance for language. Some REA studies indicated that this asymmetry did not exist among children with learning disabilities, although other studies found REA in children with and without learning disabilities (Singh & Beale, 1992). Ultimately, the findings overall have been inconclusive; however, there is a risk that educational decisions may be made based on only a partial understanding of studies such as these described. As a professional with expertise in auditory perception, the educational audiologist must monitor research studies with vigilance in order to help other service providers and educators interpret research data cautiously, especially in regard to curriculum decisions.

STUDENTS WITH MENTAL RETARDATION

Approximately 2% of the school-age population are individuals with mental retardation (Evans, 1991). Individuals may have mental retardation requiring varying degrees of support. Mental retardation is one type of **developmental disability**.

The American Association on Mental Retardation (1992) defines mental retardation as:

> *Mental retardation* refers to substantial limitations in present functioning. It is characterized by significantly subaverage intellectual functioning, existing concurrently with related limitations in two or more of the following applicable adaptive skill areas: communication, self-care, home living, social skills, community use, self-direction, health and safety, functional academics, leisure, and work. Mental retardation manifests before age 18. (p. 1)

As for students with other disabilities, PL 101-476, the Individuals with Disabilities Education Act of 1990 (IDEA) mandates that educational services be provided to persons with mental retardation in inclusive settings whenever possible (Amado, 1993).

Students with HI and Mental Retardation

Educational audiologists can expect to see a higher rate of hearing impairment (at least 10%) in persons with mental retardation than in the general school-age population (American Speech and Hearing Association, 1983; Lloyd, 1976). Because of the wide variance in eligibility criteria, an actual incidence rate for hearing impairment among individuals with mental retardation is probably higher. HI has been considered by Kropka and Williams (1986) to be "a relatively common condition" (p. 39) among persons with mental retardation. The high incidence rate is related to "specific medical classifications and chromosomal deficits" (American Speech and Hearing Association, 1982, p. 549). In other words, conditions that contribute to mental retardation also affect sensorineural hearing status. For example, genetic disorders such as Down syndrome, viral infections such as maternal rubella and cytomegalovirus, and Rh complications and low birth weight are all conditions that contribute to both HI and mental retardation.

A recent study indicates a concern for outer ear status as well. A much higher incidence of excessive and recurrent cerumen impaction has been found among persons with mental retardation (Crandell & Roeser, 1993).

Responsibilities of the Educational Audiologist for Students with HI and Mental Retardation

As for all students with hearing impairment, the educational audiologist is responsible for developing a program to monitor consistent amplification use for individuals with HI and mental retardation. Cerumen management, especially for persons who use earmolds (American Speech-Language-Hearing Association, 1992) is an additional aspect of hearing-health management as is monitoring for the possibility of a conductive loss due to cerumen impaction. The National Joint Committee on the Communicative Needs of Persons with Severe Disabilities (1992) described a set of skills needed by the audiologist who serves individuals with HI and mental retardation. Some of these skills include:

1. Experience with aided and unaided modes of communication (including posture, gestures, and speech)
2. The ability to conduct assessments in consideration of cognitive, motor, and sensory functioning
3. The ability to identify communication needs of activities of daily living (ADL), as well as communication needs of the individual's educational, vocational, and recreational environments

Other service providers may not be aware of how much aural (re)habilitation can help an individual with HI and mental retardation. Therefore, the educational audiologist may need to become an advocate for such an individual.

The need for advocacy regarding an individual's development of communication skills is "perhaps more true for persons with severe disabilities than for anyone else, for these individuals are among those with the fewest personal resources and the most need for interdependence with others" (Beukelman & Mirenda, 1992, p. 258).

Sound field amplification has been shown to help students with mental retardation cope with the detrimental effects of classroom noise (Flexer, Millin, & Brown, 1990). This is a useful option to consider for students with mild hearing loss who may not use personal amplification.

STUDENTS WITH VISUAL IMPAIRMENT

By the term "students with visual impairment," we mean, for the purposes of this section, students who have visual difficulties that are not correctable with lenses. The term "legally blind" is used in schools to indicate an individual with a visual impairment that interferes with the learning process. Students of audiology already know that hearing impairment can range in severity from mild to profound; it is probably not a surprise then to learn that visual impairments also range in severity. Approximately 80% of persons classified as legally blind actually have some degree of residual vision (Barraga, 1983). Persons with residual sight or who are **partially sighted**, possess visual acuity of 20/70 to 20/200 after correction.

Evaluation of an individual's vision considers the following:

- Visual acuity (the clarity of vision). Figure 4.2 depicts the range of visual impairment discussed above.
- Visual field (the total area in which objects are visible without shifting one's gaze). Individuals may have decreased vision in the peripheral or central parts of the visual field (sometimes called "blind spots") or have hemispheric losses (indicating loss in the left or right half of the visual field).
- Light and color sensitivity
- Oculomotor functioning (the coordination of the eye muscles)

Written materials for learners with visual impairments may be provided in large print formats or in braille, or by way of technologies that magnify, modify, or use synthetic speech to access words on computer screens (Franklin & Newman, 1992; Terzieff & Antia, 1986).

Students with HI with Visual Impairment

The combination of visual and hearing impairments is referred to as deaf-blindness or dual sensory impairment. Since 94% of affected individuals have some residual hearing and/or vision, the term "deaf-blind" may be considered inappropriate (Fredericks & Baldwin, 1987; Merchant, 1992).

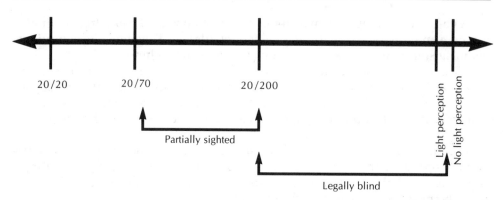

Figure 4.2. Continuum depicting the range of visual impairment. (From Beukelman, D., & Mirenda, P. [1992]. *Augmentative and alternative communication: Management of severe communication disorders in children and adults*, p. 292. Baltimore: Paul H. Brookes Publishing Co.; reprinted by permission.)

Estimates of the number of school-age children with visual and hearing impairments have been described as "notoriously inconsistent" (Sobsey & Wolf-Schein, 1991, p. 119) because of the wide range of criteria used for eligibility. Estimates indicate that approximately 4,200 students in public schools have deaf-blindness (Fredericks & Baldwin, 1987).

Of the individuals in the U.S. with deaf-blindness, approximately half have Usher's syndrome, a genetic condition in which hearing impairment is typically present at birth, and the visual impairment is a progressive loss of vision as a result of retinitis pigmentosa. Persons with Usher's syndrome typically begin to develop night blindness by age 10 and develop additional visual problems (tunnel vision, cataracts, or problems with glare) during adolescence. Other etiologies for deaf-blindness are maternal rubella and acquired deaf-blindness due to head trauma or infection. Students with deaf-blindness may demonstrate emotional or behavior problems due to the sensory deficits. Self-stimulating or self-injurious behaviors such as screaming or eye-gouging can result, and the purpose of these behaviors "appears to be either an attempt to intensify their impaired senses or to provide a general tactile-kinesthetic stimulation" (Sobsey & Wolf-Schein, 1991, p. 126). These learners are taught to substitute for these types of behaviors with more socially acceptable activities through an exercise program to encourage general body movement or with appropriate vocalizations.

Interventions for these individuals often involve training in the localization of stationary and moving sound sources and training in other auditory information that can be obtained from environmental feedback (Jones, 1988; Jose, 1983). **Coactive movement** (teacher and student performing activities together), a structured routine to build sets of expected activities, and the use of **characterization** (learning to recognize a person by an individual detail such as a bit of jewelry or clothing) are typical teaching strategies. Communication may be enhanced by teaching the one-handed American alphabet (fingerspelling into the hand) or the more difficult Tadoma method. In the Tadoma method, the individual with deaf-blindness places his or her thumb on the speaker's lips and the palm and fingers on the throat to interpret the speaker's voiced communication.

Responsibilities of the Educational Audiologist
for Students with Deaf-Blindness

Because the majority of students with deaf-blindness have some degree of residual hearing (Goetz, Guess, & Stremel-Campbell, 1987), the foremost responsibility of the audiolgoist is to ensure optimal amplification. The audiologist also collaborates with the specialist in visual impairment, because many adaptive pieces of equipment for mobility and orientation depend on audition. For example, these students are often taught to use electronic travel aids, which provide auditory cues at key locations; obviously, it is essential that students be able to hear these cues to the best of their abilities.

STUDENTS WITH EMOTIONAL DISORDERS

The federal definition of serious emotional disturbance (SED) by which a free appropriate public education was mandated for children with emotional disorders has been in existence since the passage of IDEA's precursor, PL 94-142 (The Education for All Handicapped Children Act):

> The term means a condition exhibiting one or more of the following characteristics over a long period of time and to a marked degree, which adversely affects educational performance: (a) an inability to learn which cannot be explained by intellectual, sensory, or health problems; (b) an inability to build or maintain satisfactory interpersonal relationships with peers and teachers; (c) inappropriate types of behavior or feelings under normal circumstances; (d) a tendency to develop physical symptoms or fears associated with personal or school problems. (*Federal Register* 46 [January 16, 1981], p. 3866)

It should be noted that revisions of this definition and eligibility criteria are under discussion (Mattison, 1992).

A learner with an emotional disorder often has difficulties coping with "the stresses of everyday life" (Heart, DeRuiter, & Sileo, 1986, p. 6). Emotional disorders range from mild to severe and can present with inappropriate or maladaptive behaviors that range from intense withdrawal to aggression, with subsequent socialization difficulties (Clarizio, 1992). Psychotropic drugs are often used to help children who display insomnia, hostility, extreme mood swings, or destructive behaviors. There is also a high prevalence of communication disorders in children with an emotional disorder (Prizant & Audet, 1990). Intervention in the classroom includes "affective education programs," which focus on developing an understanding of the student's feelings and attitudes (Abrams, 1992).

Some learners with an emotional disorder have been diagnosed as having autism. Because autism is frequently misunderstood, and because recent interventions have attracted the interest of audiologists, a brief discussion of autism is in order at this point.

Autism

Autism is still one of the least understood of developmental disabilities. Not that long ago, in the 1970s, parents (particularly mothers) of children with autism were unfairly held responsible for the inability of their children to develop emotional attachments. Research has established a relationship between autistic behavior and apparent damage to the central nervous system (CNS); that is, withdrawal behaviors and lack of affect are probably symptoms secondary to CNS trauma (Siefert,

1990). Auditory brainstem response (ABR) and magnetic resonance imaging (MRI) procedures have suggested cortical and subcortical abnormalities (Priven & Berthier, 1990; Thivierge, Bedard, Cote, & Maziade, 1990). Drug therapies are presently being tried to effect changes in behavior (Price & Volkar, 1992; Ratey, Grandin, & Miller, 1992).

Children with autistic disorder exhibit impairment in social interaction marked by the behaviors below:

- Withdrawal from or failure to be involved with reality
- Failure to develop oral communication
- Either oversensitivity or lack of response to stimuli, especially auditory stimuli
- Pathological resistance to changes in surroundings and routines
- Stereotypic and self-stimulating body movements such as rocking and hand flapping (Autism Society of America, 1990; Szatmari, 1992)

Among individuals with autism, social development becomes significantly impaired due to lack of apparent empathy with the emotional states of others, especially peers (Autism Society of America, 1990; Kamps, Leonard, Vernon, Dugan, & Delquadri, 1992; Szatmari, 1992; Volkar, Carter, Sparrow, & Cicchetti, 1993; Yirmiya, Sigman, Kasari, & Mundy, 1992). Interventions have been designed to help children with autism develop social skills and peer relationships (Goldstein, Kaczmarek, Pennington, & Shafer, 1992; Strain, Kerr, & Ragland, 1979).

Two innovative approaches that attempt to address the communication problems of persons with autism are **facilitated communication** and **auditory integration training**, both of which are briefly described below.

Facilitated Communication Facilitated communication (FC) utilizes the presence of a teacher, aide, or other person (the facilitator) to enable an individual with autism to communicate in written form. Individuals may point to a keyboard template, or use a computer or typewriter to spell out communications. Facilitators are taught to guide the arm movement of the individual initially, and then to fade out the physical assistance to promote independent use of the communcation strategy (Biklin, 1993).

Facilitated communication has received much attention and has generated a great deal of controversy among researchers and practitioners. Many professionals and parents have been very vocal in their support for the use of this procedure, feeling that, for the first time, their children have a way of communication and self-expression. However, research continues to indicate that the facilitators are unknowingly guiding the arm of their clients to produce certain words (Wheeler, Jacobson, Paglieri, & Schwartz, 1993).

Auditory Integration Training Another approach that is of particular interest to audiologists is AIT. Because some children with autism demonstrate an oversensitivity to auditory stimuli, a therapy was developed to attempt auditory desensitization. Participants in AIT receive auditory input from headphones over a 10-day period, in two 1/2-hour sessions, morning and afternoon. Input (typically music of all types) is filtered to completely or partially eliminate frequencies for which individuals indicate hyperacuity according to an audiogram (Fox, 1993). Effects for some individuals with autism include reductions in self-stimulating behaviors, echolalia, distractibility, and impulsivity, and an improvement in language development (Madell, 1994).

Reasons why AIT is effective are far from clear. Most persons who provide AIT are not communication specialists. Some audiologists have become qualified to provide AIT in order to study the effects of this therapy (Madell, 1994). It is possible that AIT helps children with autism who have associated central auditory processing disorders.

Students with HI and Emotional Disorders

Research regarding learners with hearing impairment and emotional disabilities (apart from studies considering the emotional impact of HI itself) is virtually nonexistent. It does appear that students with SED may have underdeveloped communication skills and consequently have less ability to solve problems and conflicts with language (Rosenthal & Simeonsson, 1991). Because we know that often students with HI already have deficits in these areas, it is likely that a concomitant emotional disorder can exacerbate these difficulties.

Responsibilities of the Educational Audiologist for Students with HI and an Emotional Disorder

The educational audiologist first needs to ascertain whether the student with SED has a hearing impairment. This is of particular concern for a child with autism because his or her lack of response to auditory stimuli may be assumed incorrectly to be related only to the diagnosis of autism (Seifert, 1990). It is vital to emphasize to school colleagues that it cannot be assumed that no hearing impairment exists without confirming results from accurate behavior or auditory brainstem response (ABR) testing. In fact, recent studies have shown a significantly higher prevalence of hearing impairment among children with autism than among the general school-age population. Klin (1993) reviewed several studies that used ABR testing to detect brainstem abnormalities and found that an unexpectedly high number of subjects with autism demonstrated previously undetected peripheral hearing loss (Skoff et al., 1986; Student & Sohmer, 1978; Taylor, Rosenblatt, & Linschoten, 1982).

> An undetected hearing loss "may exacerbate maladaptive behaviors, augment frustration, and add an additional hurdle on the path of these children's development of social and communication skills" (Klin, 1993, p. 29).

Because behavior management is an important focus for students with all types of SED (Steinburg & Kintzer, 1992), the educational audiologist needs to be sure that a student with HI and an emotional disorder can hear what is expected of him or her. Teachers and aides require technical support and information from the educational audiologist in order to conduct behavior management programs effectively. Specifically, the educational audiologist needs to advise education personnel regarding the effects of noise on the student and on the limitations of hearing aids for amplification of speech sounds.

In addition to staff support, audiologists in schools must assume responsibility for closely monitoring research regarding therapies such as AIT. People involved with children with disabilities may feel a desperation for "cures" that might influence them to make decisions based on data that are not fully substantiated.

RECENT ISSUES: FETAL ALCOHOL
SYNDROME, PRENATAL DRUG EXPOSURE, AND AIDS

It is always a challenge to stay current with the research investigating newly identified concerns in education. Only very recently has information been made available on health concerns such as the effects of fetal alcohol syndrome (FAS), prenatal drug exposure, and acquired immunodeficiency syndrome (AIDS). As with all
such issues, practitioners have the professional obligation to actively keep track of
these and related concerns in order to incorporate current research into educational planning. These three recently identified health conditions are briefly considered here.

Fetal Alcohol Syndrome

Fetal alcohol syndrome has been associated with a high likelihood of hearing impairment (Joint Committee on Infant Hearing, 1991). Approximately 5,000 infants
are born each year who are diagnosed with FAS—1 in every 750 live births (Sparks,
1992). Physical characteristics may include: short stature; droopy eyelids that make
eyes appear slanted, or eyes that are widely spaced; absent philtrum; flat, wide nose
bridge and/or small upturned nose; and large or malformed ears.

In addition to these physical and facial anomolies, there are probable detrimental effects on the central nervous system. These detrimental effects may present
as learning difficulties due to poor attending abilities and as a severe lack of prag-
matic or problem-solving skills. Memory deficits, impulsivity, and frequent temper
tantrums can negatively affect the school performance of an individual with FAS.

A related condition is fetal alcohol effects (FAE), which may present with
fewer physical characteristics but affects three times as many children as FAS (approximately 15,000 a year). An individual with FAE may have difficulty with coordination, concentration, and emotional lability (Crist, 1992).

Prenatal Drug Exposure

Infants with a history of prenatal cocaine exposure are also at risk of having a hearing impairment, because cocaine acts as a vasoconstrictor to the placenta (i.e., it
decreases the blood flow supply and reduces the amount of oxygen). Cocaine ap-
parently can also damage the central nervous system of the fetus; the neurological
deficits are suspected to result in emotional and/or learning disabilities (Saari,1991;
Shih, Cone-Wesson, & Reddix, 1988).

AIDS

Little information is available regarding AIDS and children with HI. It is known
that medications used to treat AIDS can be ototoxic. In addition, lesions from Ka-
posi's sarcoma, which may be present in individuals with AIDS, can occur in the
ear canal and contribute to conductive hearing loss. Other infections secondary to
AIDS such as meningitis can also result in hearing impairment ("AIDS-related sensory deficits," 1993).

CONCLUSION

These brief overviews of individuals with disabilities in addition to HI are intended to provide some basic information regarding how other disabilities can interact to affect an individual with hearing impairment, as well as to emphasize that **correlation with other service providers is essential**. Working with other service providers is essential when an additional disability interacts with a hearing impairment in an individual and affects a learner's academic achievement.

Another important responsibility of the educational audiologist is continuing education (self-directed or formal) in order to remain current with research in audiology and other related disciplines. Any therapy, intervention, or curriculum that incorporates principles of audition must be monitored by the educational audiologist to ensure that the learning strategies are based on proven theory rather than on trends or faulty assumptions.

Finally, it is worth the risk of repeating the obvious to strongly emphasize that amplification for individuals with disabilities should be considered according to the same criteria as for all children without other disabilities. Furthermore, additional follow-up is required for students with HI and additional disabilities to monitor for the possibility of overstimulation and overamplification.

Learning the Language

Review the following concepts from this chapter and discuss with a colleague.

- Discrepancies between achievement and potential
- Dyslexia
- Visual, perceptual, and auditory perceptual disorders
- CAPD
- Attention-deficit/hyperactivity disorder (AD/HD)
- partial sight/low vision
- DSI
- coactive movement teaching
- FC
- AIT
- FAS and FAE

Educational Audiology in Action
Suggested Learning Activities

Project 1. Interview some school professionals who have a specialty in a field other than hearing impairment. Find out:

What kind of training and practicum experiences did they have before they were hired?

What drew them to their career choice?

What changes have they experienced or observed in education since they began working in their field?

What training did they receive regarding learners with HI?

Of the students they serve, how many also have HI?

How often are they able to consult with an educational audiologist or a teacher of the HI?

How does HI seem to interact with other disabilities?

Project 2. Obtain permission to observe a student with HI and an additional disability. Before your observation, make a list of behaviors, difficulties, and strategies you would expect to be appropriate to the age of the student you are observing. After a 2-hour observation, review your list. Did you see what you expected to see? If there were discrepancies, how would you account for them?

Recommended Readings

Baron, J., & Baron, S. (1992). *There's a boy in here.* New York: Simon and Schuster.

A mother and her adult son write about their shared memories of his childhood and adolescence living with autism. The son describes his perceptions of the people and world around him, and his observations regarding the range of therapies he experienced.

Franklin, K., & Newman, K. (1992). Persons with visual and dual sensory impairments. In D. Beukelman & P. Mirenda, *Augmentative and alternative communication: Management of severe communication disorders in children and adults* (pp. 291-307). Baltimore: Paul H. Brookes Publishing Co.

This highly informative chapter describes types of visual impairment and intervention strategies for persons with combined visual and hearing impairments (dual sensory impairment).

Ratey, J., Grandin, T., & Miller, A. (1992). Defense behavior and coping in an autistic savant: The story of Temple Grandin, Ph.D. *Psychiatry, 55*(4), 383-391.

A first-hand account of the experience of autism. Temple Grandin indicates that she adapted autistic behaviors as a defense against a "flood of stimuli."

Sacks, Oliver. (1993). An Anthropologist on Mars. *The New Yorker,* Dec. 27, 1993– Jan. 3, 1994, pp. 106–125.

Dr. Sacks reports his observations during a visit with Temple Grandin, who vividly describes her experiences with and strategies for living with autism.

References

Abrams, B. (1992). Values clarification for students with emotional disabilities. *TEACHING Exceptional Children, 24*(3), 28–33.

AIDS-related sensory deficits focus of California conference. (1993, March 16). *Advance*, p. 3.

Alpin, D. (1991). Identification of additional learning difficulties in hearing impaired children. In D. Martin (Ed.), *Advances in cognition, education and deafness* (pp. 39–48). Washington, DC: Gallaudet University Press.

Amado, A.N. (Ed.). (1993). *Friendships and community connections between people with and without developmental disabilities.* Baltimore: Paul H. Brookes Publishing Co.

Aman, M., & Rojahn, S. (1992). Pharmacological intervention. In N. Singh & I. Beale (Eds.), *Learning disabilities: Nature, theory, and treatment* (pp. 478–525). New York: Springer-Verlag.

American Association on Mental Retardation. (1992). *Definition, classification, and systems of supports* (9th ed.). Washington, DC: Author.

American Psychiatric Association. (1994). *Diagnostic and statistical manual of mental disorders* (4th ed. rev., DSM-IV). Washington, DC: Author.

American Speech and Hearing Association. (1982). Serving the communicatively handicapped mentally retarded individual: Position statement. *Asha, 24,* 547–553.

American Speech and Hearing Association. (1983). *The hearing impaired mentally retarded: Recommendations for action.* Washington, DC: Social and Rehabilitiative Services, Department of Health, Education, and Welfare.

American Speech-Language-Hearing Association. (1990). What are central auditory problems in children? *Asha, 32*(8), 53–54.

American Speech-Language-Hearing Association. (1992). External auditory canal examination and cerumen management. *Asha, 34*(March, Suppl. 7), 22–24.

Autism Society of America. (1990). *Autism fact sheet* (NIH publication no. 83-1877). Bethesda, MD: Department of Health and Human Services.

Barraga, N. (1983). *Visual handicaps and learning* (rev. ed.). Austin, TX: Exceptional Resources.

Beukelman, D., & Mirenda, P. (1992). *Augmentative and alternative communication: Management of severe communication disorders in children and adults.* Baltimore: Paul H. Brookes Publishing Co.

Biklin, D. (1993). *Communication unbound.* New York: Teachers College Press.

Bullard, C., & Schirmer, B. (1991). Understanding questions: Hearing impaired children with learning problems. *Volta Review, 93,* 235–245.

Bunch, G., & Melnyk, T. (1989). A review of the evidence of a learning disabled-hearing impaired subgroup. *American Annals of the Deaf, 134,* 297–300.

Chermak, G., & Musiek, F. (1992). Managing central auditory processing disorders in children and youth. *American Journal of Audiology, 1*(3), 61–65.

Clarizio, H. (1992). Social maladjustment and emotional disturbance: Problems and positions I. *Psychology in the Schools, 29*(4), 331–341.

Cone-Wesson, B., & Spingarn, A. (1990). Effects of maternal cocaine abuse on neonatal ABR: Premature and small-for-date infants. *Journal of American Academy of Audiology, 1*(1).

Crandell, C., & Roeser, R. (1993). Incidence of excessive/impacted cerumen in individuals with mental retardation: A longitudinal investigation. *American Journal on Mental Retardation, 97*(5), 568–574.

Crist, D. (1992). Fetal alcohol syndrome. *Health Journal,* p. 20–21.

Donahue, M., Pearl, R., & Bryan, T. (1980). Learning disabled children's conversational competence: Responses to inadequate messages. *Applied Pyscholinguistics, 1,* 387–403.

Education for All Handicapped Children Act of 1975, PL 94-142. (August 23, 1977). Title 20, U.S.C. 1401 et seq: *U.S. Statutes at Large, 89*, 773–796.

Elliot, R., & Powers, A. (1988). Preparing teachers to serve the learning disabled hearing impaired. *Volta Review, 90*, 13–18.

Evans, I. (1991). Testing and diagnosis: A review and evaluation. In L. Meyer, C. Peck, & L. Brown (Eds.), *Critical issues in the lives of people with severe disabilities* (pp. 25–44). Baltimore: Paul H. Brookes Publishing Co.

Federal Register 46 (January 16, 1981), 3866.

Flexer, C., Millin, J., & Brown, L. (1990). Children with developmental disabilities: The effect of sound field amplification on word identification. *Language, Speech, and Hearing Services in Schools, 21*, 177–182.

Forness, S. (1992). Response to stimulant medication across six measures of school-related performance in children with ADHD and disruptive behavior. *Behavioral Disorders, 18*(1), 42–53.

Fox, S. (1993, April 6). Audiologists take on autism with auditory training. *Advance*, pp. 10–11.

Franklin, K., & Newman, K. (1992). Persons with visual and dual sensory impairments. In D. Beukelman & P. Mirenda, *Augmentative and alternative communication: Management of severe communication disorders in children and adults* (pp. 291–307). Baltimore: Paul H. Brookes Publishing Co.

Fredericks, H., & Baldwin, V. (1987). Individuals with sensory impairments: Who are they? How are they educated? In L. Goetz, D. Guess, & K. Stremel- Campbell (Eds.), *Innovative program design for individuals with dual sensory impairments* (pp. 3–12). Baltimore: Paul H. Brookes Publishing Co.

Goetz, L., Guess, D., & Stremel-Campbell, K. (Eds.). (1987). *Innovative program design for individuals with dual sensory impairment*. Baltimore: Paul H. Brookes Publishing Co.

Goldstein, H., Kaczmarek, L., Pennington, R., & Shafer, K. (1992). Peer-mediated intervention: Attending to, commenting on, and acknowledging the behavior of preschoolers with autism. *Journal of Applied Behavior Analysis, 25*, 289–306.

Heart, B., DeRuiter, J., & Sileo, T. (1986). *Teaching mildly and moderately handicapped students*. Englewood Cliffs, NJ: Prentice Hall.

Hocutt, A., McKinney, J., & Montague, M. (1993). Issues in the education of students with attention deficit disorder. *Exceptional Children, 60*(2), 103–106.

Joint Committee on Infant Hearing. (1991). 1990 position statement. *Asha, 33*(Suppl.5), 3–6.

Jones, C. (1988). *Evaluation and educational programming of deaf-blind/severely multi-handicapped students*. Springfield, IL: Charles C Thomas.

Jose, R. (Ed.). (1983). *Understanding low vision*. New York: American Foundation for the Blind.

Kamps, D., Leonard, B., Vernon, S., Dugan, E., & Delquadri, J. (1992). Teaching social skills to students with autism to increase peer interactions in an integrated first grade classroom. *Journal of Applied Behavior Analysis, 25*, 281–288.

Kelly, D. (1993, February 15). Appropriate intervention for ADD begins with accurate diagnosis, informed parents. *Advance*, p. 5.

Klin, A. (1993). Auditory brainstem response in autism: Brainstem dysfunction or peripheral loss? *Journal of Autism and Developmental Disorders, 23*(10), 15–35.

Kropka, B., & Williams, C. (1986). The epidemiology of hearing impairment in people with a mental handicap. In D. Ellis (Ed.), *Sensory impairments in mentally handicapped people* (pp. 35–60). San Diego: College-Hill Press.

LaSasso, C. (1985). "Learning disabilities"—Let's be careful before labeling deaf children. *Perspectives of Teachers of the Hearing Impaired, 3*(5), 2–4.

Laughton, J. (1989). The learning disabled, hearing impaired student: Reality, myth, or overextension? *Topics in Language Disorders, 9*(4), 70–79.

Leong, C. (1976). Lateralization in severely disabled readers in relation to functional cerebral development and synthesis of information. In R. Knights & D. Bakker (Eds.), *Neurophysiology of learning disorders: Theoretical approaches* (pp. 221–231). Baltimore: University Park Press.

Lewis, R., & Doorlag, D. (1991). *Teaching special students in the mainstream*. New York: Macmillan.

Lloyd, L. (1976). *Communication assessment and intervention strategies.* Baltimore: University Park Press.

Madell, J. (1994) Auditory integration training. *American Journal of Audiology, 3*(1), 14–18.

Mattison, R. (1992). Distinguishing characteristics of elementary schoolboys recommended for SED placement. *Behavioral Disorders, 17*(2), 107–114.

Mauk, G., & Mauk, P. (1992). Somewhere, out there: Preschool children with hearing impairment and learning disabilities. *Topics in Early Childhood Special Education, 12*(2), 175–195.

Maxon, A., & Smaldino, J. (1991). Hearing aid management for children. *Seminars in Hearing, 12*(4), 365–379.

McBurnett, K., Lahey, B., & Pfiffner, L. (1993). Diagnosis of attention deficit disorders in DSM-IV: Scientific basis and implications for education. *Exceptional Children, 60*(2), 108–117.

Mencher, G., & Gerber, S. (Eds.). (1983). *The multihandicapped hearing impaired child.* New York: Grune & Stratton.

Merchant, J. (1992). Deaf-blind handicapping conditions. In P. McLaughlin & P. Wehman (Eds.), *Developmental disabilities* (pp. 113–119). Boston: Andover Medical Publishers.

National Joint Committee for the Communicative Needs of Persons with Severe Disabilities. (1992). Guidelines for meeting the communication needs of persons with severe disabilities. *Asha, 34*(Suppl. 7), 1–8.

National Joint Committee on Learning Disabilities. (1991a). Learning disabilities: Issues in definition. *Asha, 33*(Suppl. 5), 18–20.

National Joint Committee on Learning Disabilities. (1991b). Providing appropriate education for students with learning disabilities in regular education classrooms. *Asha, 33*(Suppl. 5), 15–17.

Obrzut, J., Hynd, G., Obrzut, A., & Leitgeb, J. (1980). Time-sharing and dichotic listening asymmetry in normal and learning disabled children. *Developmental Psychology, 17*, 118–125.

Patterson, G. (1986). Performance models for antisocial boys. *American Psychologist, 41*, 432–444.

Pearson, D., & Lane, D. (1991). Auditory attention switching in hyperactive children. *Journal of Abnormal Child Psychology, 19*(4), 479–492.

Powers, A., Elliot, R., & Funderburg, R. (1987). Learning disabled hearing impaired students: Are they being identified? *Volta Review, 89*, 99–105.

Price, L., & Volkar, F. (1992). Clomipramine in autism: Preliminary evidence of efficacy. *Journal of the American Academy of Child and Adolescent Psychiatry, 31*(4), 746–750.

Prickett, H., & Prickett, J. (1992). Vision problems among schools and programs for deaf children: A survey of teachers of deaf students. *American Annals of the Deaf, 137*, 56–60.

Priven, J., & Berthier, M. (1990). Magnetic resonance imaging evidence for a defect of cerebral cortical development in autism. *American Journal of Psychiatry, 147*(6), 734–739.

Prizant, B., & Audet, L. (1990). Communication disorders and emotional/behavioral disorders in children and adolescents. *Journal of Speech and Hearing Disorders, 55*(2), 179–192.

Ratey, J., Grandin, T., & Miller, A. (1992). Defense behavior and coping in an autistic savant: The story of Temple Grandin, Ph.D. *Psychiatry, 55*(4), 383–391.

Ratner, V. (1988). New tests for identifying hearing impaired students with visual perceptual deficits: Relationship between deficit and ability to comprehend sign language. *American Annals of the Deaf, 133*, 336–343.

Reid, R., Maag, J., & Vasa, S. (1993). Attention deficit hyperactivity disorder as a disability category: A critique. *Exceptional Children, 60*(3), 198–214.

Rosenthal, S., & Simeonsson, R. (1991). Communication skills in emotionally disturbed and nondisturbed adolescents. *Behavioral Disorders, 16*(3), 192–199.

Roth, V. (1991). Students with learning disabilities and hearing impairments: Issues for the secondary and postsecondary teacher. *Journal of Learning Disabilities, 24*, 391–397.

Saari, L. (1991, March 10). Tormented offspring. *San Diego Union,* p. D-1.

Sanders, D. (1993). *Management of hearing handicap: Infant to elderly* (3rd ed.). Englewood Cliffs, NJ: Prentice Hall.

Schildroth, A., & Hotto, S. (1993). Annual survey of hearing impaired children and youth: 1991–92 school year. *American Annals of the Deaf, 138*, 163–168.

Seifert, C. (1990). *Theories of autism.* Lanham, MD: University Press of America.

Shaywitz, S., & Shaywitz, B. (Eds.). (1992). *Attention deficit disorder comes of age: Toward the twenty-first century.* Austin, TX: PRO-ED.

Shih, L., Cone-Wesson, B., & Reddix, B. (1988). Effects of maternal cocaine abuse on the neonatal auditory system. *International Journal of Pediatric Otorhinolaryngology, 15,* 245–251.

Singh, H., & Beale, I. (1992). *Learning disabilities: Nature, theory, and treatment.* New York: Springer-Verlag.

Skoff, B., Fein, D., McNally, B., Lucci, D., Humes-Bartho, M., & Waterhouse, L. (1986). Brainstem auditory evoked potentials in autism. *Psychophysiology, 23,* 462.

Smith, D., & Robinson, S. (1986). Educating the learning disabled. In R. Morris & B. Blatt (Eds.), *Special education: Research and trends* (pp. 222–248). New York: Pergamon.

Smoski, W., Brunt, M., & Tannahill, J. (1992). Listening characteristics of children with central auditory processing disorders. *Language, Speech, and Hearing Services in Schools, 23,* 145–152.

Sobsey, D., & Wolf-Shein, E. (1991). Sensory impairments. In F. Orelove & D. Sobsey, (Eds.), *Educating children with multiple disabilities: A transdisciplinary approach* (2nd ed.) (pp. 119–153). Baltimore: Paul H. Brookes Publishing Co.

Spafford, C., & Grosser, G. (1993). The social misperception syndrome in children with learning disabilities: Social causes versus neurological variables. *Journal of Learning Disabilities, 26*(3), 178–189.

Sparks, S. (1992). *Children of prenatal substance abuse.* San Diego: Singular Publishing Group.

Steinberg, Z., & Kintzer, J. (1992). Classrooms for emotional and behavior disturbed students: Facing the challenge. *Behavioral Disorders, 17*(2), 145–156.

Strain, P., Kerr, M., & Ragland, E. (1979). Effects of peer-mediated social initiations and prompting/reinforcement procedures on the social behavior of autistic children. *Journal of Autism and Developmental Disability, 9,* 41–54.

Student, M., & Sohmer, H. (1978). Evidence from auditory nerve and brainstem evoked responses for an organic brain lesion in children with autistic traits. *Journal of Autism and Developmental Disorders, 8,* 13–19.

Swanson, J., McBurnett, K., Wigal, T., Pfiffner, L., Lerner, M., Williams, L., Christian, D., Tamm, L., Willcutt, E., Crowley, K., Clevenger, W., Khouzam, N., Woo, C., Crinella, F., & Fisher, T. (1993). Effect of stimulant medication on children with attention deficit disorder: A "review of reviews." *Exceptional Children, 60*(2), 154–161.

Szatmari, P. (1992). A review of the DSM-III-R criteria for autistic disorder. *Journal of Autism and Developmental Disorders, 22*(4), 507–523.

Taylor, M., Rosenblatt, B., & Linschoten, L. (1982). Auditory brainstem response abnormalities in autistic children. *Canadian Journal of Neurological Science, 9,* 429–433.

Terzieff, I., & Antia, S. (1986). Children with sensory impairments: Perspectives on development. In R. Morris & B. Blatt (Eds.), *Special education: Research and Trends* (pp. 303–343). New York: Pergamon.

Thivierge, J., Bedard, C., Cote, R., & Maziade, M. (1990). Brainstem auditory evoked responses and subcortical abnormalities in autism. *American Journal of Psychiatry, 147*(12), 1609–1613.

Toro, P., Weissberg, R., Guare, J., & Liebenstein, N. (1990). A comparison of children with and without learning disabilities on social problem-solving skill, school behavior, and family background. *Journal of Learning Disabilities, 23,* 115–120.

Trace, R. (1993a, August 2). CAPD diagnosis requires comprehensive assessment. *Advance, 7,* 13.

Trace, R. (1993b, August 2). Researchers, clinicians discuss a "healthy" diversity of approaches to CAPD. *Advance,* 10–11, 13.

Volkar, F., Carter, A., Sparrow, S., & Cicchetti, D. (1993). Quantifying social development in autism. *Journal of American Academy of Child and Adolescent Psychiatry, 32*(3), 627–632.

Waldron, K. (1992). *Teaching children with learning disabilities: Strategies for success.* San Diego: Singular Publishing Group.

Wheeler, D., Jacobson, J., Paglieri, R., & Schwartz, A. (1993). An experimental assessment of facilitated communication. *Mental Retardation, 31*(1), 49–60.

Yirmiya, N., Sigman, M., Kasari, C., & Mundy, P. (1992). Empathy and cognition in high-functioning children with autism. *Child Development, 63*(1), 150–160.

Zentall, S. (1993). Research on the educational implications of attention deficit hyperactivity disorder. *Exceptional Children, 60*(2), 143–153.

Zurif, E., & Carson, G. (1970). Dyslexia in relation to cerebral dominance and temporal analysis. *Neuropsychologia, 8*, 351–361.

5

Serving Students as a Team Member

IN THE LAST FEW YEARS, the manner in which school services have been provided to students with disabilities has changed dramatically. In the 1980s, services were still provided virtually as self-contained entities: each professional worked independently of others, with little or no coordination or interaction among disciplines. Today there is a strong emphasis on collaboration and teaming—processes that require distinct skills that enable individuals to work effectively with colleagues.

In this chapter, we examine the topic of collaboration from two perspectives: **with whom** the educational audiologist collaborates and **how** the process is achieved. The first part of this chapter concerns with whom you collaborate. As a member of a **team** of service providers, the educational audiologist must be familiar with the different areas of expertise that the other team members bring. A general "job description" for a variety of team members is provided as part of this examination. However, because many areas of expertise tend to overlap, the reader is cautioned to remember that these descriptions are intended to be neither binding or exhaustive. It quickly becomes apparent that many education-related disciplines are undergoing great changes and are in the process of redefining themselves as educational reforms are realized in practice. It is somehow reassuring to know that most specialties in education are undergoing similar growing pains. Professionals in education want to avoid preconceptions of a colleague's expertise that could lead to pigeonholed expectations and unintentionally reduce the range of assistance and expertise that a professional may be very able to provide.

Specific qualifications of practitioners are not provided because these vary greatly according to state and local regulations. Rather, the suggestion is offered, perhaps as part of a team-building exercise, to interview colleagues at some length to find out the variety of background, education, training, experience, licenses, and professional certification of each team member.

How to collaborate with team members is a topic of high priority among educators and support personnel everywhere in the U.S. The second part of this chapter provides descriptions of three team configurations, including the one that most effectively facilitates the collaborative process.

EDUCATORS AS TEAM MEMBERS

Following is a general job description for the educators most directly involved with a child with HI with whom you will be working: teachers of the hearing impaired, regular classroom teachers, and resource specialists.

Teachers of Learners with Hearing Impairment

A teacher with expertise in educating children with hearing impairment may have a master's degree, or, at the least, specialized training (college credits and field experience) in addition to a B.A. and general education teacher training. The expertise of the teacher of students with hearing impairment focuses on the implications of HI on academic and language development. However, not all training programs provide a strong background regarding the use of amplification or how to develop listening skills (Sexton, 1991).

The role of the teacher of students with hearing impairment is evolving from that of a teacher in a segregated classroom to that of program manager (Luetke-Stahlman & Luckner, 1991). Many teachers still conduct a special day class; that is, a classroom with a small teacher–student ratio, which serves as the primary classroom for children with HI. However, many teachers of students with hearing impairment are also consulting with regular-education teachers whose classes include children with hearing impairment, perhaps for the first time (Luckner, 1991). Some teachers of students with HI may also work in itinerant positions. An **itinerant teacher** travels among several schools, teaching and providing consultative services to teachers and to students attending regular education classes in their local schools.

Regular Education Teachers

The role of the regular education teacher in the education of children with disabilities continues to be broadened and redefined. In addition to adapting to the changes of the educational reform movement, the regular education teacher is being asked to accommodate individual students with a variety of learning differences in a single, inclusive classroom. Many regular education teachers admit feeling uncomfortable with the new expectations for a variety of reasons, including a lack of training in the specialized skills they now need and a lack of essential technical assistance and support from their school districts. Many teachers may understandably feel less than professional and less than competent with these new situations and so may feel threatened or insecure or resentful of new demands. Teachers have also indicated a concern about the level of accountability they are held to when teaching students with disabilities, particularly when they do not have appropriate experience or training (Chorost, 1988; Lass, Tecca, & Woodford, 1987; Martin, Bernstein, Daly, & Cody, 1988).

Regular education teachers certainly are correct to expect assistance from related support personnel (audiologists, SLPs, teachers of students with HI) when a child with HI is placed in their classroom. Teachers are most receptive to accommodating the needs of a child with a disability when they fully participate in the decision-making, implementation, and evaluation of a student's placement (Luckner, Rude, & Sileo, 1989; Myles & Simpson, 1989). Teachers have also indicated strong interest in receiving information and support in a timely fashion (Luckner, 1991).

Resource Teachers

Many children, with and without disabilities, require additional or concentrated support in a specific academic area, typically reading or math. Resource teachers (sometimes called RSP specialists) provide this type of concentrated, small-group instruction that augments the classroom instruction. Resource support personnel (RSP) services formerly were exclusively provided in a separate classroom as a "pull-out" program. Now, however, the RSP is more likely to work in the regular classroom, in a small group that includes not only students with an identified disability, but also students at risk or borderline in mastering a particular skill. This is an effective "prereferral" strategy that meets the individual needs of several students in a single setting (Pugach & Johnson, 1989; Welsh et al., 1990). Prereferral activities are typically developed within teams of special-education and regular-education teachers as a means of serving students who demonstrate minor, temporary, or inconsistent academic difficulties. Effective prereferral intervention reduces the risk of overreferrals for special education services (Pugach & Johnson, 1989; Welsh et al., 1990).

SUPPORT PERSONNEL AS TEAM MEMBERS

In addition to the professional educators described, a child with hearing impairment receives services from a variety of other professionals, depending on his or her individual needs. The roles and responsibilities of some of these support personnel are described in the following section.

Speech-Language Pathologists

The speech-language pathologist (SLP) evaluates a child's communication skills and designs and provides intervention to develop these skills. By virtue of their shared educational background in communication disorders, the SLP is one of the most dependable allies of the educational audiologist. However, it is important to remember that not every SLP has a strong background in the communication needs of children with hearing impairment, apart from theory. For example, although most students with HI receive speech and language intervention at some point during their school careers, SLPs have indicated little or no experience in inspecting hearing aids (Lass et al., 1989; Subtelney, Webster, & Murphy, 1980).

The SLP is becoming actively engaged in the collaboration process in schools (Conner & Welsh, 1993). Most SLPs working in schools are involved in some classroom service delivery, using the same small-group instruction method that was described for the RSP specialist. SLPs may also teach the entire class a unit on a language goal, modeling the lesson for the classroom teacher, or teach a unit in cooperation with the teacher, each integrating his or her goals into the lesson. This technique is referred to as co-teaching (Montgomery, 1992; Russell & Kaderavek, 1993).

School Nurses

At the beginning of the 20th century, school nurses were employed to conduct "medical inspections" and to teach good habits in hygiene and health (Struthers, 1917). Today, the school nurse is fully involved in a wide range of health issues, including:

- Screenings (for vision, hearing, and scoliosis, for example)
- Provision of medical services, from routine first aid to dispensing of medications to the treatment of acute and chronic conditions
- Control of infectious conditions such as head lice, influenza, ringworm (Lewis & Thomson, 1986; Synoground & Kelsey, 1990)

Many school nurses are licensed audiometrists, qualified to conduct **hearing screening** programs under the supervision of an audiologist (Johnson, Stein, & Lass, 1992). School nurses are available to provide medical treatment at the school site, and are responsible for the maintenance of health records. Nurses also conduct vision screenings, which are very important for children who are particularly dependent upon visual input. School nurses can be valuable liaisons between the school and the health community, often knowing doctors who are associated with nonprofit or low-cost community ear, nose, and throat (ENT) clinics or who provide other medical services to the school community.

School Psychologists, Counselors, and Social Workers

The **school psychologist** is responsible for the administration and interpretation of a battery of psychometric assessments, primarily standardized intelligence, psychosocial, and aptitude evaluations. The traditional role of the school psychologist has been to test a child and explain the test results in response to concerns expressed by parents and/or teachers; support the explanation; and to provide advice to parents and teachers about how to help the child with learning, social, or behavioral difficulties (Weiner & Davidson, 1990). However, as discussed in terms of other specialties within education, the field of school psychology currently sees itself at a crossroad. While many practitioners want to maintain the role of tester and child behavior expert, others are interested in expanding their expertise into a variety of other domains, in order to actively participate in educational reform (Cole & Seigel, 1990; Phillips, 1990). Generally at the present time, the school psychologist devotes most of his or her workday to referral-test-placement activities related to individuals who require special education services. A proposed restructuring of educational services would make it possible for the school psychologist, for example, to practice "intervention assistance" for regular-education teachers in behavior management techniques. The school psychologist could also expand into the areas of personnel development and team building, interpersonal communications, social and basic life skills, and multicultural concerns, as well as share information with other school personnel on family systems, gender issues, or friendship formation, for example (Kaufmann, 1988; Medway, 1992; Shinn, 1986; Yssledyke, Reynolds, & Weinberg, 1984).

The conventional responsibilities of the **school counselor** have been twofold. First, as an academic advisor, the counselor provides information about college admissions, course selection, vocational training, and job placement. Second, as a crisis manager or interventionist, the counselor is expected to provide on-site assistance to students experiencing interpersonal problems with teachers, peers, or family (Thompson, 1992). Because of dramatic social changes in society, counselors are finding themselves more involved in curriculum development in the areas of health and physical development, self-concept, and social issues (Worzbyt & O'Rourke, 1989). Counselors are also serving as liaisons in the partnerships growing between schools and business and industry. As in other disciplines, the need for developing collaborative and team-building skills is emphasized in the professional literature of the school counselor.

Social workers are involved in social issues, ranging from financial assistance to discrimination to interpersonal or family conflicts. A most important role of a school social worker in the life of a child with a hearing impairment is to be the liaison with other community agencies. The social worker, for example, often coordinates arranging for testing or medical services, or for financial assistance so that a student can obtain hearing aids.

The social worker is also the most likely person to contact regarding suspected child abuse and neglect. Audiologists in schools have been advised since 1984 that all states mandate that service providers in education must report suspected abuse or neglect. Those service providers who do not report suspected abuse or neglect risk the penalty of a fine or a misdemeanor or criminal charge. Immunity from such liability is provided those who report in good faith (Tower, 1992). Each school district has its own policy regarding such procedures, and audiologists are expected to be familiar with these procedures (Holvoet & Helmstetter, 1989).

Social workers have expertise in many other issues that can adversely affect a student's life. Such issues include substance abuse or family difficulties such as divorce, illness, separation, adoption, inadequate childcare, teenage pregnancy, homelessness, or parental unemployment. Social workers are skilled in developing interventions that provide their clients with skills and resources to cope with the conditions of their environment (Forman, 1987; Jansson, 1990; Monkman, 1991; Schultz & Heuchert, 1983; Steele & Raider, 1991).

It is likely that the services of school social workers are underutilized. For example, Wang, Reynolds, and Walberg (1991) suggested that the expertise of social workers can facilitate many aspects of an individual's transition from "special programming" to a fully inclusive classroom. The school social worker's expertise in group dynamics and in the coping and adaptive behaviors of individuals and groups can help teachers, service providers, and students work effectively with the change in service delivery. It has also been recommended that school social workers collaborate with special educators regarding a student's IEP and decisions regarding the least restrictive environment by providing in-depth profiles regarding time-on-task, group functioning, and emotional and behavior concerns (Drisko, 1993; Monkman, 1991; Rogoff & Constable, 1991). However, because of strained or limited resources, school social workers may not be able to provide this type of consultative support, and may be available only for crisis intervention (A. Sholander, personal communication, August 23, 1993). As with other school-related disciplines, the involvement of social workers in the various aspects described above depends on their particular job description as developed by the employing school district.

Psychologists, counselors, and social workers agree that they share much expertise (Gibelman, 1993). It is critical to know all the ways in which team members can contribute to student programming—in other words, do not assume any limitations.

Occupational Therapists, Physical Therapists, and Adaptive Physical Education Teachers

The **occupational therapist** (OT) is a health professional who applies goal-directed activity to assess and treat people with various disabilities (Hopkins & Smith, 1993). In an educational setting, the occupational therapist uses activity and adapted surroundings to facilitate the student's independent living skills and to maximize the student's ability to participate in the educational process. OTs provide services to students with disabilities that affect their large and small motor functioning, such as muscular dystrophy, moderate-to-severe cerebral palsy, severe juvenile rheumatoid arthritis, and paraplegia (American Occupational Therapy Association, 1987; Kramer & Hinojosa, 1993; Powell, 1994).

Occupational therapy focuses on activities of daily living (ADL) (Griswold, 1994). Typical goals of occupational therapy include improving a student's motor skills so that he or she can interact more independently with the environment and adapting the physical classroom to allow the student to function independently and effectively. The occupational therapist sometimes is assisted by a certified occupational therapist assistant (COTA), who has an associate's degree in the discipline.

The **physical therapist** (PT) is also concerned with a student's motor functioning, specifically, the student's mobility (Tecklin, 1989). A PT provides services to children with disabilities that affect the large muscle groups, such as cerebral palsy, scoliosis, spina bifida, and pulmonary disorders. PTs and OTs may have common treatment goals, but the treatment modalities will differ. For example, a common objective might be to establish trunk stability. The PT may see trunk stability as prerequisite to large muscle activity such as sitting and walking; the OT may see it as a prerequisite to sitting, in order to use the arms for writing and other small muscle activities (i.e., occupation). The therapy and exercises may appear similar, but the PT uses heat, ultrasound, and water therapy and emphasizes mobility, and the OT uses activities that emphasize adaptability (Pratt & Allen, 1989; Royeen & Coutinho, 1991).

The **adaptive physical education** (APE) teacher is responsible for a student's physical fitness, development of spatial awareness, and eye-hand/eye-foot coordination (Cratty, 1989; Winnick, 1990). The APE teacher adapts and modifies developmental activities, exercises, and games, so that an individual with disabilities is actively involved in physical education with his or her peers. The APE teacher uses group activities to promote fitness, in contrast to the PT and OT, who prescribe individual intervention programs (Churton, 1987; Royeen & Coutinho, 1991). APE teachers have some background on disabilities; however, the information they receive may be less than accurate. For example, a current APE textbook advises that "deafness may be persistent or intermittent and most commonly caused by inner-ear infections" (Jowsey, 1992, p. 270).

The three professions of occupational therapy, physical therapy, and adaptive physical education readily acknowledge that there is overlap in the practice of their fields. Because a PT must be referred by a physician, the PT often functions in a medical setting, while an OT is not required to be referred by a physician, and so is more often found in an educational setting (Pratt & Allen, 1989). Collaboration and communication is always sought in order to coordinate and support each professional's goals for the students they jointly serve.

Paraprofessionals and Volunteer Service Providers

Classroom Aides Job descriptions for classroom aides typically have involved clerical responsibilities (grading papers and compiling homework), but recently there has been much growth in the involvement of classroom aides in more complex operations in the classroom. Depending on the needs of the classroom teacher, the aide may become involved in formal assessment and initial instruction (often called pre-tutoring), modifications of materials, and one-to-one instruction (Jones & Bender, 1993).

Sign Language Interpreters A sign language interpreter conveys speech within listening range to a student with a hearing impairment. The interpreter stays personally removed from any resulting dialogue. However, most interpreters in schools are also expected to function as an aide or tutor to a student with HI. Qualifications for the position of interpreter vary across the country, and very few school districts have the luxury of choosing from a pool of applicants certified by the Registry of Interpreters for the Deaf (RID). It is important to know that the supervision and evaluation of interpreter skills is often not regulated. If a student with HI is experiencing some problems in a mainstream setting, it is advisable to verify that the interpreter's skills are adequate to meet the individual's needs. Evaluation may be conducted by a person designated as the coordinator of sign language interpreting services, if the coordinator has fluent signing skills. Otherwise, evaluation must be obtained from outside the district (e.g., from a university program or from another district with qualified signers).

Interpreters must be careful not to overexert themselves. Because of the limited and repetitive motions involved in interpreting, they are at risk of an occupational injury, carpal tunnel syndrome. This syndrome is associated with overuse of nerves in the wrist, which can become compressed, causing numbness and tingling (Stedt, 1992).

Notetakers and Tutors Typically, students in a learner's class volunteer as notetakers for a learner with HI. NCR (no carbon required) paper may be provided to a notetaker so that after a lecture the notetaker and student with HI each have a copy. (A third copy could be maintained in a notebook for general class use for students who were absent or who missed part of the notes.)

The use of tutors for a student with HI depends on individual needs and school resources. Peer tutoring (i.e., one-to-one review of material with a student of the same age or slightly older) is frequently used as a means to support learning, both for the tutor and the learner being tutored (Gartner & Lipsky, 1990; Jenkins & Jenkins, 1985; Reissman, 1988).

All paraprofessionals and volunteer service providers should be informally consulted on a routine basis regarding the student's progress. These individuals often have insights from their direct contact regarding a learner's progress that can help in developing quality services for the individual.

SHARING INFORMATION WITH TEAM MEMBERS

The educational audiologist has a wealth of information regarding the needs of students with HI that he or she will want to share with the service providers such as those described above. Some relevant concerns regard the functional limits of hearing aids, the effects of noise on speech discrimination, and issues involved in testing a student with HI. While other concerns are addressed in specific chapters of this book, the issue of testing is presented here as an example of an issue of shared concern among team members. First, basic principles of testing a student with HI are described. Next, the chapter concludes with recommendations on **how** to effectively share this information with team members.

> The educational audiologist is responsible for ensuring that all assessments, formal and informal, fairly reflect the abilities of the student with HI.

Of greatest concern are the standardized tests that are used to place students into special education programs and to monitor their annual progress. Because so many testing instruments are language-based, a student with HI may demonstrate learning abilities and intelligence levels on such tests at much lower levels than he or she actually possesses. For that reason, all oral tests (such as the Stanford-Binet Intelligence Scale [Thorndike, Hagen, & Sattler, 1986]) are considered inappropriate for students who are deaf or who have a severe hearing impairment (Vess & Gregory, 1985). Nonverbal instruments such as the Leiter International Performance Scale (Leiter, 1948) are recommended, although the results must be interpreted with caution because there are no standardized norms. Although there is much information regarding cognitive evaluation of persons with HI (e.g., Bradley-Johnson & Evans, 1991; Zieziula, 1982), it has not been made widely available to school psychologists. Research in the cognitive evaluation of students with HI is typically disseminated in the literature of communication disorders and Deaf culture, and so it is usually out of the mainstream of psychology literature (Braden, 1992). The educational audiologist must ascertain that the school psychologist is aware of methods of cognitive evaluation of persons with HI.

The Impact of HI on Testing Across Disciplines

The educational audiologist must ensure that each educator and service provider complies with the following requirements for testing a student with HI:

1. The testing environment must be an optimal listening environment for the student with HI. Hearing aids or FM systems must be functioning properly; the environment must have minimal background noise; and the student must be free of middle ear infections, upper respiratory infections, or other health conditions that can compromise residual hearing.
2. The student must understand the tasks required of him or her. If the student's first language is sign, an interpreter must be used unless the tester is proficient in sign. Written instructions are not appropriate; "understanding checks" must be conducted routinely.
3. The student must wear glasses if prescribed.
4. The tester is also advised to use several short sessions to avoid student fatigue, to use several measures as a reliability check, and to use classroom observation as part of the assessment.

These conditions must be adapted to all individual testing situations. For example, APE teachers typically test children in highly reverberant gymnasiums, or outside in the schoolyard. Both sites present obvious environmental factors that may compromise the testing. The APE teacher may not realize that, although she is giving instructions in a loud voice, she is also turning in several directions, and a child may be hearing only wind noise in his hearing aids. The regular education teacher may not realize that the vocabulary he is using may be above the level of the child's language development. The RSP teacher may not know that a student with HI expends extraordinary energy in concentration and processing; fatigue, then, is a legitimate concern at the end of a school day and must be considered when scheduling a time for testing. The educational audiologist must ensure that all team members are advised of all of the factors that can have a negative effect on the accurate academic and cognitive testing of a child with a HI.

Summary

The newly employed educational audiologist may be astonished at the number of persons involved in the education of a learner with HI. Obviously, the level of involvement of each professional is determined by the needs of each student. Additionally, the involvement of particular individuals changes over time, intensifying at some points of a student's academic career and diminishing at other times. Services to students may become increasingly indirect. For example, the educational audiologist consults with a regular-education teacher, who then directly provides the necessary service in the class (Frassinelli, Superior, & Meyers, 1983). Some highly specialized skills such as electroacoustic hearing aid analysis will always be a direct audiological service provided by the educational audiologist to the student. Some needed services can readily and appropriately be **shared services**, such as daily hearing aid inspection.

WORKING ON A TEAM

One of the most satisfying and invigorating aspects of working in the school setting is the opportunity to interact with a wide range of service providers. This professional interaction requires ongoing evaluation in terms of the efficacy and efficiency of service provision. Why? Because the **process** of service delivery (through effective team interaction) often determines if the desired **outcomes** (student success) are achieved. If service delivery were an equation, it might appear as presented in Figure 5.1.

The **teaming** or process component of the equation can take several forms. The following section discusses three team configurations: multidisciplinary, interdisciplinary, and transdisciplinary.

The first two team configurations, multidisciplinary and interdisciplinary, are described because they are the approaches most often used in school settings. However, the transdisciplinary model provides the approach considered most effective by educators for achieving desired student outcomes, and so will be discussed at length.

STUDENT SERVICES   +   TEAMING   =   STUDENT SUCCESS

(product)   (process)   (outcomes)

Figure 5.1. Components of effective service delivery.

Multidisciplinary Team Approach

In a multidisciplinary team approach, professionals from several disciplines all serve the same student, but they do so independently of each other. Assessments of the individual student's needs and subsequent interventions or therapies based on assessment findings are conducted in isolation. Following is an example of how a multidisciplinary team works:

1. The speech-language pathologist (SLP) tests Samantha in order to measure her speech and language development. He arranges with the regular education teacher to have Samantha meet twice a week with three other students in his therapy room to work on articulation goals and language deficits.
2. The resource specialist (RSP) conducts tests to measure Samantha's reading skills. She arranges to have Samantha work twice a week with a small group of children in her office in order to develop vocabulary and reading comprehension.
3. The adaptive physical education (APE) teacher conducts tests to measure Samantha's level of physical fitness and coordination. She arranges to have Samantha work in the gym once a week on strengthening large muscles, on increasing stamina, and in improving her hand–eye coordination.
4. The itinerant teacher of the HI measures Samantha's skills in speechreading and her use of residual hearing. She arranges to see Samantha individually once a week to work on her ability to discriminate speech in noise.
5. The regular education teacher follows the plans of instruction and testing developed at the beginning of the year by the team members.

Characteristics of the Multidisciplinary Approach:

- Each assessment is conducted separately from other assessments.
- Each intervention or therapy is independent of and unrelated to the others.
- No communication is shared among professionals.
- Services for Samantha are disjointed, fragmented, and uncoordinated.

Some professionals may argue that the multidisciplinary approach is efficient. However, with so many assessments and interventions being conducted, Samantha is missing a great deal of classroom instruction, so the argument for efficiency is weak. Actually, this approach serves the needs of the professionals rather than the needs of the student. Professionals may also claim that this approach allows one to fully exercise one's area of expertise. The concern to protect one's field of expertise is called a "turf issue" and is not appropriate when it interferes with the necessity to provide the best possible services for an individual learner.

Interdisciplinary Approach

In the interdisciplinary approach also, team members independently assess and serve the learner. However, an effort is made to maintain communication among professionals so that each knows what others are doing. Let us consider how this approach to service delivery and teaming works for our first-grade student, Samantha:

1. The SLP, the RSP, the APE teacher, and the itinerant teacher of the HI all assess independently, as described for the multidisciplinary team.
2. All professionals, including the regular education teacher, meet to report and discuss the assessment results. All professionals exchange information and are apprised of the findings of the other assessments. They discuss the implications of the assessments relative to their own, in order to obtain a complete picture of Samantha's development, and to interpret the results in light of the professional expertise of each team member.
3. Each professional plans and implements appropriate interventions and therapies independently, as with the multidisciplinary team. Progress reports may or may not be shared among team members during the school year.

Characteristics of the Interdisciplinary Approach:

- Each assessment is conducted separately from other assessments.
- Each intervention or therapy is independent of and unrelated to the others.
- Communication is shared among professionals.
- Services for Samantha may or may not be disjointed, fragmented, and uncoordinated, depending on how interested the various professionals are in capitalizing on the benefits of the shared communication.

The approach of the interdisciplinary team is descriptive of the typical IEP process and IEP meeting for students with HI. Each professional assesses the student's skills and abilities independent of other disciplines and then reports the findings at the IEP meeting. Annual goals are described at these meetings, but typically the method of meeting these goals (the manner of implementation) does not get addressed. Each professional is independently responsible for seeing that the discipline-specific goals are met. For example, the SLP is accountable for language goals and the RSP for reading goals.

Because there is communication among the professionals serving a student, the likelihood of contradictory plans and goals is reduced. The opportunity to seek information from other disciplines increases. Some coordination of therapies or interventions is possible, if team members are interested. The difference between the interdisciplinary approach and the multidisciplinary approach is that professionals are aware of the results from the assessments conducted by the other professionals as well as their overall goals and programs. In the final analysis, however, following this approach, Samantha is likely to still undergo disjointed weeks of pull-out programs that are not likely to be coordinated with her classroom instruction or with each other.

Transdisciplinary Approach

In a transdisciplinary approach to service delivery, all professionals strive to learn enough about the disciplines of the other professionals in order to provide a coordinated service plan. The following example, again for Samantha, demonstrates how a transdisciplinary team approach might serve this student:

1. To the greatest extent possible, assessments are combined or coordinated in order to provide information to several team members at one time (arena assessment). Or, team members from various disciplines will train each other to conduct basic assessments in order to share the responsibility for assessment.
2. Team members meet to report and discuss the assessment results.
3. Decisions for intervention are reached by group consensus. Implementation of interventions is a team responsibility and is conducted in a coordinated fashion. The RSP, the SLP, and itinerant teacher of the HI routinely meet with the regular education teacher to discuss the concepts, vocabulary, and content currently being taught in class; these are then incorporated into various interventions.
4. Interventions may be conducted within the context of the regular classroom. Team members are trained by other members to integrate specific goals into each intervention in order to support and enhance the others.

Characteristics of the Transdisciplinary Approach:

- Assessments are blended or shared as much as possible.
- Each intervention or therapy is coordinated and integrated with others as much as possible.
- Communication is ongoing and of high priority to professionals.
- Services for Samantha are consistent and supportive of her classroom instruction and conducted within her class as much as possible.

The transdisciplinary approach "attempts to break the traditional rigidity of discipline boundaries and to encourage a teaching/learning process between team members. It supports the development of a staff that functions with greater unity . . . ." (Servis, 1978, p. 81).

The process by which members of the transdisciplinary team interact is **collaboration**. Collaboration in a transdisciplinary team has been found to provide benefits for both the student and the team members. The student benefits from a consistent, coordinated, and integrated program that provides maximum instruction time by reducing or eliminating pull-out sessions. Team members benefit from increasing their knowledge and skills, from a sense of support in their decision-making (often called "shared ownership"), and in their development of innovative ideas (Beninghof & Singer, 1992; Miller, 1993). With the increasing diversity of the student population, it is felt that no one educator can keep pace with the information explosion in the field; a transdisciplinary approach can contribute to professional growth by pooling content, knowledge, and skills (Thousand, Villa, Paolucci-Whitcomb, & Nevin, 1992). This professional growth ultimately benefits the student.

> Collaborating with others as part of a transdisciplinary team "is an interactive process that enables people with diverse expertise to generate mutually defined problems. The outcome is enhanced, altered and produces solutions that are different from those that the individual team members would produce independently." (Idol, Paolucci-Whitcomb, & Nevin, 1986, p. 1)

BARRIERS TO PROFESSIONAL AND TEAM COLLABORATION

Some issues have been identified as barriers to collaboration or to using the transdisciplinary team approach to serving students. One of the most pressing barriers to collaboration is the matter of **time**. The transdisciplinary team approach may seem to require an inordinate amount of time to meet, discuss, share, train, meet again, evaluate, and meet again. There is undeniably some inconvenience in scheduling meetings among professionals with very crowded calendars. However, with attention and respect for each team member's needs, it is not an insurmountable problem. Many practitioners have reported that, in fact, the effort spent working proactively to avoid student problems through careful planning is no more time consuming than addressing problems reactively after they arise.

Another possible barrier to collaboration is the issue of **role release**. Earlier, the concept of professional "turf" issues was introduced. Many persons have a strong personal identification with the profession in which they trained, and so feel uncomfortable in sharing their expertise with others. Such reluctance is understandable: for example, teachers have a long history of working in isolation, and specialists have enjoyed a certain degree of prestige with respect to their areas of expertise. In collaboration, however, all team members must be willing and comfortable with "surrendering" some of their expertise (or their turf) by sharing it with others, thereby strengthening the overall professionalism of the team. This is termed **reciprocity**, which is defined as providing all team members with access to all information and with the opportunity to be part of the complete process of problem identification, problem solving, and evaluation of outcomes. For some professionals, this is easier said than done. Sharing information and skills for them is equated with sharing power and control, and not all persons are initially secure or comfortable with that concept. Reciprocity may represent an undermining of traditional professional authority and identity (Johnson & Pugach, 1992). Ten components of reciprocity are identified in Table 5.1.

A suggestion to address this reluctance to share and collaborate includes conveying to all team members that they each are free to accept, reject, table, modify, or mediate any recommendations made by the team. The responsibility for problem solving must be seen as one to be shared. Furthermore, as a respected professional, no team member is forced to do something he or she is not willing to do. If team members support the expressed team mission statement to provide comprehensive

Table 5.1. Ten components of reciprocity

1. Job sharing
2. Flexibility
3. Reaching group consensus
4. Sharing ideas and information
5. Recognizing needs of colleagues, students, district, school
6. Supportive decision making
7. Mutual respect and trust
8. Complementary efforts (division of labor)
9. Each person has a voice
10. Widespread participation

From West, J., Idol, L., and Cannon G. (1989). *Collaboration in the schools: An inservice and preservice curriculum for teachers, support staff, and administrators (instructor's manual)*. Austin, TX: PRO-ED; reprinted by permission.

and effective programs to students with special needs, they should be able to set aside personal agendas for the sake of quality education for their students.

Team members are encouraged to maintain efforts in the face of difficulties with collaboration. "Adopting this approach is not an event: it is a process of change that occurs over time" (Ferguson, 1992, p. 361). A helpful checklist for team behaviors is found in Figure 5.2.

Checklist for Team Behaviors

Task-Accomplishing Behaviors	Relationship-Building Behaviors

Initiating
___ Establishing goals, objectives, or tasks
___ Suggesting procedures, ways of operating

Seeking Information
___ Asking for facts, ideas, opinions, beliefs

Giving Information
___ Offering facts, ideas, opinions, beliefs

Clarifying
___ Probing for meaning
___ Explaining ideas

Building
___ Elaborating on other's ideas

Paraphrasing and Summarizing
___ Restating what someone has said
___ Reviewing the ideas that have been offered
___ Pulling varied ideas together into a whole

Problem Solving
___ Offering alternatives
___ Considering advantages and disadvantages
___ Making proposals
___ Testing for group agreement
___ Deciding how to decide
___ Identifying who will do what by when
___ Summarizing the decision

Managing
___ Sharing leadership appropriately
___ Using group time well
___ Regularly evaluating its performance

Listening
___ Attending to others
___ Not interrupting
___ Responding to what's been said

Encouraging
___ Acting friendly, open, and accepting
___ Soliciting participation
___ Praising and supporting others

Gatekeeping
___ Facilitating everyone's participation
___ Observing where the group is in its process
___ Testing group satisfaction with the process

Harmonizing
___ Willingness to differ
___ Recognizing instead of avoiding issues/conflicts
___ Working through conflicts
___ Relieving tension; laughing
___ Yielding when necessary to achieve group objective

Figure 5.2. Checklist for team behaviors (© 1993 PHOENIX International; reprinted by permission.)

MODELS OF PROFESSIONAL
INTERACTION IN ONE-TO-ONE RELATIONSHIPS

The previous sections examined the collaborative process by which professionals can effectively interact in a group or team. There are parallels to the ways in which professionals interact with one another. This section discusses the types of interactions most often observed to take place between an educational audiologist and another education specialist—for our purposes, a regular education classroom teacher.

West and Idol (1987) described 11 different models of professional interaction and consultation found in the fields of mental health, law, education, and business. Two of these models are of interest to the educational audiologist, one as a point of departure from previous experience (the expert model), and the other model as a goal for educators (the collaborative model).

Expert Model

The **expert model** of professional behavior and interaction is that typically found in a medical or clinical setting. In the expert model, a patient or client identifies a health problem, seeks out a trained expert for a diagnosis, and generally follows the recommended solutions to the health problem. The professional is accustomed to being sought out, to receiving respect and appreciation for his or her training and expertise, and to obtaining compliance with his or her recommendations from the patient.

The expert model describes the setting in which clinical audiology is practiced: an individual experiencing hearing difficulties seeks out, or is referred to, the expert/audiologist. The patient expects to be evaluated and to obtain a diagnosis. If the audiologist recommends hearing aids or steps to conserve hearing health, the patient knows this is an expert recommendation and gives it serious consideration.

This model of service delivery describes the majority of graduate training experiences in most audiology programs—and appropriately so, as part of a medical or clinical program. Because it is an inherent part of the traditional graduate training experience, it is not surprising that audiologists initially applied this approach in school settings.

In order for this expert model to be effective in schools, the audiologist would have to be confident that all appropriate school personnel are informed about each student's hearing impairment and its implications for education. In addition, following the expert model, school personnel would actively seek out the expertise of the educational audiologist and would follow the audiologist's recommendations in order to provide the optimal environment for each student with HI.

Even with limited experience in a school setting, the reader can probably guess that the expert model does not work well in schools. **More typically, educational personnel are not aware of the nature of hearing impairment, its impact on education, or the role of the educational audiologist.** As a result, support and pursuit of the educational audiologist's recommendations to school personnel often lack enthusiasm and sustained commitment.

Collaborative Model

Because of experiences with the expert model such as have just been described, educational audiologists came to realize that the expert model that they learned in graduate school is not an appropriate model for the educational setting. Many educational audiologists are trying another approach with much success. This approach is the **collaborative model** and follows the same premise as the collaborative approach in teaming.

In the collaborative model or approach, the goal is not to have an expert provide the solution to a problem. Rather, the goal of collaboration is to develop a shared ownership of a problem where a pair or team of professionals—not a single expert—is responsible for identifying problems and for implementing recommendations that are beneficial to the student. Collaboration operates on a perceived parity or the mutual acknowledgment of each professional's expertise (Thousand et al., 1992). For example, when planning services for a learner with HI, the educational audiologist serves as a specialist in hearing impairment, and the classroom teacher is respectfully recognized as a curriculum and child development specialist. Table 5.2 shows a comparison of the expert and collaborative models.

Two Scenarios: Expert Model and Collaborative Model

To illustrate how these models differ, let us compare them through the following two scenarios.

Scenario one takes place in a mainstream classroom in which the educational audiologist wants to ensure that the hearing aids of a student with HI are inspected daily. Operating in an expert model or approach, the educational audiologist may drop by the classroom unannounced and approach the classroom teacher with the information that PL 94-142 mandates hearing aid inspection; leave a kit containing a battery tester, a stethoset, and/or an instruction sheet; and a telephone number in case any questions arise.

The teacher may respond in a variety of ways, all of which are reasonable: he or she may be annoyed with having to deal with yet another accommodation; intimidated by being responsible for technology with which he or she is unfamiliar; or

Table 5.2. Comparison of features of expert and collaborative models of professional interaction

Model	Goals	Steps	Responsibilities
Expert	To alleviate short-term problem	No steps	Teacher identifies problem Expert solves problem
Collaborative	To develop parity between the regular education teacher and the educational audiologist, resulting in shared ownership of concerns for students with HI	1. Gain mutual acceptance 2. Assess problem(s) 3. Formulate goals matched to assessment outcomes 4. Implement intervention procedures 5. Evaluate results of intervention	Emphasize mutuality and parity with respect to each other's expertise; all stages reflect shared responsibility

Adapted from West, Idol, and Cannon (1989).

interested but overwhelmed, putting the information aside for another time to think it over. A frustrated educational audiologist and unchecked hearing aids are the result of this encounter.

This approach was less than successful because the teacher had not identified a problem and sought out an expert. Instead, an expert simply told the teacher what he or she should do in the classroom instead of consulting with him or her. There was a mismatch in how the two professionals viewed the situation.

Now let us consider making a "paradigm shift"; that is, another way of doing something (Kuhn, 1970), and use a different set of assumptions about professional interaction. In a collaborative approach, we assume that we will be working **with** other professionals rather than independently. Working collaboratively, we assume that each person brings to the situation a variety of expertise and background. We also assume that other professionals have as little information about our field as we do about theirs and that we are all interested in sharing responsibility for providing the student with HI the best education possible. With these assumptions, how do professionals work together to achieve their goals? Let us consider another way to look at the same scenario.

Scenario two takes place in the same mainstream classroom setting. Following the collaborative approach, the educational audiologist would call to schedule a mutually convenient meeting with the regular education teacher so that both professionals could focus on the whole child. The meeting may begin with the educational audiologist asking open-ended questions about the student's performance and the teacher's concerns. As the teacher identifies concerns, the educational audiologist can offer pertinent information about the student's hearing impairment, thereby providing the teacher with a better understanding of the difficulties of listening in a noisy classroom setting, with a realistic expectation of speechreading abilities, and with the value of visual cues in providing important information to the student. Because amplification is of primary concern to the student and the educational audiologist, the teacher's familiarity with the operation of hearing aids would be determined. Because the hearing aids need to be checked daily, the audiologist says, "We do need to work together to be sure Monty's aids are OK every day. You can imagine how hard it would be for him if they weren't! And actually, it's required by law. How would you recommend we go about this?" The teacher is asked for recommendations as to: 1) the most convenient time of day to check the aids, 2) the most appropriate place to perform the check, 3) the best way to maintain a monitoring/recordkeeping system, and 4) the best place to keep spare batteries, the battery tester, and similar equipment. The teacher identifies what will work best in the context of her classroom and class schedule, and the educational audiologist provides the technical assistance to support those decisions. Follow-up meetings can be arranged in the ongoing communication between them in order to discuss new concerns or to modify the initial arrangements.

By giving the classroom teacher enough time to discuss potential concerns, by acknowledging the teacher's expertise in education and classroom management and about the student in question, and by seeking input for shared solutions to concerns, the educational audiologist builds a foundation of professional trust, respect, and parity that can often result in a stronger commitment to workable solutions—and the student—on the part of the teacher.

Skills for collaboration:
1. An atmosphere of acceptance of differences in expertise and skills
2. Acceptance of differences in viewpoints and approaches
3. Willingness to not know everything
4. An ability to call on colleagues for assistance and advice
5. Nonthreatening opportunities for discussion in colleagues' areas of expertise
(Howard, 1982)

THE PROCESS OF CHANGING THE
APPROACH TO PROFESSIONAL INTERACTION

Because it is a departure from the status quo (that is, the interdisciplinary team approach), learning to collaborate as part of a transdisciplinary team means adjusting to changes in assumptions and methods. Changing the process of personal and professional interactions does not happen overnight, nor does it develop effortlessly or painlessly. Because of the experiences with the expert model of most audiology training programs, the audiologist new to the school environment may feel the stress of change as much as an educator with 20 years experience with the status quo.

Stages of Professional Development

The process of adjusting to the roles and demands of a new position can take its toll. Parsons and Meyers (1984) identified four stages of professional development and the concerns encountered at each stage:

Survival Stage   In this first stage, the professional wonders: How will my performance be assessed? How will I relate to the staff? What are the routines? How can I best demonstrate competency?

Consolidation Stage   In this second stage, the professional feels: I am demonstrating basic competency with fundamental requirements. I am clear about job expectations. I can identify some skills that I need to develop and I am working on some of these.

Renewal Stage   In this third stage, the professional can state: I have mastered basic skills and have performed them competently for some time. I am becoming bored with the routine, and I am looking for new approaches and ideas being developed in the field.

Maturity Stage   In the fourth stage, the professional asserts: I am integrating, modifying, and evaluating new ideas and approaches with confidence. I am continuing to grow professionally, and I am satisfied with my accomplishments.

During this process of professional development, the need to accommodate to changes occurs whether or not one is in the appropriate stage of professional development to meet the demands of change.

Stages of Professional Development in the Collaborative Process

Adjusting to an innovation such as the collaborative process follows the same stages of professional development outlined above.

Survival Stage In this first stage, the professional wonders: How will this change affect my responsibilities? With this change, how will my competency be evaluated?

Consolidation Stage In this second stage, the professional feels: I understand the basics of this change and can implement it on at least a surface or routine level. I can also identify some problems with the change that I would like to address.

Renewal Stage In the third stage, the professional states: I have mastered this change and have used it competently for some time. I am interested to know if there are ways to refine this change to better suit the needs of the field and my students.

Maturity Stage In this fourth stage, the professional asserts: I have incorporated this change into fundamental aspects of the way that I work. I have found ways to modify and integrate some finer points of this innovation, and I feel that these have contributed to my professional growth.

Some Final Words on Change

It is helpful to know that with each change or adjustment to an innovation, there is some degree of internal conflict and, possibly, some interpersonal conflict as well (Fisher & Ury, 1991). Such conflicts are to be expected and are part of the process. In a series of journal entries, educators recorded their experiences in adjusting to a change in their educational program and made similar observations (Red & Shainline, 1987). These observations can be summarized as follows:

- Change is a process that requires time, reflection, and ongoing effort.
- Conflict is inevitable, and some discomfort should be expected and, in fact, is fundamental to the process of change.
- Theory evolves into practice. After cycles of reflection, effort, and evaluation, the innovation gradually becomes part of professional service delivery. Fullan (1991) suggested that significant change in an educational setting takes a minimum of 2–3 years.

These comments are intended to provide new practitioners with some insight into the adjustment process they and their colleagues are likely to experience with the introduction of an innovation in the delivery of services.

CONCLUSION

This chapter has focused on topics not typically addressed in audiology training. However, because these topics—teaming and collaboration—are part of the energetic dialogue in the field of education, these topics are highly important in the training of the educational audiologist. Audiologists working in educational settings find that the application of the expert model approach has proven to be ineffective in the educational setting. At the same time, related disciplines began to examine methods of teaming and service delivery, and the process of collaboration was explored and implemented. The time and effort required to effectively collaborate with all team members is resulting in a satisfying payoff in benefits for both the service providers and the students who receive their services.

Learning the Language

Review the following concepts from this chapter and discuss with a colleague.

- Itinerant teacher
- OT
- PT
- APE
- Indirect and direct services
- Multi-/inter-/transdisciplinary teams
- Collaboration
- Role release
- Expert model
- Reciprocity

Educational Audiology in Action
Suggested Learning Activities

Project 1. Review literature from related educational disciplines.

Choose a related educational specialty discussed in this chapter, and review journals from its professional literature. Look at articles from the last 2 years. Is this discipline concerned with the impact of educational reforms? If so, what are the strategies proposed to help professionals in this discipline meet the challenges of these reforms? Some journals to review:

Adapted Physical Education Quarterly
Exceptional Children
Focus on Exceptional Children
Journal of School Health
Journal of School Psychology
Journal of Special Education
Language, Speech, and Hearing Services in Schools
Psychology in the Schools
Remedial and Special Education
School Counselor
School Psychology Review
Social Work in Education
TEACHING Exceptional Children
Volta Review

Project 2. With permission, observe a student study team meeting.

Which disciplines are represented on this team? Does the team configuration resemble a transdisciplinary approach? If so, are characteristics of collaboration observable? Is reciprocity honored? Is responsibility shared for decisions and implementation of plans? Is there comfort in role release among team members?

Project 3. Interview any special education service provider with more than 10 years experience in his or her field.

What was the field like when he or she first entered the profession, and how is it different today? What changes has he or she observed and experienced in the field? What are his or her reactions to these changes? Have some changes seemed easier to adapt to than others? How so? How does this professional describe the process of change that has taken place in his or her professional experience?

References

American Occupational Therapy Association. (1987). *Guidelines for occupational therapy services in school systems.* Rockville, MD: American Occupational Therapy Association.

Beninghof, A., & Singer, A. (1992). Team teaching: An inservice training activity. *TEACHING Exceptional Children, 24*(2), 58–61.

Braden, J. (1992). Intellectual assessment of deaf and hard of hearing people: A quantitative and qualitative research synthesis. *School Psychology Review, 21,* 82–94.

Bradley-Johnson, S., & Evans, L. (1991). *Psychoeducational assessment of hearing impaired students: Infancy through high school.* San Diego, CA: Singular Publishing Group.

Chorost, S. (1988). The hearing impaired child in the mainstream: A survey of the attitudes of regular classroom teachers. *Volta Review, 90,* 7–12.

Churton, M. (1987). Impact of the Education of the Handicapped Act on adapted physical education: A 10-year review. *Adapted Physical Activity Quarterly, 4,* 1–8.

Cole, E., & Siegel, J. (Eds.). (1990). *Effective consultation in school psychology.* Toronto: Hogrefe and Huber.

Conner, T., & Welsh, R. (1993). Teams and teamwork: Educational settings. *Asha, 35*(7), 35–36.

Cratty, B. (1989). *Adapted physical education in the mainstream* (2nd ed.). Denver: Love Publishing Co.

Drisko, J. (1993). Special education teacher consultation: A student-focused, skill defining approach. *Social Work in Education, 15,* 19–28.

Ferguson, M. (1992). Implementing collaborative consultation. *Language, Speech, and Hearing Services in Schools, 23,* 361–362.

Fisher, R., & Ury, W. (1991). *Getting to yes: Negotiating agreement without giving in* (2nd ed.). New York: Penguin Books.

Forman, S. (Ed.). (1987). *School-based affective and social interventions.* New York: Haworth Press.

Frassinelli, L., Superior, K., & Meyers, J. (1983). A consultative model for speech and language intervention. *Asha, 25*(11), 25–30.

Fullan, M. (1991). *The new meaning of educational change* (2nd ed.). New York: Teachers College Press.

Gartner, A., & Lipsky, D.K. (1990). Students as instructional agents. In W. Stainback & S. Stainback (Eds.), *Support networks for inclusive schooling: Interdependent integrated education* (pp. 81–93). Baltimore: Paul H. Brookes Publishing Co.

Gibelman, M. (1993). School social workers, counselors, and psychologists in collaboration: A shared agenda. *Social Work in Education, 15,* 45–53.

Griswold, L. (1994). Ethnographic analysis: A study of classroom environments. *American Journal of Occupational Therapy, 48*(5), 397–402.

Holvoet, J., & Helmstetter, E. (1989). *Special problems of students with special needs: A guide for educators.* Boston: College-Hill Press.

Hopkins, H., & Smith, H. (1993). *Occupational therapy* (8th ed.). Philadelphia: J.B. Lippincott.

Howard, J. (1982). The role of the pediatrician with exceptional children and their families. *Exceptional Children, 48,* 316–322.

Idol, L., Paolucci-Whitcomb, P., & Nevin, A. (1986). *Collaborative consultation.* Rockville, MD: Aspen Publishers, Inc.

Jansson, B. (1990). *Social welfare policy: From theory to practice.* Belmont, CA: Wadsworth Publishing Co.

Jenkins, J., & Jenkins, L. (1985). Peer tutoring in elementary and secondary programs. *Focus on Exceptional Children, 17*(6), pp. 1–12.

Johnson, C., Stein, R., & Lass, N. (1992). Public school nurses' preparedness for a hearing aid monitoring program. *Language, Speech, and Hearing Services in Schools, 23,* 141–144.

Johnson, L., & Pugach, M. (1992). Continuing the dialogue: Embracing a more expansive understanding of collaborative relationships. In W. Stainback & S. Stainback (Eds.), *Controversial issues confronting special education: Divergent perspectives* (pp. 215–222). Newton, MA: Allyn & Bacon.

Jones, K., & Bender, W. (1993). Utilization of paraprofessionals in special education: A review of the literature. *Remedial and Special Education, 14*(1), 7–14.

Jowsey, S. (1992). *Can I play too? Physical education for physically disabled children in mainstream schools.* London: David Fulton Publishers.

Kaufmann, J. (1988). A revolution can also mean returning to the starting point: Will school psychology help special education complete the circuit? *School Psychology Review, 17,* 490–494.

Kramer, P., & Hinojosa, J. (1993). *Frames of reference for pediatric occupational therapy.* Baltimore: Williams & Wilkins.

Kuhn, T. (1970). *The structure of scientific revolutions.* Chicago: University of Chicago Press.

Lass, N., Tecca, J., & Woodford, C. (1987). Teachers' knowledge of, exposure to, and attitudes toward hearing aids and hearing aid wearers. *Language, Speech, and Hearing Services in Schools, 18,* 86–91.

Lass, N., Woodford, C., Pannbacker, M., Carlin, M., Saniga, R., Schmitt, J., & Everly-Myers, D. (1989). Speech-language pathologists' knowledge of, exposure to, and attitudes toward hearing aids and hearing aid wearers. *Language, Speech, and Hearing Services in Schools, 20,* 115–132.

Leiter, R. (1948). *Leiter International Performance Scale.* Chicago: Stoelting Co.

Lewis, K., & Thomson, H. (1986). *Manual of school health.* Menlo Park, CA: Addison-Wesley Publishing.

Luckner, J. (1991). Mainstreaming hearing impaired students: Perceptions of regular education teachers. *Language, Speech, and Hearing Services in Schools, 22,* 302–307.

Luckner, J., Rude, H., & Sileo, T. (1989). Collaborative consultation: A method of improving services for mainstreamed students who are hearing impaired. *American Annals of the Deaf, 134*(5), 301–304.

Luetke-Stahlman, B., & Luckner, J. (1991). *Effectively educating students with hearing impairments.* New York: Longman.

Martin, F., Bernstein, M., Daly, J., & Cody, J. (1988). Classroom teachers' knowledge of hearing disorders and attitudes about mainstreaming hard of hearing children. *Language, Speech, and Hearing Services in Schools, 19,* 83–95.

Medway, F. (1992). The rapprochement of social psychology and school psychology: An historical analysis. In F. Medway & T. Cafferty (Eds.), *School psychology: A social psychological perspective* (pp. 5–25). Hillsdale, NJ: Lawrence Erlbaum Associates.

Miller, D. (1993). Teams and teamwork. Strategies for improvement. *Asha, 35*(7), 45–46.

Monkman, M. (1991). The characteristic focus of the social worker in the public schools. In R. Constable, J. Flynn, & S. McDonald (Eds.), *School social work: Practice and research perspectives* (2nd ed., pp. 30–49). Chicago: Lyceum Books.

Montgomery, J. (1992). Perspectives from the field: Language, speech and hearing services in schools. *Language, Speech, and Hearing Services in Schools, 23,* 363–364.

Myles, B., & Simpson, R. (1989). Regular educators' modification preferences for mainstreaming mildly handicapped children. *Journal of Special Education, 22,* 479–491.

Parsons, R., & Meyers, J. (1984). *Developing consultation skills.* San Francisco: Jossey-Bass.

Phillips, B. (1990). *School psychology at a turning point.* San Francisco: Jossey-Bass.

Powell, N. (1994). Content for educational programs in school-based occupational therapy from a practice perspective. *American Journal of Occupational Therapy, 48*(2), 130–137.

Pratt, P., & Allen, A. (1989). *Occupational therapy for children* (2nd ed.). St. Louis: C.V. Mosby.

Pugach, M., & Johnson, L. (1989). Prereferral interventions: Progress, problems, and challenges. *Exceptional Children, 56*(3), 217–226.

Red, C., & Shainline, E. (1987). Teachers reflect on change. *Educational Leadership, 44,* 38–40.

Reissman, F. (1988). Transforming the schools: A new paradigm. *Social Policy, 19*(1), 2–4.

Rogoff, M., & Constable, R. (1991). The least restrictive environment: Its implementation and school social workers. In R. Constable, J. Flynn, & S. McDonald (Eds.), *School social work: Practice and research perspectives* (2nd ed., pp. 233–244). Chicago: Lyceum Books.

Royeen, C., & Coutinho, M. (1991). The special education administrator's perspective. In W. Dunn (Ed.), *Pediatric occupational therapy: Facilitating effective service provision* (pp. 309–317). Thorofare, NJ: SLACK, Inc.

Russell, S., & Kaderavek, J. (1993). Alternative models for collaboration. *Language, Speech, and Hearing Services in Schools, 24,* 76–78.

Schultz, E., & Heuchert, C. (1983). *Child stress and the school experience.* New York: Human Services Press.

Servis, B. (1978). Developing IEPs for physically handicapped students: A transdisciplinary viewpoint. *TEACHING Exceptional Children, 10,* 78–82.

Sexton, J. (1991). Team management of the child with hearing loss. *Seminars in Hearing, 12,* 329–339.

Shinn, M. (1986). Does anyone care what happens after the refer-test-place sequence: The systematic evaluation of special education program effectiveness. *School Psychology Review, 15,* 49–58.

Stedt, J. (1992). Interpreter's wrist: Repetitive stress injury and carpal tunnel syndrome in sign language interpreters. *American Annals of the Deaf, 137,* 40–43.

Steele, W., & Raider, M. (1991). *Working with families in crisis: School-based intervention.* New York: Guilford Press.

Struthers, L. (1917). *The school nurse: A survey of the duties and responsibilities of the nurse in the maintenance of health and physical perfection and the prevention of disease among school children.* New York: G.P. Putnam.

Subtelney, J., Webster, P., & Murphy, L. (1980). Personnel preparation for teaching speech to the hearing impaired: Current status and recommendations. In J. Subtelney (Ed.), *Speech assessment and speech improvement for the hearing impaired* (pp. 366–388). Washington, DC: Alexander Graham Bell Association.

Synoground, S., & Kelsey, M. (1990). *Health care problems in the classroom.* Springfield, IL: Charles C Thomas.

Tecklin, J. (1989). *Pediatric physical therapy.* Philadelphia: J.B. Lippincott.

Thompson, R. (1992). *School counseling renewal: Strategies for the twenty-first century.* Muncie, IN: Accelerated Development.

Thorndike, R., Hagen, E., & Sattler, J. (1986). *Stanford-Binet Intelligence Scale.* Chicago: Riverside Publishing Co.

Thousand, J., Villa, R., Paolucci-Whitcomb, P., & Nevin, A. (1992). A rationale for collaborative consultation. In W. Stainback & S. Stainback (Eds.), *Controversial issues confronting special education: Divergent perspectives* (pp. 223–232). Newton, MA: Allyn & Bacon.

Tower, C. (1992). *The role of educators in the prevention and treatment of child abuse and neglect.* Washington, DC: U.S. Department of Health and Human Services.

Vess, S., & Gregory, L. (1985). Best practices in the assessment of hearing impaired children. In A. Thomas & J. Grimes (Eds.), *Best practices in school psychology* (pp. 473–483). Kent, OH: National Association of School Psychologists.

Wang, M., Reynolds, M., & Walberg, H. (1991). Integrating second-system children: Alternatives to segregation and classification of handicapped children. In R. Constable, J. Flynn, & S. McDonald (Eds.), *School social work: Practice and research perspectives* (2nd ed., pp. 156–166). Chicago: Lyceum Books.

Weiner, J., & Davidson, I. (1990). The in-school team experience. In E. Cole & J. Siegel (Eds.), *Effective consultation in school psychology* (pp. 19–32). Toronto: Hogrefe and Huber.

Welsh, M., Judge, T., Anderson, J., Bray, J., Child, B., & Franke, L. (1990). Collaborative options-outcome planner: A tool for implementing prereferral consultation. *TEACHING Exceptional Children, 22*(2), 30–31.

West, J., & Idol, L. (1987). School consultation (Part 1): An interdisciplinary perspective on theory, models and research. *Journal of Learning Disorders, 20,* 388–408.

West, J., Idol, L., & Cannon, G. (1989). *Collaboration in the schools: An inservice and preservice curriculum for teachers, support staff, and administrators (instructor's manual).* Austin, TX: PRO-ED.

Winnick, J. (Ed.). (1990). *Adapted physical education and sports.* Champaign, IL: Human Kinetics Books.

Worzbyt, J., & O'Rourke, K. (1989). *Elementary school counseling: A blueprint for today and tomorrow.* Muncie, IN: Accelerated Development.

Ysseldyke, J., Reynolds, M., & Weinberg, R. (1984). *School psychology: A blueprint for training and practice.* Minneapolis: National Psychology Inservice Training Network.

Zieziula, F. (Ed.). (1982). *Assessment of hearing impaired people: A guide for selecting psychological, educational and vocational tests.* Washington, DC: Gallaudet College Press.

6

Educational Audiology Across the Lifespan

Infants and Toddlers

FEDERAL FINANCIAL SUPPORT OF EDUCATIONAL services for infants and toddlers at risk for or with disabilities began in 1986 with PL 99-457, the Education for the Handicapped Act (EHA) Amendments of 1986. (Remember, in 1990 this law was renamed, under PL 101-476, the Individuals with Disabilities Education Act [IDEA].) Part H of PL 99-457 (later expanded in PL 102-119, the Individuals with Disabilities Education Act Amendments of 1991) provides funds to states to develop early intervention programs for children at risk for developmental delay or with disabilities from the ages of birth through 2. As mentioned in Chapter 1, audiologists were identified as one of the ten appropriate service providers for infants and toddlers with disabilities.

This role as service provider for infants and toddlers widened the scope of practice for audiologists in education because PL 94-142, the original Education for All Handicapped Children Act of 1975, addressed learners from age 3 to 21 years only. This broadened scope of practice challenges educational audiologists and the other identified professionals to develop new skills in order to serve infants and toddlers in educational settings (Rousch & McWilliams, 1990).

> Educational audiologists who serve infants and toddlers with hearing impairment and their families should consider themselves early interventionists and, therefore, part of an early intervention team.

In this chapter, students of educational audiology examine the responsibilities of the educational audiologist in regard to infants and toddlers, ages 0 through 2, with hearing impairment. These responsibilities extend far beyond the traditional application of clinical expertise. Knowing how to assess the level of hearing impairment, or how to provide appropriate amplification, is an application only of the science to the artful science of early intervention audiology. An educational audiologist who serves infants and toddlers with hearing impairment, as part of a transdisciplinary team, **actually serves the child and the family, not just the child**. Different service delivery methods are required when the child and the family are both the focus of service. The art, then, of early intervention is understanding the needs of a particular family, serving the child in the context of his or her family, and, most important, developing trust and respect with family members.

Students and practitioners alike face the exciting challenge of developing the new skills needed to be an effective early interventionist. This chapter first provides a description of the clinical responsibilities of the educational audiologist in serving infants and toddlers. Next, three basic areas of early intervention practice are presented: 1) serving children in the context of their families; 2) developing the document that describes and organizes early intervention services, the individualized family service plan (IFSP); and 3) serving as a collaborating team member on a transdisciplinary early intervention team and participating in the process of the IFSP.

CLINICAL RESPONSIBILITIES OF THE EDUCATIONAL AUDIOLOGIST IN SERVING INFANTS AND TODDLERS

Since the passage of PL 99-457, the Education of the Handicapped Act Amendments of 1986, the following set of definitions and responsibilities for audiologists serving infants and toddlers and their families have been provided:

i.   Identification of children with hearing impairment, using at risk criteria and appropriate screening techniques;
ii.   Determination of the range, nature, and degree of hearing loss and communication functions, by use of audiological evaluation procedures;
iii. Referral for medical and other services necessary for the habilitation or rehabilitation of children with auditory impairment;
iv.   Provision of auditory training, aural rehabilitation, speech reading and listening device orientation and training, and other services;
v.   Provision of services for prevention of hearing loss; and
vi.   Determination of the child's need for amplification, including selecting, fitting, and dispensing appropriate listening and vibrotactile devices, and the evaluation of the effectiveness of these devices. (*Federal Register*, June 22, 1989, Sec. 303.12, p. 26312)

Items ii through vi are traditional clinical responsibilities of the audiologist, and training for these skills is provided in virtually all audiology programs. Item i, however, the identification of children with hearing impairment, is of special concern to educational audiologists. This concern is addressed in the following section.

Identification of Children with Hearing Impairment

The efficacy of early intervention programs ultimately depends on the timely identification of disabling conditions. No matter how carefully planned or expertly developed, services are underutilized when infants with hearing impairment are not identified as soon as possible. If identification procedures are not *significantly* improved, many infants and toddlers with hearing impairment will not benefit from available programs. Educational audiologists are among the professionals most qualified to improve the current disappointing status of early identification of hearing impairment.

Hearing impairment is one of the more common handicapping conditions in children. Approximately 120,000 infants are born in the U.S. each year with moderate-to-severe hearing impairment. This is 2.5%–5% of all live births (Joint Committee on Infant Hearing, 1991). Because of its invisible nature, hearing impairment often is not identified until later. In the U.S., the mean age of identification of HI is 2.5 years (Gustason, 1989; Welsh & Slater, 1993). Infants with a severe or profound hearing impairment still babble and coo until approximately 6 months, because their verbal play is an activity enjoyed initially for its tactile stimulation. However, after the age of 6 months, because they perceive no auditory feedback to their verbalizations, these behaviors begin to fade out. Only then do parents and caregivers begin to register their concern.

> **One parent remembers**: "Why didn't he jump when the door slammed? Why did he look so surprised when I came up from behind him, even though I had been calling his name? Although he looked like he understood, he wasn't talking. I was afraid he was, you know, maybe retarded. But my neighbor said boys always talk later than girls."

Impact of Hearing Impairment on Learning

Although hearing status is often mistakenly assumed to be divided between hearing and deaf, **the great majority (92%–94%) of children with HI have mild, moderate** or **moderately severe impairment** and are more accurately considered to be "hard of hearing." The remaining 6%–8% of children with HI have profound hearing impairment or are deaf (Flexer, Wray, & Ireland, 1989). Children who are hard of hearing typically develop the usual speech and language milestones, but at a delayed rate, and with a variety of deviances. Superficially, a toddler may appear to develop normally, and his or her hearing impairment can go undetected until he or she is screened in kindergarten. Deaf children, however, typically demonstrate such significant delay that the diagnosis occurs much earlier—although still not as early as is optimal, as is discussed shortly.

Regardless of the degree of hearing impairment, the educational impact on a child is significant. Early studies that examined the effect of severe hearing impairment found that deaf children typically demonstrated marked deficits in language development and concomitant delay in academic progress (Cooper & Rosenstein, 1966; Grant, 1987; Groht, 1958; Ling, 1976; Quigley & Power, 1972; Schmidt, 1968).

Children with less severe hearing impairment also experience difficulties in language development. Vocabulary deficits, delayed syntax development, and inappropriate use of morphological markers and figurative speech are noticeable characteristics of the language of students who are hard of hearing.

The impact of hearing impairment on spoken and written language development has a direct relationship to a child's cognitive development. As Sanders (1982) pointed out:

> Deprived of the ability to hear spoken language, or able to hear it only in a very distorted manner, the child with a profound or severe hearing impairment will experience serious difficulty in acquiring linguistic skills. . . . Language competency is a critical factor in . . . cognitive development, speech perception and learning abilities within an auditory environment. (p. 161–162)

Students with hearing impairment often repeat grades, have depressed math skills, and have reading levels that plateau at the fourth- or fifth-grade level. One study (Davis, Shepard, Stelmachowitz, & Gorga, 1981) measured the reading abilities of 1,250 students with hearing impairment in Iowa and noted a leveling off of reading skills at a fourth-grade level by age 16. Pertinent to our interest in early identification is this finding: **Only 29 of these 1,250 students had been identified as having a hearing impairment before the age of 3.**

The Benefits of Early Identification

The sooner a hearing impairment is identified and remediated with amplification, the more the child seems to benefit. Several studies support the efficacy of early intervention, particularly for children with hearing impairment. Watkins (1987) observed four groups of infants with hearing impairment and reported superior communication and social skills in the two groups that were in a home intervention program, compared with the two groups that were not. Another study reported similar positive effects on linguistic attainment from home intervention programs (White & White, 1987).

Longitudinal studies indicate that the intervention programs that showed the longest duration of gain were those that started at birth and involved the parents (Greenstein, Greenstein, & McConville, et al., 1976; Levitt, McGarr, & Geffner, 1987; Schweinhart & Weikart, 1980).

Hearing-health professionals recognize the professional ethic to strive for the earliest intervention possible. Ross (1990) pointed out that "even the incomplete and intermittent deprivation of sound can have a deleterious effect when it occurs during the first few years of a child's life" (p. 73). Animal studies have consistently shown that auditory deprivation results in structural changes in the auditory pathways and neurons, and in physiological aberrations in the processing of complex sound patterns (Webster & Webster, 1977).

In addition to the need to stimulate the auditory nerves, Northern and Downs (1984) addressed the concept of "critical learning periods" in a child's life, and the early plasticity of the brain, which requires stimulation in the first 3 years of life if auditory perceptions and oral language learning are to occur. For effective early intervention, Ross (1990) encouraged developing "a sense of urgency, and the feeling of irreplaceable time being squandered" (p. 74). Most hearing health professionals would agree with Dunst (1986), who suggested that it is necessary to move past generalized discussions of efficacy and explore specific variables that are most effective in early intervention.

Delays in Early Identification

In the United States, the average age in which hearing loss is identified is 2.5 years. Some countries, notably those with socialized medicine, have obtained an identification rate of up to 100% by a child's first birthday (Gustason, 1989; Hitchings & Haggard, 1983).

The U.S. does not yet have a federal plan to make early identification of hearing loss a priority. In response to concerns regarding delays in identification, former Surgeon General C. Everett Koop issued the following challenge to hearing health professionals: by the year 2000, 90% of all children with a significant hearing impairment will be identified by 12 months of age (*Healthy People 2000*, 1990). As with many other health issues, this challenge is to be addressed by policies developed at the state level. To date, fewer than half of the states have policies concerning screening for hearing loss in newborns. Where policies do exist, most states use a High Risk Register (HRR) for screening newborns (English, 1992).

   High Risk Register (HRR) for Early Identification of HI   Ideally, all newborn children, or neonates, are screened for hearing impairment. In 1993, the National Institute on Deafness and Other Communication Disorders (NIDCD) of the National Institutes of Health (NIH) recommended universal hearing screening for all infants within their first 3 months of life. Recommended screening procedures include otoacoustic emission (OAE) and auditory brainstem response (ABR) testing (Giebel & Redemann, 1992; Goldberg, 1993). Many states currently utilize some form of High Risk Register to help identify children at risk for HI (Welsh & Slater, 1993). The following sections detail components of a comprehensive High Risk Register. Part A of the High Risk Register consists of criteria to be applied to infants from 0 to 28 days of age. Part B is particularly relevant to educational audiologists involved in identifying hearing impairment in infants and toddlers, from 29 days to 2 years of age, through parent information programs and community coordination.

   High Risk Register: Part A   Table 6.1 is a listing of the criteria recommended by the Joint Committee on Infant Hearing (1991) to determine risk of hearing impairment. Part A lists 10 criteria used to identify neonates at risk for hearing impairment. This information is typically collected by hospital personnel through a review of hospital medical records, by physical observation of the neonate, and by interviewing the mother. If a neonate has one or more of the risk factors, the HRR recommends an ABR evaluation prior to hospital discharge, and no later than 3 months of age.

   Mahoney and Eichwald (1986) described a highly effective use of the HRR for neonates that was developed for the state of Utah. High risk factors observed for each child are entered into birth records, and a computerized search begins the process of identification and follow-up evaluation. The average age of identification of hearing impairment in infants and toddlers in Utah is 11 months—compared to the national average of 30 months. The cost of this program has been estimated at $1 per live birth.

   Students of educational audiology are strongly encouraged to consider the first project outlined in Educational Audiology in Action at the end of this chapter to find out how their state uses Part A of the HRR (Table 6.1).

   High Risk Register: Part B   Part B of the HRR consists of criteria for screening infants from age 29 days to 2 years, after hospital discharge. Part B is intended to help identify infants who were not at risk at birth. For example, if a child is born with a health condition that indicates risk (such as low birth weight or jaundice) in a state that uses a HRR, a hearing test is typically administered before release from the hospital. However, 50% of all infants with hearing impairment experience unremarkable deliveries and evidence good postnatal health; therefore, because they

Table 6.1.　Criteria to determine risk of hearing impairment in infants and toddlers

A.　Risk criteria for sensorineural hearing impairment in neonates (birth–28 days):
　1.　Family history of congenital or delayed onset childhood sensorineural hearing imparment.
　2.　Congenital infection known or suspected to be asssociated with sensorineural hearing impairment such as toxoplasmosis, syphilis, rubella, cytomegalovirus, and herpes.
　3.　Craniofacial anomalies including morphologic abnormalities of the pinna and ear canal, absent philtrum, low hairline, etc.
　4.　Birth weight less than 1,500 grams (approx. 3.3 lbs).
　5.　Hyperbilirubinemia at a level exceeding indication for exchange transfusion.
　6.　Ototoxic medications including but not limited to the aminoglycosides used for more than 5 days (e.g., gentamicin, tobramycin, kanamycin, streptomycin) and loop diuretics used in combination with aminoglycosides.
　7.　Bacterial meningitis.
　8.　Severe depression at birth, which may include infants with Apgar scores of 0–3 at 5 minutes, or those who fail to initiate spontaneous respiration by 10 minutes, or those with hypotonia persisting to 2 hours of age.
　9.　Prolonged mechanical ventilation for a duration equal to or greater than 10 days (e.g., persistent pulmonary hypertension).
　10.　Stigmata or other findings associated with a syndrome known to include sensorineural hearing loss (e.g., Waardenburg or Usher's syndrome).

B.　Risk criteria for sensorineural hearing impairment in infants (29 days–2 years):
　1.　Parent/caregiver concern regarding hearing, speech, language and/or developmental delay.
　2.　Bacterial meningitis.
　3.　Neonatal risk factors that may be associated with progressive sensorineural hearing loss (e.g., cytomegalovirus, prolonged mechanical ventilation, and inherited disorders).
　4.　Head trauma, especially with either longitudinal or transverse fracture of the temporal bone.
　5.　Stigmata or other findings associated with a syndrome known to include sensorineural hearing loss (e.g., Waardenburg or Usher's syndrome).
　6.　Ototoxic medications including but not limited to the aminoglycosides used for more than 5 days (e.g., gentamicin, tobramycin, kanamycin, streptomycin) and loop diuretics used in combination with aminoglycosides.
　7.　Children with neurodegenerative disorders such as neurofibromatosis, myoclonic epilepsy, Werdnig-Hoffman disease, Tay-Sachs disease, infantile Gaucher's disease, Nieman-Pick disease, any metachromatic leukodystrophy, or any infantile demylinating neuropathy.
　8.　Childhood infectious diseases known to be associated with sensorineural hearing loss (e.g., mumps, measles).

From Joint Committee on Infant Hearing. (1991). 1990 position statement. *Asha, 33,* (Suppl. 5), 3–6; reprinted with permission.

did not exhibit a risk factor, they leave the hospital without a hearing evaluation. The hearing impairment is then noticed by parents and caregivers over the course of time. Research has consistently indicated that parents begin to suspect hearing loss before a child's first birthday (Bergstrom, 1984; Luterman, 1970; Ross, 1990) and that parents' suspicions have proven to be a reliable indicator of the existence of a hearing impairment (McCormick, Curnock, & Spavins, 1984).

When parents are concerned about a hearing impairment, they are most likely to consult their family doctor ("Burson-Marstellar public information survey," *Asha,* 1987). In order to provide assistance and direction about the identification of hearing impairment to family physicians, pediatricians, and parents, the Joint Committee on Infant Hearing (1991) compiled Part B of the High Risk Register, which is intended to be used as part of the routine protocol of well-baby checkups or other office visits throughout the first 2 years of life.

The inclusion of Part B of the HRR widens its focus from the original 1982 version, which considered only neonates. However, readers are reminded that Part B is only the first step in the process of early identification of hearing impairment in infants from ages 29 days to 2 years. For optimal early identification of hearing impairment, pediatricians and other early interventionists must be convinced of the value of this screening tool—and this greatly depends on their interactions and relationships with educational audiologists. Enlisting support within a community to include Part B in routine well-baby screening protocol requires focused and consistent effort on the part of the audiologist.

Students in educational audiology are encouraged to consider the second project described in Educational Audiology in Action at the end of this chapter to investigate implementation and evaluation of Part B of the HRR in their state or region (Bess, 1993).

> **One family's experience:** Ms. A. was painfully aware that her son Martin was not talking by his second birthday, but since he was her first child, she was unsure of the implications. "Later we went home to the Philippines, and my mother was wondering why he wasn't talking, and I told her that all the children in the United States talk late. . . . My girlfriend had told me that some talk at three years old." As a Navy wife, she had to relocate frequently, and so was isolated from her more experienced family members. In addition, she had not been able to develop friendships with parents of typically developing children. Physicians did not indicate concern when Martin was brought in for checkups and innoculations. Without professional help, she had no access to information regarding normal language development.
>
> By the time the diagnosis of a severe bilateral loss was confirmed for Martin, Mr. and Ms. A had a second child. Susan was tested immediately, and was found to have a moderate bilateral loss. Ms. A is sure that if she had known of her first child's hearing loss in time, she would have chosen to have no more children. She does not feel up to caring for two children with hearing impairment, and often feels overwhelmed, frightened, and resentful that information was not more readily available to her.

Summary

PL 99-457, the Education of the Handicapped Act Amendments of 1986, was enacted concurrent with the challenge to identify hearing loss at the earliest age possible. The challenge to educational audiologists as early interventionists is to become actively involved in developing policies and programs in states and regions that do not yet have effective early identification programs.

BEYOND CLINICAL RESPONSIBILITIES: WORKING WITH FAMILIES

Up to this point, we have been considering traditional audiology concerns for infants and toddlers: early identification leading to timely early intervention services. As indicated in the introduction to this chapter, however, the audiologist in the school setting is required to have additional expertise in serving children in the context of their families through developing the Individualized Family Service Plan and working with a team. These areas are discussed in the second part of this chapter.

PL 99-457, the Education of the Handicapped Act Amendments of 1986, recognized that the typical and appropriate environment for intervention with infants and toddlers was most often within the context of their families. This is an important concept to consider because prior to PL 99-457, early intervention had typically not considered the family as a whole. Services were child-centered, and families were not included in services.

> Because infants and toddlers are inextricably dependent on their families, it is now recognized that the **child in the context of the family rather than just the child should be the focus of services**. This approach is driven by the assumption that involvement of the family is a more powerful and effective method of intervention for the child than intervention directed to the child alone.

This **family-centered** approach required that professionals change their focus from a **child-centered** approach. The process of changing to a **family-centered service delivery system** has been difficult for many professionals. The family-centered approach to services differs markedly from the model driving earlier training and past role expectations. Typical training in graduate audiology programs does not teach the skills that are needed to work with families. So, educational audiologists join other professionals in meeting the challenge of developing new skills, often with an initial sense of discomfort with the unfamiliar. It is reassuring to know that all professionals working in early intervention are going through the same process of adjustment to a family-centered system of services.

> A family-centered service system encourages the early interventionist to surrender the accustomed role of child expert, and, instead, to support the family as the primary decision-maker regarding intervention.

A recent study demonstrated the challenges of adjusting to a family-centered service system. Early interventionists were asked to rate the typical level of family interactions that occurred in their programs, and also to describe their perceptions of ideal levels of family interaction (Bailey, Buysse, Edmondson, & Smith, 1992). These professionals rated their observations on a 10-point scale, with 1 indicating that professionals make all decisions and 10 indicating that the family make all decisions, lead team meetings, write the IFSP, and plan and coordinate assessments. Differences between the real and the ideal were notable. Typical real interactions averaged a score between 4 and 5, and ideal interactions were rated between 7 and 8. When asked to identify possible barriers to the ideal level of family involvement, 70% indicated that families, as well as the existing system, presented barriers. In other words, it was felt that many families were also struggling to adjust to their new role as active participants in their child's education. In addition, the current system of service delivery was not facilitating the new focus of family-centered services.

Professionals themselves have also indicated the need for informed direction as they adjust to the family as the focus of service delivery. After working many years with a service delivery system that focused on the child, professionals in the field of special education have asked for support in learning to provide family-centered services. Typically, support begins with learning about how the family functions as a system, and with developing skills in collaboration and team membership.

The following section provides an overview of how family systems function, the development of family-centered services, and the role of the educational audiologist in providing family-centered services.

Family Systems Theory

Family systems theory starts with the assumption that a family may be defined as two or more individuals who: 1) state they are a family, and 2) assume obligations to family members that are generally considered as appropriate to family support (Hartman, 1981).

Family systems theory developed to examine the interactive roles each family member plays in the family dynamic. Family systems theory operates on the premise that circumstances that affect one family member ultimately affect all family members and the family system to some degree. McGoldrick and Gerson (1985) provided this observation: "The physical, social and emotional functioning of family members is profoundly interdependent, with changes in one part of the system reverberating in other parts of the system" (p. 5). Consider these examples: A parent receives word to expect a lay-off notice soon. The entire family becomes affected by the sudden concern for financial security, the anxiety of finding a new job, and the need to economize until income is stable. A high school senior is notified that a college far from home has accepted her. While the student experiences excitement and considers possible homesickness, her parents address the cost of tuition, housing, and transportation. In addition, parents and siblings both begin to adjust to a family member moving out of the home. Even a relatively personal incident, such as the decision to start a diet, affects the rest of the family.

Components of the Family System In order to understand such interdependency, educational audiologists working as early interventionists must understand what makes up the family system. Components of the family system include: family structure, family resources, family interaction, family functions, and family lifecycle.

Family Structure While acknowledging that every family is unique, it is fair to say that every family can also be described by certain characteristics, such as family size, structural formation, socioeconomic status, education, cultural background and religion, and even geographic location. These characteristics all contribute to how a family is structured. The characteristics of an infant or toddler with a disability, including the type of disability and the degree of severity, is also part of the description of a family's structure.

The individual family structure may help to determine the best way in which professionals can provide services. A close, extended family may wish to include grandparents, aunts, uncles, or cousins in the child's educational plans. A family with a strong religious affiliation may want to seek support from its religious community. A family from a particular culture may prefer working with professionals from a similar background.

Family Resources   Each family has strengths or strategies to draw on when facing a challenge. These strengths and strategies comprise their family resources and can include physical and mental health, the support of extended family and friends, religious background, and a variety of coping strategies. By coping strategies we mean ways that individuals and families relieve the stress of a situation. Coping strategies have been identified as:

Temporarily ignoring the problem by becoming involved in other activities, such as going for a walk or reading a book. This brief respite allows time to adjust to a difficult or upsetting situation. This coping strategy is called passive appraisal.

Reconsidering a problem in a different light in order to make it more tolerable. For example, a parent may say to herself, "At least Julio is healthy. A hearing problem is not as serious as leukemia, like what happened to my cousin's daughter." This coping strategy is called reframing a problem or concern.

Seeking spiritual support through comfort in one's belief system

Seeking social support from friends and family through practical and emotional assistance

Seeking formal support by way of assistance from agencies and professionals (Olson et al., 1983)

Families vary widely in the ways in which they cope with challenges. Educational audiologists need to recognize and be sensitive to a family's particular coping styles and to work within those styles in order to help families grow in their adjustment to the new family member with HI.

> "It's not that I regret having Ashley, but I didn't expect this. I never smoke, I don't drink, I hardly even took Tylenol during my pregnancy. I was doing everything I could, eating all those healthy foods. So when I learned about Ashley being deaf, it came like a shock. It still is. I pray all the time to be able to handle this."

Family Interaction   Family interaction is the process by which a family deals with the events of daily life. Family interaction is how families accomplish the "work" of a family: providing affection and support, resolving problems, sharing household chores, and making plans for the future. The way family interactions take place can be defined by three characteristics: family attachment, family adaptability, and family communication. The continuum of each characteristic is shown in Figure 6.1.

Attachment describes the levels of dependence within a family. Emotional support of family members is appropriate and healthy, but a family may become too closely bonded, or "enmeshed," while individual needs are suppressed. An enmeshed family often depends almost exclusively on family members for all emotional and practical support. At the other end of the continuum is a family whose members live parallel lives but who draw little emotional support from the family unit. This type of family is described as "disengaged." A disengaged family shares the same residence, but members typically feel they are on their own in a crisis

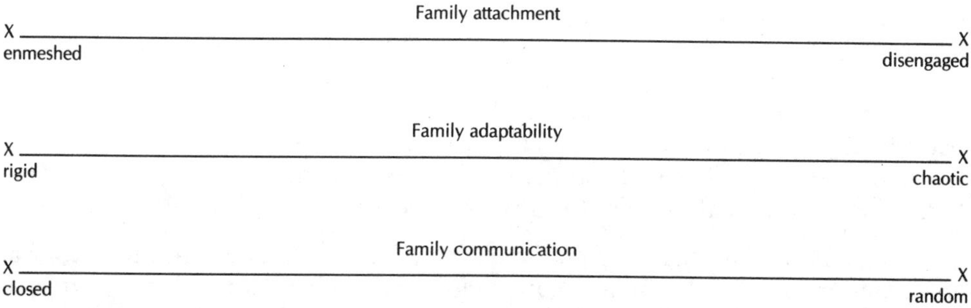

Family attachment

X ———————————————————————————————— X
enmeshed   disengaged

Family adaptability

X ———————————————————————————————— X
rigid   chaotic

Family communication

X ———————————————————————————————— X
closed   random

Figure 6.1. Continua of family interactions.

when they may need help or support. Most families fall somewhere in the middle of the continuum, meeting the challenge of providing emotional support while promoting independence among individual family members. In order to provide useful services to families with a infant or toddler with a disability, the early interventionist needs to determine the level of attachment in a particular family, to ensure that the interventions match the family's style. For example, a very close or enmeshed family may prefer to have only immediate family members involved in the intervention, whereas a less attached family is probably comfortable with the involvement of strangers.

Adaptability is a measure of the family's ability to adapt to change or to a stressful situation. Adaptability is also described as a continuum, from rigid to chaotic. A rigid family maintains interactions in accordance with predetermined roles and expectations, such as "breadwinner" and "caregiver." A rigid family may not adjust easily to the unexpected challenges of an infant or toddler with HI. At the other extreme, a chaotic family functions with few or inconsistent rules and with little leadership or direction within the family. A chaotic family may have no set mealtimes or bedtime routines or may not stay in the same residence for very long. In a chaotic family, discipline strategies may be unpredictable, varying from one day to the next. Again, most families fall somewhere in the middle, striving to function along a consistent set of expectations while demonstrating flexibility when needed.

As specialists in communicative disorders, audiologists may feel on familiar ground with the **communication** aspect of family life. However, here we are considering how a family communicates, which is not typically addressed in clinical training programs. Family communication concerns how effectively and honestly family members communicate information and feelings to one another. The communication continuum extends from closed, where problems are not discussed and feelings are ignored or over-intellectualized, to random, where all issues are discussed with high levels of emotion. A balance between these two extremes enables a family to share common concerns when a child with a disability becomes part of the family.

Family Functions   The purpose of the family is to serve the collective and individual needs of its members. According to Turnbull and Turnbull (1986), these needs are met through performing the following functions:

Economic (generating income, paying bills)
Domestic/health care (running the household, purchasing and preparing food)
Recreational (leisure activities for the family and for individuals)
Socialization (developing and maintaining friendships; learning social skills)
Self-identity (developing a sense of belonging, self-image)
Affection (providing love and companionship, expressing emotions)
Educational/vocational (developing a work ethic, saving for college)

It is important to realize that a family may focus only on certain functions at any given time, and a decision as to which functions have priority can change at any moment. A family may also choose to focus on a function that is not considered a priority by a professional. Differences in a family's and a professional's functional priorities can become a source of tension or animosity if a professional does not respect a family's right to determine its own course. It is imperative for a professional in early intervention to withhold personal judgment regarding family decisions, as long as the children are not in danger of abuse or neglect.

It is also critical to understand that an early intervention professional is not expected to become involved in every facet of a family's life. For example, an educational audiologist is not responsible for helping a family member find a job or otherwise generate income. An educational audiologist would, however, be responsible for helping to obtain financial assistance from public and private agencies to cover the cost of hearing aids. Educational audiologists regularly need to ask themselves: "Am I staying within the mandates and professional ethics of my field? Am I developing a relationship with this family that is supportive and within professional boundaries?" Maintaining a professional attitude with families is an ongoing challenge to all early interventionists.

Family Life Cycle   A family, by nature, is in a constant state of change. A family adjusts to the birth of a new baby, members take new jobs or return to school, a family may have to relocate, family members become ill, and family members die. These above are examples of changes that occur in a family, and change often increases stress in a family. In addition to these changes, there are also broader stages in a family's life cycle. Stages in the life cycle of a family with children include: 1) childbearing years, 2) school-age years, 3) adolescence, 4) young adulthood, 5) post-parental, and 6) aging. It is quite common for a family to have to be involved in more than one stage at a time. When moving to a new life stage, a family can expect to experience some stress from the changes that mark the transition.

Stages in the family life cycle are often defined by rituals determined by society to mark the transition. Weddings, religious initiations, graduations, and retirement are symbols of significant changes in a family. However, for a family with a child with a disability, such transitions may not be as ritualized or as well defined, and may instead remind family members that the future is not predictable, and the next appropriate stage may not be so apparent.

Summary   Understanding family systems theory can assist the educational audiologist in determining the most compatible ways of effectively interacting with a family. Insight into a family's particular structure, resources, interaction, functions, and life cycle are invaluable in helping a family to become part of the IFSP team.

THE INDIVIDUALIZED FAMILY SERVICE PLAN

The focus of this chapter shifts now from discussion of professional responsibilities and family systems theory to discussion of the combination of the two, which is the process by which professionals and families collaborate to provide services to an infant or toddler with a disability. In the following section, the individualized family service plan (IFSP) is described, both as a contract and as a process for developing partnerships between families and professionals.

The following section answers the question, "What does an IFSP look like?" Subsequent sections consider first, how to develop an IFSP, and second, what an IFSP team is. Because educational audiologists are now involved in IFSP teams, it is vital that we understand our role in the team process.

IFSP: The Document

The individualized family service plan (IFSP) is the written document that PL 99-457 specified is necessary to outline the plan for services for infants and toddlers and their families. The IFSP can be considered as the equivalent of the individualized education program (IEP) that applies to children from age 3 to 21 years. While the IEP focuses on the **child's** skills and goals, the IFSP considers the **child within the context of the family**.

The IFSP is intended to be very flexible, and it is developed collaboratively with the family. Not only is the family's first language used for the written IFSP, but, as much as possible, the family's actual words are used to indicate concerns and priorities. Professionals are reminded to recognize and avoid jargon that may intimidate family members or remove them from their sense of ownership in the development of their plan.

A sample IFSP form is shown in Figure 6.2. Every early intervention program devises its own version of the IFSP that reflects its programmatic focus. Readers are reminded that an IFSP is not an unalterable contract, but one that changes frequently as goals are met and adjusts to the family's changing concerns for their child's development.

Components of the IFSP Although the IFSP is a living document, it must still meet some requirements in order to comply with PL 101-476 (IDEA). Specifically, the IFSP must include the following:

1. A description of the child's current levels of development—physical, cognitive, speech and language, psychosocial, and self-help—obtained by objective criteria (i.e., standardized tests)
2. A statement of the family's concerns, priorities, and resources as they relate to the development of their child with disabilities
3. A statement of outcomes expected to be achieved by the child and family with the help of appropriate professionals. Procedures, timelines, and criteria, and review/evaluation processes are also defined
4. A description of the specific early intervention services to be provided, including frequency, location, and method of service delivery
5. A projected date for initiation of services, and the anticipated duration of these services

INDIVIDUALIZED FAMILY SERVICE PLAN (IFSP)
HAPPY VALLEY EDUCATION AREA

Child's Name_____   Date of Birth_____
Parent(s) Name_____   Phone_____
Address_____

Referred By_____   Date referral received_____

Family Members (Name, relationship, age):

_____
_____
_____
_____
_____

IFSP Team: (* indicates family members)

	Name	Agency	Phone
Service coordinator:			
Lead service provider:			
Others (indicate title):			

_____
_____
_____
_____
_____
_____
_____

Description of Family Resources:

Figure 6.2. An example of an IFSP form.

Summary of Child's Present Level of Functioning:

Physical health:

Problem-solving (cognitive) abilities:

Communication:

Social abilities

Self-help abilities:

Fine motor skills:

Gross motor skills:

Complete medical records and test results are attached.

(continued)

Figure 6.2. *(continued)*

Statement of family's present concerns regarding their child:

Identify the priority of the above concerns by numbering #1, #2, etc.

Expected Outcomes of Services:

Outcome

#1

#2.

#3.

(continue on Page 3/supplement if needed)

I agree to the implementation of the proposed outcomes and actions. I understand that I am able to make changes in this Individualized Family Service Plan at any time.

_____

Parent's signature   Date

Figure 6.2. (continued)

Outcome #_____
    To be met by_____
    Starting_____
    How often_____
    Where_____

Date	Description of Service	Action Taken

6. The name of the service coordinator responsible for implementing and coordinating services among agencies and professionals
7. A description of a transition plan to appropriate preschool services at age 3, as necessary

Some concern is usually expressed regarding the physical format of the IFSP. The National Early Childhood Technical Assistance System (NEC*TAS) indicated that although

> the purpose of the IFSP is to identify and organize families' goals for their children and themselves . . . the IFSP—the written product itself—is possibly the least important aspect of the entire IFSP process. Far more important are the interaction, collaboration, and partnerships between families and professionals that are necessary to develop and implement the IFSP. (1989, p. 1)

The development of partnerships between families and professionals is an **ongoing process** that cannot be hurried or assumed. As mentioned, the IFSP process is addressed in a later section. For now, we turn to a description of the components of the IFSP document.

Child Assessment   The first requirement of the IFSP is a comprehensive description of the child's current levels of development. Early interventionists agree that the child assessment mandated for the IFSP does not consist of a one-time collection of data at the time of intake but is an ongoing process of assessment, determined by the family's concerns in the child's development.

Information sources for the child's physical development may include a physician's report, as well as reports from occupational and physical therapists, vision impairment and mobility specialists, and audiologists. When the infant or toddler has a hearing impairment, the educational audiologist must ensure that full and accurate information about hearing levels is presented and is comprehensible to all members of the IFSP team. A report written in everyday language that describes the results of audiometric measurements and recommendations for amplification, speech, language, and auditory training, and medical follow-up facilitates the understanding of the child's hearing abilities by all the members of the IFSP team.

Numerous assessments are available for measuring the child's cognitive and communication development, psychosocial and self-help skills, and motor development. Subtests of the following instruments, normed for children from birth to age 3, are often used:

- Battelle Developmental Inventory (Newborg, Stock, Wnek, Guidubaldi, & Svinicki, 1984)
- Bayley Scales of Infant Development (Bayley, 1969)
- Brigance Inventory of Early Development (Brigance, 1978)
- Early Learning Accomplishment Profile (also known as E-LAP) (Glover, Preminger, & Sanford, 1978)
- Hawaii Early Learning Profile (also known as HELP) (Furuno, O'Reilly, Hosaka, Inatsuka, Allman, & Zeisloft, 1979)

Although some of these instruments provide suggested testing modifications to accommodate the needs of children with hearing impairments (such as the use of sign language), none are normed for infants and toddlers with hearing impairment.

Cautious and informed interpretation of the results of these instruments is an important responsibility of the educational audiologist. Audiologists are strongly urged to develop a working knowledge of these and other assessments in order to provide appropriate interpretation of the findings in relation to the child's hearing levels. The audiologist must address the following concerns regarding the assessment process and results:

1. Did the child have optimal amplification? Was a listening check of the hearing aid(s) or FM system conducted?
2. Were there health complications (such as middle ear infections) that may have compromised the child's ability to hear and, therefore, respond?
3. Was the test administered in a setting with good lighting that was also free of background noise and visual distractions?
4. If the infant or toddler is developing sign language skills, was the tester familiar with child-level approximations of signs?

The educational audiologist is responsible for ensuring that assessments are administered and interpreted with a fair consideration of the child's hearing impairment.

Family Concerns, Priorities, and Resources   In the early conceptualization of the IFSP, there was interest in designing formalized and structured assessments for families, which included rating scales and other efforts to standardize measurements. Examples of these instruments include F-COPES-Family Crisis Oriented Personal Scales (McCubbin, Olson, & Larsen, 1981), and the Parenting Stress Index (Abidin, 1986). Implied in the use of this type of assessment, however, is a pathological orientation that focuses on issues that **families** may not have identified as problematic (Slentz & Bricker, 1992). There is also a likelihood that the use of such instruments has a negative impact on the developing relationship between the family and professionals. Positive relationships are less likely to occur when assessment is seen as an invasion of privacy or a measure of fault-finding. Families have been reported to feel uncomfortable and even threatened by such processes of assessment (Slentz, Walker, & Bricker, 1989). Certainly the sharing of personal information with virtual strangers—who are not responding with reciprocity—is not a normalizing process. (The principle of normalization was discussed in Chapter 2. Briefly, it advocates that professionals help persons with disabilities "obtain an existence as close as to the normal as possible" [Wolfensberger, 1972, p. 26].) Families with typically developing children do not experience the intrusion of family assessment; therefore, to be treated as normal, the family with a child with a disability should also not be expected to undergo assessment.

It would appear, then, that extending the practice of child assessment to the lives of families is inappropriate, and recently an emerging concensus has developed that assessment information should be obtained from parents and other family members in the form of informal discussions (Hanson & Lynch, 1989). An initial, focused interview and a brief needs assessment help to establish family priorities and provide a starting point for intervention. One purpose of this form of assessment is to develop a trusting relationship between professionals and families, with the intent to address only intervention concerns. Formal assessments of families, then, should be avoided altogether or used with great caution (Bailey & McWilliam, 1990).

PL 99-457, the Education of the Handicapped Act Amendments of 1986, originally required identification of a family's "strengths and needs." This language was replaced in the reauthorization of the law, PL 102-119, the Individuals with Disabilities Education Act Amendments of 1991, by the phrase "resources, priorities, and concerns." This change better reflects the intent of the law, which is not to assess the family per se but to help identify issues that a family decides are "relevant to its ability to enhance the development of its child" (National Early Childhood Technical Assistance System [NEC*TAS], 1989, p. 18).

Bailey et al. (1986) identified three goals for family interviews, which support the intent to identify resources, priorities, and concerns. 1) To assist a family in coping with its child's needs. These address issues specific to the child's disability, such as learning to perform a daily hearing aid listening check and studying information on communication options (e.g., Cued Speech, American Sign Language, aural/oral approach). 2) To help the family understand their child's development within the family. A family may request basic information regarding child development or on the impact of a hearing loss on the child's speech and language development. 3) To help promote positive parent–child relationships. It is well documented that parents of children with disabilities are often less responsive to their children, starting a cycle of minimal interaction or overly directive interactions.

In addition, there are two issues to consider regarding family interviews. First is the concern for a family's privacy, which is actualized by avoiding overly intrusive procedures, as has been discussed. Second, sensitivity to the family's culture is an integral part of good family interview techniques. Most early intervention programs have represented middle-class, English-language, Anglo-Saxon cultural values. These values can influence practitioner views on such family issues as childrearing, the roles of family members, and perceptions of disabilities. Given the dramatic demographic changes in the U.S., professionals are strongly advised to stay current regarding the interest in the importance of the cultural differences in this country, including those of the Deaf culture (e.g., Anderson & Grace, 1991; Christensen & Delgado, 1993; Crago & Eriks-Brophy, 1993; Grant, 1993; Padden & Humphries, 1988; Rodriquez & Santiviago, 1991). All interviews and other interactions with a particular family should be conducted with an appreciation and respect for differences among cultures, including views of and recommendations for early intervention. Students in educational audiology are strongly encouraged to refer to the sources in the Recommended Readings section of this chapter in order to develop multicultural competencies as part of their ongoing professional responsibilities.

Expected Child and Family Outcomes   The description of expected child outcomes is very similar to the long-term goals that are developed in an individualized education program (IEP). The description of expected child outcomes is a statement of positive changes that the family expects to occur for their child. A child outcome describes both the expected result of intervention and the process for achieving the expected outcome. For example, Maria's family is interested in increasing the intelligibility of her speech. The formulated outcome indicates that Maria will increase her articulation skills (the expectation) and will receive speech therapy twice a week and use amplification a minimum of 8 hours per day in order to self-monitor her speech (the process).

The determination of **family outcomes**, however, is approached differently. Nowhere is it mandated that parents attend programs, establish performance goals, or meet any other expectations of professionals. To describe family outcomes, it is essential to move away from the behavioral objectives that are typical for children. Obviously, behavioral objectives are inappropriate to formulate for families. Rather, it is appropriate to describe family goals in terms of what families can expect from professionals. For example, a family goal might be stated: "The family indicates an interest in respite care and information regarding child-discipline strategies. Therefore, Ms./Mr. Professional will follow up on those interests by providing pertinent information within 3 weeks of the date of this meeting." It is also inappropriate to indicate that family members are expected to meet goals, and family outcomes should be written in the form of suggestions. For example, "Because the family expresses interest in sharing experiences with other parents, Mr. and Mrs. Wong will be given information about the weekly meetings of the local Parent-to-Parent support group. Members of the family may choose to attend meetings at their convenience."

The above examples demonstrate the principle of **family-guided** services in action. While the focus of assessment and intervention is always on the child, the *direction and implementation* of these services are guided by family concerns. The perceived needs of the child should always be identified by the family as the result of ongoing conversations with professionals, and child-related outcomes must be guided by the parents' values and priorities (Beckman & Bristol, 1991). Furthermore, professionals are reminded that suggested goals and outcomes should be placed within a family systems framework that recognizes that any outcome recommended for the child will affect other members of the family to some degree.

Description of Services   The description of services consists of one or more statements regarding the type of interventions, the frequency of the services, and the way services are delivered; for example, "two sessions per week with the occupational therapist, 45 minutes visit per session, conducted in the home, with one session per month conducted as a group session."

The level of family involvement and participation in services, however, is determined by the families themselves. In addition, the family determines the level of intervention (e.g., the number of visits by the occupational therapist per week) because the intervention directly affects the family's life.

Services offered by an educational audiologist might include, but are not limited to, hearing aid maintenance and direct instruction toward the development of listening skills, and speech and language (oral and/or signed) skills. If the infant or toddler has additional disabilities, the educational audiologist may provide other transdisciplinary services after being trained by the appropriate professional, or the educational audiologist may train another service provider to conduct hearing aid checks or to develop listening skills.

Service Coordinator   The IFSP must include the designated service coordinator who is responsible for implementing and coordinating the services with the family and professionals across agencies. The service coordinator is usually the professional or family member most closely associated with the family's needs. For a family with a child with a hearing impairment, an audiologist and a teacher of the hearing impaired (certified for infants and toddlers) are both professionals likely to serve as service coordinator. One person usually performs this role in order to simplify communications with families. In the past, many families have complained of the inconvenience of dealing with several persons in several different agencies in order to obtain services.

The original language of PL 99-457, the Education of the Handicapped Act Amendments of 1986, used the term "case manager" instead of service coordinator. More recently, professionals have felt that referring to an infant or toddler and his or her family as a "case" that required "managing" did little to promote positive relations with families (Lynch, Jackson, Mendoza, & English, 1991). The term service coordinator came into usage with PL 102-119, the Individuals with Disabilities Education Act Amendments of 1991.

The job of the service coordinator involves more than orchestrating family and child services across agencies (Bailey, 1989; Dunst & Trivette, 1989).

> Although one of the main roles of the case manager [service coordinator] is to coordinate interagency services, one of the other roles referred to in the law [PL 99-457] is to **develop the capabilities of the family in order to become active decision-makers for the child** . . . The ultimate goal of the case manager [service coordinator] is to help families develop the skills that they need to serve as their own case coordinator in the future. (Lynch, Mendoza, & English, 1990, p. 56)

The service coordinator may function as a resource person, advocate, enabler, mobilizer, and listener, which involve skills that extend far beyond the organizational abilities typically expected in the past (Cegelka & Mendoza, 1988).

Transition Plan The IFSP specifies the arrangements for the toddler's transition from the early intervention program to a preschool program. It is recommended that transition plans include an introductory stage of the projected placement approximately 6 months before the child's third birthday, and a follow-up stage lasting 6 months beyond the actual program change. Transition services need to include discussion and an exchange of information with the parents regarding program options, and continuing discussion regarding the needs of the child and family during the transition (Lynch, Mendoza, & English, 1990; McGonigel & Johnson, 1991).

PL 102-119, the Individuals with Disabilities Education Act Amendments of 1991, included an important new component of transition planning. PL 102-119 allows for extending the use of IFSPs for children 3–5 years of age. As a result, parents can choose to continue the educational plan with which they are familiar (the IFSP) or adopt the individualized education program (IEP) that will guide their child's education after the age of 5. This option is intended to facilitate for families the toddler's transition to preschool programs.

> **A parent's first contact:** During the first trimester of pregnancy, Ms. Barnes experienced mild symptoms of an illness tentatively diagnosed as rubella. This component of prenatal health history was identified by the High Risk Register (HRR) as a cause for concern for the hearing health of her newborn daughter, Isabella. The neonate was assessed with ABR testing and was found to have a severe bilateral hearing loss.

Before the mother and child were discharged, the audiologist at the hospital provided Ms. Barnes with information regarding amplification and financial resources. Ms. Barnes was also given the names, telephone numbers, and addresses of audiologists who served infants and toddlers in the local educational program. Ms. Barnes consented to have her name referred to these audiologists. When one of the educational audiologists, Mr. Mendoza, received the referral, he wrote a letter to Ms. Barnes encouraging her to contact him at her convenience.

Ms. Barnes did not contact Mr. Mendoza right away. She wanted to rest, and to talk to immediate and extended family members for advice. After 3 months, she felt that her family had too little information or experience about Isabella's hearing impairment, and she was ready to seek outside help. She called Mr. Mendoza for an appointment. When she mentioned that her energy level was still low, he offered to visit at her home for the appointment.

During their first visit, Mr. Mendoza saw that Ms. Barnes was unsure of her position as a parent and that she was uncomfortable about the prospect of the intrusion of outsiders into her family life. Mr. Mendoza hoped to clarify several points:

- The extent of participation in an educational plan was entirely up to the family, as they deemed appropriate for Isabella and themselves. An educational plan would be very flexible and reflect the family's priorities and concerns for the infant.
- Because Isabella's disability was a hearing impairment, an educational audiologist was one choice for a service coordinator. If Ms. Barnes wanted someone else as service coordinator, such as a speech-language pathologist or a teacher of the hearing impaired, she just had to ask and the director of the early intervention program would make every effort to meet her request.
- To help simplify educational plans for her child, the service coordinator would ensure that all involved service providers would work together for her daughter, while guaranteeing strict confidentiality.
- The one strong recommendation Mr. Mendoza made was for amplification to be obtained as soon as possible. Mr. Mendoza used an analogy to describe Isabella's development: just as leg muscles must exercise in order to develop, so must the auditory system be stimulated in order to develop residual hearing.

In addition to providing information and talking, the educational audiologist listened and answered many questions. Ms. Barnes had virtually no experience with hearing impairment, so her questions ranged from hearing aids to sign language to concerns regarding her baby's intelligence.

Ms. Barnes felt overwhelmed by this first meeting because there was so much to understand and remember. After Mr. Mendoza left, however, she realized she had already learned that she had the right to choose options for her child, she had the right to choose the person who would coordinate these options, and any interested family member could be involved in Isabella's educational plans.

Most important, Ms. Barnes was given the name and telephone number of a mother in the group Parents Together. This woman also had a daughter with a hearing impairment and might be the best person to understand what Ms. Barnes was going through. There was much to think about and decide upon in the near future, but Ms. Barnes realized two things: there was help available for her daughter, and she and her family could be involved in providing this help.

IFSP: The Process

The needs of an infant or toddler and the concerns of the family can be expected to be continually changing. Figure 6.3 shows the process of ongoing evaluation and reconsideration of the choices made in a child's educational plan. Steps 2, assessment; 3, program planning; 4, implementation and monitoring; and 5, review, evaluation, and transition will be repeated as many times as necessary according to the changing needs of the child and family.

The relationships between families and professionals change also, perhaps from a distant or even distrustful position to one of trusting partnership. The IFSP document may be amended or adjusted many times. It is hoped that each change marks an improvement in the relationship between family and professionals.

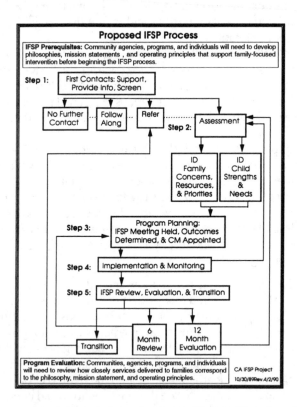

Figure 6.3. Proposed IFSP process. (From Lynch, E., Mendoza, J., & English, K. [1990]. Implementing individualized family service plans in California: Final report. Sacramento: California State Department of Developmental Services; reprinted by permission.)

In discussions regarding relationships between families and service providers, the term "empowerment" has been criticized as overused. Indeed, it may be inappropriate if interpreted to mean **bestowing power upon families**, when, in fact, **this power of self-determination is already theirs by right!** A more appropriate term might be "enablement," by which we mean creating opportunities for families to apply their resources and skills to the interests of their child and to acquire new skills as needed. Professionals who interact with families in an enabling way ensure that a family maintains its sense of control and is able to recognize positive changes in the child with a disability as a result of their own resources and decisions.

The antithesis of enablement includes the following behaviors on the part of professionals:

- Encouraging family dependence upon the professional
- Promoting the surrender of control of the child's future to "experts" by allowing parents to see themselves as unqualified to make good choices for their child
- Undermining the confidence of family members in order to enhance the authority or prestige of the professional

Professionals dedicated to enabling families must watch for any inclinations in themselves toward these behaviors. Remembering that the ongoing process of the the IFSP is one of partnership building and of family enablement helps keep the professional focused on the intent of PL 99-457. The Education of the Handicapped Act Amendments of 1986 were enacted to ensure that families are supported in their efforts to meet the needs of their children in the context of individual family concerns and priorities.

The IFSP Team

The IFSP process depends on the effective collaboration by all members of the IFSP team. The reader will remember that the three models typically used in teaming with other professionals were discussed in Chapter 5. As in Chapter 5, the three team configurations—multidisciplinary, interdisciplinary, and transdisciplinary—are each examined as they would function for a particular child and family.

How a Multidisciplinary Team Serves Tony and His Family   Tony, age 15 months, has mild cerebral palsy and a moderate bilateral hearing impairment. His family has chosen Mr. Quincy, an early childhood specialist, as their service coordinator:

1. The audiologist fits Tony with bilateral hearing aids, teaches the family how to conduct daily listening checks, and makes an appointment for a routine 6-month evaluation. Copies of all reports are sent to Mr. Quincy and Tony's parents.
2. A speech-language pathologist (SLP) conducts an assessment and recommends a home visit once per week in order to teach articulation skills to Tony and stimulate his language development. Copies of all reports are sent to Mr. Quincy and Tony's parents.
3. An occupational therapist (OT) conducts an assessment and recommends weekly home visits to provide appropriate support. Copies of all reports are sent to Mr. Quincy and Tony's parents.

4. Mr. Quincy conducts an assessment and asks to visit the family once a month in order to observe Tony's overall development.

As an example of how the multidisciplinary IFSP team functions, during one of the home visits by the OT, Tony's grandmother mentions that there is an increasing problem with feedback from his right hearing aid. The OT mentions this concern in the next report to Mr. Quincy.

The result of this IFSP team process is that four service providers work independently of each other. Only Mr. Quincy is fully aware of the extent of services being provided. Services are consistent and organized, but not integrated. In addition, the family does not appear to be considered part of the team because they have no opportunity to contribute to the decision-making process.

How an Interdisciplinary Team Serves Tony and His Family This team does not differ much from the multidisciplinary team approach. The four service providers each conduct individual assessments as above, but they do meet together routinely with the family to share the results. Each specialist still provides services independently, but each is aware of what the others are doing. For example, during a home visit by the SLP, Tony's grandmother reports a hearing aid problem. The SLP suggests they call the audiologist, and the SLP later directly contacts the audiologist to pass on the concern.

The result of this process is that the four professionals work independently but are teaming because they meet and talk with each other. Problems can be directed to the appropriate professionals because all are able to meet on occasion.

How a Transdisciplinary Team Serves Tony and His Family In the transdisciplinary approach, the four service providers meet with the family to determine the most efficient way to provide services. Two or three home visits a week from as many professionals is disruptive to the family. Therefore, the family requests that one professional is chosen to serve as the lead service provider. The family identifies "Tony talking normally" as their highest priority and wants the speech-language pathologist to coordinate services. Therefore, the SLP agrees to be the lead professional and to visit the family's home once a week. However, during that visit, other concerns identified in the IFSP meeting need to be addressed, so each professional teaches the SLP an effective level of proficiency in his or her discipline. For example, the audiologist teaches how to conduct a hearing aid check and provides a stethoscope, battery tester, and a small troubleshooting chart. The OT teaches the SLP large muscle exercises for Tony and provides a chart to monitor progress. Mr. Quincy teaches the SLP to use a screening test to monitor developmental milestones. The SLP incorporates speech, language, and listening goals into interactions with Tony while demonstrating to the family how to incorporate all goals into daily family life. For example, during a home visit, the SLP can troubleshoot a minor hearing aid problem and show the family how to do the same.

As a result, the intervention services are convenient for the family and integrated across disciplines to address the needs of the child. The family and professionals continue to expand their skills regarding Tony, and the family is as involved in the intervention as they choose.

Responsibilities of the Educational Audiologist as a Member of a Transdisciplinary IFSP Team As a member of a transdisciplinary IFSP team, the educational audiologist shares information, skills, and responsibilities with other service providers. These responsibilities include: 1) teaching rudimentary audiological skills to all team members, so that all develop competency in audiogram interpretation, hearing aid use, FM systems, and development of listening skills, among others; 2) learning similar skills in kind from other team members, such as basic developmental screening procedures or stages in language development.

A prerequisite for membership on this type of team is the willingness to surrender the role of sole expert in order to benefit from shared expertise among team members. As mentioned previously, this type of role release may be difficult for some professionals, especially for those who strongly identify with a self-image of expertise in a particular area (Landerholm, 1990).

The development of team skills also involves recognizing families as essential members of the IFSP team, to the level of involvement they choose. As the National Early Childhood Technical Assistance System (NEC*TAS) (1989) firmly stated:

> Respect for family autonomy and for the primacy of family beliefs and values dictates that, except in those rare instances that involve child abuse or neglect as defined by federal and state statutes, families have the final decision in all matters regarding their children. In a truly collaborative approach to the IFSP, the right of families to make decisions for their children and themselves exist in harmony with the responsibility of professionals to share their knowledge, expertise, and concerns with families who seek early intervention services. (p. 8)

Expertise shared with other service providers must also be shared with family members to the extent that they choose.

SUMMARY

Readers will note that this chapter provides at least as much information about families as about infants and toddlers with hearing impairment. This dual focus is in keeping with the intention of PL 99-457 and PL 101-476, the Individuals with Disabilities Education Act of 1990 (IDEA), which make the family "the legitimate center of early intervention services" (National Early Childhood Technical Assistance System [NEC*TAS], 1989, p. 18). For audiologists, the educational needs of an infant or toddler with HI are clear: early identification of hearing loss, appropriate otologic management, optimal amplification, maximum speech and language stimulation, and the development of auditory skills. However, for both audiologists and other early intervention service providers, working in accord with the concerns, priorities, and resources of the child's family can be unfamiliar territory. Collaborative developing of an individualized family service plan is a new process, and a complex one. Educational audiologists involved in early intervention services will meet these new challenges by respecting the family's right to decide the course of their child's development and sharing their concerns and recommendations regarding the implications of hearing impairment.

Learning the Language

To best serve infants and toddlers with HI in educational settings, it is imperative to be able to use the language of early interventionists. Review the following vocabulary and concepts and discuss with a colleague.

- PL 99-457
- PL 102-119
- EHA
- IDEA
- Part H of EHA
- Serving children within the context of their families
- Early intervention
- Child-centered versus family-centered approach to service delivery
- The IFSP as a document
- The IFSP as a process
- Multidisciplinary, interdisciplinary, and transdisciplinary teaming

Educational Audiology in Action
Suggested Learning Activities

Project 1. Part A of the High Risk Register.

Find out if there is a program for early identification of hearing impairment in your state. The state health department can provide this information.

If yes:
1. Is a High Risk Register used?
2. Is it similar to that developed by the Joint Committee on Infant Hearing?
3. What type of program of referral and follow-up system has been established? How do families with infants with hearing impairment get referred to the local early intervention program?

If no: among professionals in your area:
1. Ask the state health department if a program is being considered or is in the process of development.
2. Find out what the speech and hearing association in your state is doing to promote an early identification program. Join a committee to provide assistance.

Project 2. Part B of the High Risk Register.

Find out if local pediatricians, health clinics, and early interventionists use Part B of the HRR to screen for hearing impairment.

If yes:
1. Find out how Part B is utilized.
2. How are referrals made for comprehensive hearing evaluations and to programs in early intervention?

If no:
1. Establish relationships among professionals in your area by seeking support for a community project that targets early identification of hearing impairment.
    a. Send a letter to a local pediatrician or director of a health clinic to introduce yourself, and explain your interest in developing a coordinated approach to early identification of hearing impairment. Include in the letter a brief description of the concerns of late identification, and how the use of Part B of the HRR might address this concern with their cooperation. Indicate that you will follow up with a telephone call.
    b. Call and ask for a brief meeting, or extend a lunch invitation, for the purpose of elaborating further on this project.
    c. For the meeting, prepare a brief description of your ideas, and ask for suggestions on how these ideas could be integrated into existing office routines. (Pos-

sibilities include: 1) asking parents to complete a short questionnaire; 2) developing a checklist with high-risk criteria for the physician or nurse to use during each exam; 3) displaying a poster in the waiting room about age-appropriate auditory and language behaviors, with the encouragement to parents to mention concerns to the physician. Look for ways to help the physician to develop ownership in this project.

Remember, physicians need to know where to make referrals. A facility that can accommodate comprehensive hearing evaluations must be prepared to receive referrals and must also be prepared to provide additional referrals to the local educational agency providing early intervention services. A tracking system must be in place to ensure that no child "falls through the cracks." If a process of following up referrals has not been established, the educational audiologist is well qualified to take on this responsibility.

Each state, district, and community differs in the availability of resources and personnel, so these suggestions obviously can be modified to fit particular circumstances. Because the focus of the community project is in the best interests of children, cooperation from professionals should not be difficult to obtain. Strategies such as a write-up in a local newspaper or a public service announcement (PSA) on television and radio can advise parents of the program, while also recognizing professional cooperation.

Project 3. Get to know your local early intervention (EI) program.

Find out how infants and toddlers with hearing impairment are being served in your community. Ask at the local office of special education for a meeting with a service provider, preferably with an educational audiologist. Obtain the following information:

1. How many infants and toddlers with hearing impairment receive services locally?

2. What kind of services do they receive? For example, are services home-based or center-based?

3. What services do educational audiologists provide?

4. How many infants and toddlers have disabilities in addition to hearing impairment? How are their particular needs served?

5. How does a family find out about the early intervention program? What is the referral process?

6. What types of assessments does the EI program use?

7. How is the IFSP developed? Does the process appear to be multidisciplinary, interdisciplinary, or transdisciplinary?

8. Ask for a copy of an IFSP form and compare it to the requirements that are discussed in this text. For example, how are family concerns indicated?

Resources

American Society for Deaf Children
("A parent-helping-parent organization")
2848 Arden Way
Sacramento, CA 95825-1373
(800) 942-ASDC

Provides information and support to families with children who are deaf or hard of hearing. Parents receive newsletters and personal contacts with other parents.

John Tracy Clinic
806 West Adams Blvd.
Los Angeles, CA 90007
(213) 748-5481

Provides a full correspondence course to parents of children with HI. Lessons are designed to show parents how to develop listening and language skills in their child. Lessons are self-paced and include discussions of family–child relationships, as well as suggested games and activities.

National Early Childhood Technical Assistance System (NEC*TAS)
500 NationsBank Plaza
137 E. Franklin St.
Chapel Hill, NC 27514
(919) 962-2001

Provides materials related to the implementation of programs and services for infants and toddlers with disabilities and their families. A free catalog of materials is available on request.

Ski*Hi Model Program
Utah State University
Logan, UT 84322-1900
(801) 752-4601

Provides information on a preschool home program for infants and toddlers from birth to 36 months.

Zero to Three/National Center for Clinical Infant Programs
P.O. Box 96529
Washington, DC 20009-6529
(800) 544-0155

Publishes an informational bulletin six times a year.

Recommended Readings

Early Intervention

Bailey, D., & Wolery, M. (1992). *Teaching infants and preschoolers with handicaps* (2nd ed.). Columbus, OH: Merrill Publishing Co.

The authors provide an historical perspective as well as a description of the current developments in early intervention. Topics include assessment and intervention strategies and program design (from both philosophical and practical considerations).

Hanson, M., & Lynch, E. (1989). *Early intervention: Implementing child and family services for infants and toddlers who are at risk or disabled.* Austin, TX: PRO-ED.

This text provides an overview of all aspects of early intervention for children from birth to age 3, starting with a history of this specialty. Most of the text addresses concerns in developing, running, and evaluating a program and in collaborating with other community agencies.

Thurman, K., & Widerstrom, A. (1990). *Infants and young children with special needs: A developmental and ecological approach* (2nd ed.). Baltimore: Paul H. Brookes Publishing Co.

The first part of the text provides information regarding typical and atypical development in children, the conditions that put infants and children at risk, and the provision of early intervention services in the least restrictive environment. The second part of the book examines asessment procedures, the IFSP, and family issues.

Multicultural Issues

Adkins, D. (Ed.). (1987). Families and their hearing impaired children. *Volta Review, 89*(5). (Published by Alexander Graham Bell Association.)

The September 1987 issue is a monograph on the topic of families. Although all of the articles are excellent, two address cultural issues to consider when serving children with hearing impairment. Both articles remind the reader that it is not just the ears that require attention and respect from professionals.

Christensen, C., & Delgado, G. (Eds.).(1993). *Multicultural issues in deafness.* New York: Longman.

This text provides chapters describing both the Deaf culture and mainstream and other cultures that interplay with deafness. Deaf children with multicultural backgrounds face unique challenges in the school environment, but usually do not have teachers well prepared for these challenges.

Lynch, E., & Hanson, M. (Eds.). (1992). *Developing cross-cultural competence: A guide for working with young children and their families.* Baltimore: Paul H. Brookes Publishing Co.

Part 1 encourages readers to consider various aspects of mainstream culture to understand how early intervention has been developed and implemented. Part 2 contains chapters written by persons from several cultures, which provide insights into some significant differences in perceptions of family, children, disability, and the role of professionals in intervention. Part 3 discusses the challenge of developing a culturally appropriate intervention process.

References

Abidin, R. (1986). *Parenting Stress Index* (2nd ed.). Charlottesville, VA: Pediatric Psychology Press.

Anderson, G., & Grace, C. (1991). The Black Deaf adolescent: A diverse and underserved population. *Volta Review, 93,* 73–86.

Bailey, D. (1989). Case management in early identification. *Journal of Early Intervention, 13*(2), 120–134.

Bailey, D., Buysse, V., Edmondson, R., & Smith, T. (1992) Creating family-centered services in early intervention: Perceptions of professionals in four states. *Exceptional Children, 58,* 298–309.

Bailey, D., & McWilliam, R. (1990). Normalizing early intervention. *Topics in Early Childhood Special Education, 10*(2), 33–47.

Bailey, D., Simeonsson, R., Winston, P., Huntington, G., Comfort, M., Isbell, P., O'Donnell, K., & Helm, J. (1986). Family focused intervention: A functional model for planning, implementing, and evaluating infant and family services in early intervention. *Journal of the Division of Early Childhood, 10,* 156–171.

Bayley, N. (1969). *Bayley Scales of Infant Development.* Chicago: Psychological Corporation.

Beckman, P., & Bristol, M. (1991). Issues in developing the IFSP: A framework for establishing family outcomes. *Topics in Early Childhood Special Education, 11*(3), 19–31.

Bergstrom, L. (1984, March). *Congenital deafness.* Paper presented at the Colorado Otology-Audiology Workshop, Aspen.

Bess, F. (1993). Early identification of hearing loss: A review of the whys, hows, and whens. *Hearing Journal, 46*(6), 22–25.

Brigance, A. (1978). *Brigance Inventory of Early Development.* North Billerica, MA: Curriculum Associates, Inc.

"Burson-Marstellar public information survey." (1987, August). *Asha,* pp. 21–24.

Cegelka, P., & Mendoza, J. (1988). *P-PACT [Parents and Professionals in Collaborative Training] training materials.* (Available from Department of Special Education, San Diego State University, San Diego, CA 92182.)

Christensen, C., & Delgado, G. (1993). *Multicultural issues in deafness.* New York: Longman.

Cooper, R., & Rosenstein, J. (1966). Language acquisition of deaf children. *Volta Review, 68*(1), 58–67.

Crago, M., & Eriks-Brophy, A. (1993). Feeling right: Approaches to a family's culture. *Volta Review, 95*(5), 123–129.

Davis, J., Shepard, N., Stelmachowitz, P., & Gorga, M. (1981). Characteristics of hearing impaired children in the public schools: Part I. Psycho-educational data. *Journal of Speech and Hearing Disorders, 46,* 130–137.

Dunst, C. (1986). Overview of the efficacy of early intervention programs. In L. Brickman & D. Weatherford (Eds.), *Evaluating early intervention programs for severely handicapped children and their families* (pp. 79–148). Austin, TX: PRO-ED.

Dunst, C., & Trivette, C. (1989). An enablement and empowerment perspective of case management. *Topics in Early Childhood Education, 8*(4), 87–102.

Education of the Handicapped Act Amendments of 1986, PL 99-457. (October 8, 1986). Title 20, U.S.C. 1400 et seq: *U.S. Statutes at Large, 100,* 1145–1177.

English, K. (1992). States' use of a high-risk register for the early identification of hearing impairment. *Asha, 34*(8), 75–77.

Federal Register. (June 22, 1989). Rules and Regulations, Department of Education, Office of Special Education and Rehabilitation Services (34, Part 303), Early Intervention Program for Infants and Toddlers With Handicaps. Washington, DC: U.S. Government Printing Office.

Flexer, C., Wray D., & Ireland, J. (1989). Preferential seating is not enough: Issues in classroom management of hearing-impaired students. *Language, Speech, and Hearing Services in Schools, 20*(1), 11–21.

Furuno, S., O'Reilly, K., Hosaka, C., Inatsuka, T., Allman, T., & Zeisloft, B. (1979). *Hawaii Early Learning Profile*. Palo Alto, CA: VORT Corporation.

Giebel, A., & Redemann, E. (1992). Screening infants and children by means of TEDAE. *Hearing Journal, 45*(11), 25–28.

Glover, E., Preminger, J., & Sanford, A. (1978). *Early Learning Accomplishment Profile (ELAP)*. Winston-Salem, NC: Kaplan Press.

Goldberg, B. (1993). Universal hearing screening of infants: An idea whose time has come. *Asha, 35*(6), 63–64.

Grant, J. (1987). *The hearing-impaired child: Birth to six*. Boston: College-Hill Press.

Grant, J. (1993). Hearing impaired children from Mexican-American homes. *Volta Review, 95*(5), 131–135.

Greenstein, J., Greenstein, B., McConville, K., & Stellini, L. (1976). *Mother–infant communication and language acquisition in deaf infants*. New York: Lexington School for the Deaf.

Groht, M. (1958). *Natural language for deaf children*. Washington, DC: Alexander Graham Bell Association.

Gustason, G. (1989). Early identification of hearing-impaired infants: A review of Israeli and American progress. *Volta Review, 91*(6), 291–295.

Hanson, M., & Lynch, E. (1989). *Early intervention: Implementing child and family services for infants and toddlers who are at risk or disabled*. Austin, TX: PRO-ED.

Hartman, A. (1981, January). The family: A central focus for practice. *Social Work*, 7–13.

Healthy People 2000: National health promotion and disease prevention objectives (1990). Washington, DC: U.S. Department of Health and Human Services.

Hitchings, V., & Haggard, M. (1983). Incorporation of parental suspicions in screening infants' hearing. *British Journal of Audiology, 17*, 71–75.

Individuals with Disabilities Education Act of 1990 (IDEA), PL 101-476. (October 30, 1990). Title 20, U.S.C. 1400 et seq: *U.S. Statutes at Large, 104*, 1103–1151.

Individuals with Disabilities Education Act Amendments of 1991, PL 102-199. (October 7, 1991). Title 20, U.S.C. 1400 et seq: *U.S. Statutes at Large, 105*, 587–608.

Joint Committee on Infant Hearing. (1991). 1990 position statement. *Asha, 33*, (Suppl. 5), 3–6.

Landerholm, E. (1990). The transdisciplinary team approach in infant intervention programs. *TEACHING Exceptional Children, 22*(2), 66–70.

Levitt, H., McGarr, N., & Geffner, D. (1987). Development of language and communication skills in hearing impaired children. *ASHA Monograph 6*.

Ling, D. (1976). *Speech and the hearing impaired child*. Washington, DC: Alexander Graham Bell Association.

Luterman, D. (1970). *Deafness in the family*. Boston: College-Hill Press.

Lynch, E., Jackson, J., Mendoza, J., & English, K. (1991). The merging of best practice and state policy in the IFSP process in California. *Topics in Early Childhood Special Education, 11*(3), 32–53.

Lynch, E., Mendoza, J., & English, K. (1990). *Implementing Individualized Family Service Plans in California: Final report*. San Diego, CA: Department of Special Education, San Diego State University.

Mahoney, T., & Eichwald, J. (1986). Model program V: A high risk register by computerized search of birth certificates. In E. Swigart (Ed.), *Neonatal hearing screening* (pp. 223–240). San Diego: College-Hill Press.

McCormick, B., Curnock, D., & Spavins, F. (1984). Auditory screening of special care neonates using the auditory response cradle. *Archives of Disease in Childhood, 59*, 1168–1172.

McCubbin, H., Olson, D., & Larsen, A. (1981). *F-COPES-Family Crisis Oriented Personal Scale*. St. Paul: Department of Family Social Science, University of Minnesota.

McGoldrick, M., & Gerson, R. (1985). *Genograms in family assessment*. New York: Norton.

McGonigel, M.J., & Johnson, B. (1991). An overview. In M.J. McGonigel, R. Kaufmann, & B. Johnson (Eds.), *Guidelines and recommended practices for the Individualized Family Service Plan* (2nd ed., pp. 1–5). Bethesda, MD: Association for the Care of Children's Health.

National Early Childhood Technical Assistance System (NEC*TAS). (1989). *Guidelines and recommended practices for the Individualized Family Service Plan.* Chapel Hill: University of North Carolina.

Newborg, J., Stock, J., Wnek, L., Guidubaldi, J., & Svinicki, J. (1984). *Battelle Developmental Inventory.* Allen, TX: DLM Teaching Resources.

Northern, J., & Downs, M. (1984). *Hearing in children* (3rd ed.). Baltimore: Williams & Wilkins.

Olson, D., McCubbin, H., Barnes, H., Larsen, A., Muxen, M., & Wilson, M. (1983). *Families: What makes them work.* Beverly Hills: Sage Publications.

Padden, C., & Humphries, T. (1988). *Deaf in America: Voices in a culture.* Cambridge, MA: Harvard University Press.

Quigley, S., & Power, D. (1972). *The development of syntactic structures in the language of deaf children.* Urbana, IL: Institute for Research on Exceptional Children.

Rodriquez, O., & Santiviago, M. (1991). Hispanic Deaf adolescents: A multicultural minority. *Volta Review, 93,* 89–97.

Ross, M. (1990). Implications of delay in detection and management of deafness. *Volta Review, 92*(2), 69–79.

Rousch, J., & McWilliams, R. (1990). A new challenge for pediatric audiology: Public Law 99-457. *Journal of American Academy of Audiology, 1,* 196; 208.

Sanders, D. (1982). *Aural rehabilitation: A management model* (2nd ed.). Englewood Cliffs, NJ: Prentice Hall.

Schmidt, P. (1968). Language instruction for the deaf. *Volta Review, 68,* 85–105, 123.

Schweinhart, L., & Weikart, D. (1980). Young children grow up: The effects of the Perry Preschool Program on youths through age 15. *Monographs of the High/Scope Education Research Foundation, 7.*

Slentz, K., & Bricker, D. (1992). Family-guided assessment of IFSP development: Jumping off the family assessment bandwagon. *Journal of Early Intervention, 16,* 11–19.

Slentz, K., Walker, B., & Bricker, D. (1989). Supporting parent involvement in early intervention: A role-taking model. In G. Singer & L. Irvin (Eds.), *Support for caregiving families: Enabling positive adaptation to disability* (pp. 221–238). Baltimore: Paul H. Brookes Publishing Co.

Turnbull, A., & Turnbull, H. (1986). *Families, professionals, and exceptionality: A special partnership.* Columbus, OH: Charles E. Merrill.

Watkins, S. (1987). Long-term effect of home intervention with hearing-impaired children. *American Annals of the Deaf, 132,* 267–275.

Webster, D., & Webster, M. (1977). Neonatal sound deprivation affects brain stem auditory nuclei. *Archives of Otolaryngology, 103,* 392–396.

Welsh, R., & Slater, S. (1993). The state of hearing impairment identification programs. *Asha, 35*(4), 49–52.

White, S., & White, R. (1987). The effects of hearing status of the family and age of intervention on receptive and expressive oral language skills in hearing impaired infants. In H. Levitt, N. McGarr, & D. Geffner (Eds.), Development of language and communication skills in hearing impaired children. *ASHA Monograph 6,* 9–24.

Wolfensberger, W. (1972). *The principle of normalization in human services.* Toronto, Ontario, Canada: National Institute of Mental Health.

7

Educational Audiology
Across the Lifespan

Preschool Through High School

THE EDUCATIONAL AUDIOLOGIST SERVING PRESCHOOL through high school students has an overriding responsibility: to **ensure that learners with HI have optimal listening and learning environments**. The audiologist fulfills this responsibility with a variety of strategies, which include:

- Investigating and improving classroom acoustics
- Monitoring the status of all amplification devices
- Supporting the development of listening skills
- Providing support for the psychosocial issues that can affect learners with HI

In addition, educational audiologists have responsibilities to **learners with normal hearing**:

- Developing and supervising effective screening programs
- Developing and implementing aggressive, long-term hearing conservation programs

This chapter discusses each of these responsibilities in detail in the following sections.

ENSURING OPTIMAL LISTENING AND LEARNING ENVIRONMENTS FOR LEARNERS WITH HI

Classroom Acoustics

There are three variables to consider in evaluating the acoustic environment of a classroom: noise levels, reverberation, and distance between teacher and student.

Noise Levels   The typical classroom has been well documented as a remarkably noisy place. Noise can be described as "any auditory disturbance that interferes with what a listener wants to hear" (Crandell, 1991, p. 19). Noise levels in active classrooms have been consistently measured at approximately 55 dBA (Bess, Sinclair, & Riggs, 1984; Finitzo, 1988; Ross & Giolas, 1971; Sanders, 1965; Watson, 1964). Other spaces in a school can be even noisier: The noise levels of an occupied gymnasium may range from 82 to 86 dBA and an occupied cafeteria from 75 to 80 dBA (Finitzo, 1988).

The casual observer may interpret this level of noise as an indication of active engagement in learning. Audiologists see such noise as a potential threat to the learning and listening environment of **all** learners, particularly learners with HI. What concerns audiologists is not only the noise level itself, but also the relative loudness of the teacher's voice, or of the **signal** providing classroom instruction. The intensity of a typical conversational voice is approximately 60 dBA (Berg, 1986). A **signal-to-noise (s/n) ratio** can be calculated by subtracting the level of noise from the level of the signal (in this case, the teacher's voice). If the signal is higher in intensity than the noise level, a positive value is obtained. If the signal is lower in intensity than the noise level, a negative value is obtained.

For most classrooms, the s/n ratio appears thus: Signal minus noise, or 60 dB − 55 dB = +5 dB.

In other words the signal—the teacher's voice that transmits vital directions, instructions, explanations, elaborations, new concepts, and vocabulary—is only 5 dB above the ambient noise level of the typical classroom (Sanders, 1965). This value describes an unacceptable learning environment when we know that **children with hearing impairment require a s/n ratio of up to +30 dB for optimal speech discrimination** (Dirks, Morgan, & Dubno, 1982; Genzel, 1971).

This s/n ratio considers only the traditional enclosed classroom. The open classroom, where instruction is conducted in several areas simultaneously, without acoustic barriers, has been declared by Berg (1986) as an "educational disaster" (p. 169) because of the unacceptably high levels of noise.

Reverberation   The level of noise is one characteristic of the acoustics of a classroom. The second variable of the acoustics is the amount of **reverberation** in the room. Reverberation refers to the prolongation of sound as sound waves reflect off the hard surfaces in a room. Reverberation is inversely related to absorption, which is the amount of sound energy absorbed by the materials in the room. **Reverberation time (RT)** indicates the amount of time it takes for a sound to decay 60 dB from its initial onset.

Excessive reverberation can interfere with speech perception by overlapping with the energy of the direct signal of the teacher's voice. For optimal perception of speech, it has been recommended that the RT of a classroom not exceed 0.3 seconds (Berg, 1987). However, the RT for most classrooms exceeds this recommendation and typically ranges from 0.4 to 1.2 seconds (Crandell, 1991; Finitzo, 1988; Ross, 1987).

RT can be quickly estimated by using the absorption coefficients found in Table 7.1 with the following formula (Berg, 1986): RT = .05 (volume of room in cubic feet) divided by the absorption value (A). Separate absorption values are obtained for all surface areas (floor, walls, ceiling) and then added together. In the example below, the average or mean value of the absorption coefficients for 500, 1,000, and 2,000 Hz are used in the calculation (Crandell, 1991). Let us consider a classroom measuring 20 feet × 30 feet × 8 feet or with a volume of 4,800 cubic feet.

Floor: carpet on concrete (average absorption coefficient = .46)
    20 × 30 × .46 = 27.6
Side walls: plasterboard (average absorption coefficient = .06)
    30 × 8 × .06 (× 2 walls) = 28.8

Table 7.1. Absorption coefficients for building materials and furnishings found in a typical classroom

Material/furnishing	Frequency			
	500 Hz	1,000 Hz	2,000 Hz	X̄
Brick, unglazed	.03	.04	.05	.04
Carpet, heavy on concrete	.30	.50	.60	.46
Concrete, painted	.06	.07	.09	.07
Linoleum	.03	.03	.03	.03
Wood floor	.10	.07	.06	.07
Acoustic ceiling tile	.90	.95	.90	.91
Curtains, medium weight	.50	.75	.70	.65
Glass window	.20	.10	.07	.12
Plywood paneling	.15	.10	.09	.11
Plaster board	.10	.05	.04	.06
Person	.47	.50	.55	.51

Adapted from: Berg (1986).

End walls: plywood (average absorption coefficient = .11)
   $20 \times 8 \times .11$ ($\times$ 2 walls) = 35.2
Ceiling: plasterboard (average absorption coefficient = .06)
   $20 \times 30 \times .06 = 36$
Total: $27.6 + 28.8 + 35.2 + 36 = 376$ (the value of A).

Thus, RT = $\dfrac{.05(4800)}{376}$ = .64 seconds

Therefore, this room has a preliminary **RT of 0.64 seconds**, which exceeds the recommended RT of 0.3 seconds. Additional calculations that consider the absorption values of windows, draperies, and other components of the room help obtain a closer estimate of the true RT of the room. Modifications of some of the surfaces (such as carpet or acoustic ceiling tile) can reduce the reverberation time to the recommended level.

There are two points to keep in mind when considering the effects of noise and reverberation on classroom listening. First, as Crandell (1991) pointed out, there is an inescapable and synergistic interaction between noise and reverberation:

> That is, the interaction of the two distortions adversely affects speech recognition greater than the sum of both effects taken independently. For example, if a listener experiences a reduction in speech recognition of 10% in a noisy listening environment and a reduction of 10% in a reverberant setting, recognition deficits may actually equate to 30 or 40% in "real-world" listening environments that contain both noise and reverberation. As with noise and reverberation in isolation, research indicates that pediatric listeners have considerably greater speech recognition problems in noise and reverberation than adult subjects. (p. 25)

Data from a classic study (Finitzo-Hieber & Tillman, 1978) support this observation. Table 7.2 compares the discrimination scores obtained from different listening conditions for students with normal hearing and students with HI who were aided.

According to this table, what are the implications of a classroom with a +6 dB s/n ratio and a RT of 1.2 seconds? Students with normal hearing can discriminate accurately approximately 54% of monosyllables, creating a significant challenge

Table 7.2.   Effects of noise and reverberation on speech discrimination

RT (seconds)	S/N ratio (dB)	Monosyllable discrimination scores (in %)	
		Children with normal hearing	Children with hearing impairment (aided)
0.4	+12	83%	60%
	+6	71%	52%
	0	48%	28%
1.2	+12	70%	41%
	+6	54%	27%
	0	30%	11%

From Finitzo-Hieber, T., & Tillman, T. (1978). Room acoustics effects on monosyllabic word discrimination ability for normal and hearing impaired children. *Journal of Speech and Hearing Research, 21,* 440–458; reprinted by permission.

for listening tasks. Learners with HI may discriminate accurately only 27% of monosyllables, which creates an unrealistic expectation for listening tasks in an arguably restrictive environment; that is, an environment that does not support learning. When recommending acoustic modifications to a classroom, it is important to emphasize that **high levels of noise and reverberation have adverse affects on all learners**.

The second point to remember regarding the effects of noise and reverberation is that there is a correlation of the impact of noise and reverberation with the age of the listener. Deleterious effects of noise and reverberation increase as the age of the listener decreases. Young children have a markedly more difficult time discriminating signals in noise, probably because of their limited language base and inexperience with making accurate guesses (Elliot et al., 1979; Yacullo & Hawkins, 1987).

Distance Between Speaker and Listener   The third variable of the acoustic environment to consider is the distance between the speaker (teacher) and the listener (students). Earlier, it was mentioned that the typical conversational noise level is 60 dB. This value is typically determined from a distance of 6 feet. As the distance between speaker and listener increases, the intensity of the signal (the teacher's voice) decreases. Each time the distance doubles, the intensity of the signal perceived by the listener decreases by 6 dB. Therefore, at 12 feet, the signal is 54 dB; at 24 feet, 48 dB. In addition, although the signal decreases in intensity, the overall noise level stays the same. The less intense signal then becomes increasingly difficult to discrminate against the consistent background noise level. The conventional recommendation of "preferential seating" is not effective when the teacher walks about the room in order to keep students on task and engaged in the learning activities (Flexer, Wray, & Ireland, 1989).

Recommendations to Improve Classroom Acoustics

The educational audiologist can usually provide three recommendations that will improve the acoustics of a typical classroom. All three recommendations will improve the signal-to-noise ratio to at least +20 dB, thereby increasing the opportunity to hear instruction clearly. The recommendations are:

1. Decrease the overall noise level in the class to 35 dBA
2. Decrease the reverberation time to 0.3 seconds
3. Decrease the distance of instruction to a maximum of 6 feet

The first recommendation, decrease the overall noise level in the classroom to 35 dBA, can be achieved by modifying the surface areas of the room, first considering modifications in the ceiling and floor because they comprise about 60% of the total surface area of the room (Crum & Matkin, 1976).

The second recommendation, decrease the reverberation time to 0.3 seconds, can be accomplished by reducing or eliminating sources of extraneous noise inside and outside the classroom. Figure 7.1 provides a checklist to help the educational audiologist identify noise sources in and outside the classroom. Using a checklist can help classroom teachers recognize sources of noise that are usually ignored.

The third recommendation, decrease the distance of instruction to a maximum of 6 feet, is best achieved with the use of FM amplification, which is described in the next section of this chapter.

Can you hear any of the following?

Inside the classroom:	Barely	Noticeably	How to make quieter
Fluorescent lights			
Fishtank filter			
Computers			
Computer printer			
Heating/cooling system			
Plumbing			
Hamster cage			
Pencil sharpener			
PA system			
Feet shuffling			
Chairs scraping			
Student voices			
Doors opening/closing			
Other			
Outside the classroom:			
Motor traffic (school buses, cars)			
Foot traffic			
Conversation			
Custodial/maintenance work			
Other			

Figure 7.1. Classroom noise source checklist.

Amplification Devices

Now that we have considered strategies to investigate and improve classroom acoustics, we turn to strategies to monitor the status of amplification devices. Three types of amplification devices require the attention of the educational audiologist: the personal hearing aid, the FM system, and sound field amplification.

Personal Hearing Aids

Monitoring Programs It probably comes as no surprise that a prescription does not ensure the successful use of hearing aids for children. Children are notoriously tough on these delicate (and expensive) instruments, and every educational audiologist has a story about aids that were thrown out of the school bus window, dropped into the lavatory toilet, or stomped flat on the playground. If the status of personal amplification devices is not agressively and consistently monitored, it has been found that 50% of personal hearing aids are inoperable or functioning inappropriately at any given time (Coleman, 1975; Gaeth & Lounsbury, 1966; Kemker, McConnell, Logan, & Green, 1979; Potts & Greenwood, 1983; Smedley & Plapinger, 1988; Zink, 1972).

The educational audiologist is responsible for ensuring that all students' hearing aids are operating properly. To meet this responsibility, a program must be effected that will support: 1) daily check procedures, 2) troubleshooting minor problems, and 3) routine electroacoustic analysis (English, 1991; Reichman & Healey, 1989).

Suggested forms for conducting a hearing aid (HA) monitoring program are provided in Figures 7.2, 7.3, and 7.4. Figure 7.2 is a sample form that provides reinforcement to young students for remembering and taking care of their aids. Each day a sticker or a star is provided in the appropriate box, and after 1 or 2 weeks (if duplicated on one sheet of paper), it is sent home with the student to let parents know that HA use at school is followed closely and is a vital part of their child's education.

Before the HA monitoring program form goes home, the information is transferred to the educational audiologist's records (Figure 7.3). The data sheet shown in Figure 7.3 provides an efficient method of tracking concerns regarding HA use or overly long repairs. Whether by this method or another that is suited to the specific environment and situation, it is essential that some system of record keeping be established.

Daily Hearing Aid Check Student: _____ Week of: _____	SUN	MON	TUES	WED	THURS	FRI	SAT
I wore hearing aids today! The batteries have been checked. The earmolds are clean.							

Figure 7.2. Form for daily hearing aid check.

Monthly Hearing Aid Checklist

Student _____

Month _____ , 19 _____

Date	Hearing Aids		No Hearing Aids		COMMENTS
	right	left	right	left	
1					
2					
3					
4					
5					
6					
7					
8					
9					
10					
11					
12					
13					
14					
15					
16					
17					
18					
19					
20					
21					
22					
23					
24					
25					
26					
27					
28					
29					
30					
31					

Figure 7.3. Form for monthly HA monitoring.

If the educational audiologist is responsible for students with HI who are in several schools across one or more districts, the HA monitoring program depends greatly on the help of teachers, aides, SLPs, school nurses, or others who are willing to be trained and to assume the responsibility for monitoring on a day-to-day basis. Minimal training includes: how to properly use a battery tester, HA stethoscope, and a wax loop; and a troubleshooting checklist such as that in Figure 7.4. As with any training, do not assume that reviewing the procedure one time is sufficient. The educational audiologist must check routinely throughout the year to ensure that the responsible adult is monitoring HA use correctly. A sample hearing and monitoring training inservice is provided in Appendix B.

Hearing Aid Use and the IEP   Consistent use and care of personal hearing aids in school should be incorporated into the goals and objectives of the IEP (Bess & McConnell, 1981; Maxon & Smaldino, 1991). Goals and objectives are written incorporating the philosophy that each student, to the best of his or her ability, will become increasingly responsible for understanding the nature of his or her hearing impairment and for self-managing amplification (Adkins, 1993; Lipscomb, von Al-

If the aid is . . .	Battery	Earmold/tubing	Other
Weak	1. Wrong type 2. Leakage occurring—replace 3. Nearly dead–replace	1. Tubing kinked 2. Almost completely clogged with wax	1. Microphone opening clogged—parent needs to take aid to audiologist
Intermittent	1. Corrosion on battery contact—try rubbing with pencil eraser (gently!) 2. Weak battery	1. Tubing knotted	1. Problems with contacts for volume control—parent needs to take aid to audiologist or hearing aid dispenser
Producing feedback (whistling)		1. Tubing punctured 2. Tubing loose from earmold or hook 3. Improper fit of earmold (has become too small?)	1. Hook loose from case 2. Volume too high—should be approximately ¾ rotation of volume control, unless dispensing audiologist indicates otherwise
Dead	1. Dead 2. Wrong type 3. Battery inserted backwards	1. Tubing blocked 2. Earmold clogged	1. Hearing aid off 2. Switch is on "T" 3. Corroded battery contacts
Distorting	Nearly dead	Tubing or earmold nearly clogged	Microphone opening closed

Note: Some problems, such as stiff tubing or a small crack in the case, do not require immediate repair but do need monitoring. The following problems need attention ASAP: static, intermittency, feedback with the earmold snugly in ear, no output with a strong battery, or any problem that directly affects the quality of the output.

If you are not able to correct the problem, be sure to notify the student's parent or primary caregiver of your findings, and ask to be advised of their steps toward repair.

Figure 7.4.   HA troubleshooting checklist.

men, & Blair, 1992). (A sample IEP incorporating such goals and objectives was presented in Chapter 2.)

The Educational Audiologist and the Hearing Aid Dispenser It is essential that the educational audiologist maintain professional relationships with hearing aid dispensers in the community. When an educational audiologist is first hired by a school district, it is suggested that he or she send an introductory letter to the dispensers who have fit the students with HI in that district. (The name, address, and telephone number of each student's dispenser should be found in each student's record.) This initial contact helps when it is necessary to collaborate to solve hearing aid problems. Similar contacts should be made with professionals who provide related services to students with HI, such as aural rehabilitation, speech and language intervention, and cochlear implant fittings. The obvious purpose in developing these relationships is to ensure that services are coordinated.

FM Systems Another source of amplification is provided by the FM system. As much as we value the consistent use of hearing aids, there are still important limitations to their use in the classroom. The hearing aid user perceives noise and signal as equally loud, because the microphone does not discriminate what sounds to amplify and what to eliminate. In addition, the distance between the speaker and the hearing aid user is important. In order to maintain a signal-to-noise ratio of +20 dB, the teacher needs to speak into the HA microphone from no farther than 12 inches (Lewis, 1994; Maxon, Brackett, & van den Berg, 1991a). As the teacher turns to talk to other students or walk to another part of the room, his or her voice fades farther away from the hearing aid user.

The most effective technology available to overcome these limitations is the FM system. Used originally for auditory training activities in classes for the deaf (and therefore sometimes called "auditory trainers"), FM technology is now being used in every educational placement for students with all levels of hearing impairment. An FM system has two components. The first is the teacher's microphone, which picks up, amplifies, and transmits the teacher's voice. Figure 7.5 shows a microphone that is secured with a lapel clip, and the rest of the FM unit is attached to a belt. A headset can also be used instead of a lapel microphone (not shown), or the entire unit can be worn with a strap around the neck lavalier style (Figure 7.6). The second component of the FM system is the student's receiver (Figure 7.7).

FM technology continues to be miniaturized: A student's receiver can now fit into behind-the-ear (BTE) cases, which also function as personal hearing aids.

In an FM system, the teacher's voice is transmitted by a frequency modulated (FM) signal to the student's receiver, which works very much like a personal radio station. The teacher's mouth is approximately 6–8 inches away from the microphone, and, because the teacher's voice is transmitted by an FM signal rather than by air waves, the student perceives this voice as consistently presented at 6–8 inches from the hearing aid microphone. Reception stays consistent up to a distance of 200 feet. FM amplification is also useful when a student attends a large-group activity, such as a presentation in an auditorium or a p.e. lesson in the schoolyard.

With an FM system, the problem of direction of the speaker is also eliminated. A hearing aid user hears best when the conversation is face-to-face, and the speech is aimed at the microphone. However, teachers are likely to move around the room

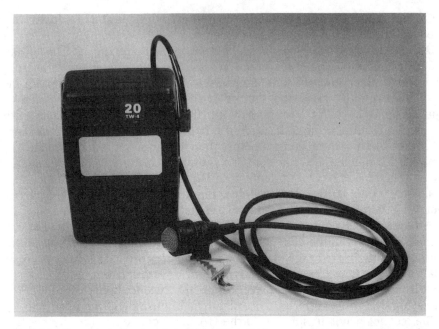

Figure 7.5.   The teacher's microphone in an FM unit. (Photograph courtesy of Telex Communications, Inc.)

Figure 7.6.   Teacher and students using FM technology. (Photograph courtesy of Telex Communications, Inc.)

Figure 7.7. Student receivers with, from front to back: 1) BTE microphones, 2) binaural cords and button transducers, 3) monaural cord and button transducer, and 4) direct audio input to hearing aids. Also pictured is a teacher's microphone (worn with a neck loop). (Photograph courtesy of Telex Communications, Inc.)

or turn to the chalkboard while continuing instruction. A large part of this speech would be lost to a hearing aid user, but a learner with an FM unit can hear every word consistently, regardless of the direction of the speaker's voice.

In addition, an FM system is designed to amplify and transmit the teacher's voice (signal) approximately **15 dB above the environmental noise**. In an FM system, the student's unit is equipped to receive two kinds of input. The first type of input is received from the teacher's microphone. In addition, the student's unit also has external microphones (mics) that function as personal hearing aids do: All sounds, including the student's own speech, are picked up, amplified, and transmitted to the student's ear. As such, three listening options are available with FM systems: 1) FM only, which is appropriate in lecture situations where the teacher is the only person talking. Virtually all competing environmental sounds are eliminated; 2) External mics only, which is appropriate when the student wants to hear classmate discussion and his or her own speech while the teacher is "off the air" (not transmitting instruction); 3) FM and external mics combined, which is appropriate when classroom activity includes both classroom discussion and teacher instruction. In this setting, the teacher's voice is transmitted 12–15 dB above the classroom discussion to enhance the signal-to-noise ratio.

These factors combine in what has been called "the FM advantage" (Flexer et al., 1989, p. 14). The FM advantage consists of overriding the negative effects of poor signal-to-noise ratio by increasing the signal, as well as eliminating the effects of distance and direction through FM transmission. There is an additional advantage to the FM system that is not insignificant: because FM equipment is always kept in the classroom, amplification is always available, unlike personal hearing aids, which may be left at home or may need repair.

FM Equipment Operation Following is a brief description of the operation of the FM system. There are several models of FM systems available, and some features are specific to certain models. However, there are generic features of most models, which are now described.

The **teacher's FM unit** consists of an antenna, an on-off switch, and a battery light to test the rechargeable battery. The microphone can transmit on 1 of the 40 channels made available by the Federal Communications Commission (FCC). Some models have universal channel options, and are able to transmit on any channel as needed.

The **student's FM unit** consists of two external mics, either on top of the unit, or at ear level with a BTE unit, with individual volume controls for each mic. Lights indicate when the battery is low, or when the unit is not receiving an FM signal, which serves as a visual reminder for the teacher to check the microphone to ensure that it is transmitting. The potentiometers for frequency response and saturation sound pressure levels operate on the same principles as those in hearing aids. (It has been observed that graduate students seem somehow intimidated by these setting options, even with coursework and experience in hearing aid fittings [L. McLean, personal communication, September 28, 1993].) It should be reassuring to know that the training received in hearing aid fittings is suitable preparation for FM fittings.

There are a variety of coupling options for the student's receiver. (See Figure 7.6 for three examples.) Custom-fit earmolds equipped with snap rings will accommodate transducers and cords attached to the unit. BTE mics allow for the reception of sound at ear level. Personal hearing aids with strong telecoil capability can be used if the student wears a telemagnetic neck loop attached to the unit. Personal hearing aids with direct audio capability can be coupled with a snap-on boot to hard wire to the unit (Hawkins & Schum, 1985; Thibodeau & McCaffrey, 1992). Headphones can also be used.

Teacher and student FM units stay charged for the length of a typical school day, and can be recharged overnight.

Issues in Using FM Systems There are two major concerns in the fitting of FM systems: 1) developing a broad base of support among all involved persons, and 2) monitoring and maintaining equipment. In the following section, recommended procedures are provided for addressing each of these concerns.

In order to address the first task, developing a broad base of support for use of the system, certain realities need to be acknowledged.

The educational audiologist's recommendation of an FM system for a student is just the beginning of the actual fitting process (Edwards, 1991b). Because the FM is not an invisible device, it may present a "visual deviance" (Flexer et al., 1989, p. 16) for the student that must be recognized and addressed as part of the planning process. To develop support to help the student feel comfortable with the system, it is helpful to refer to the recent literature on the changes in education and special education regarding team ownership of a particular situation. This approach has been found to help individuals become comfortable with a new way of doing things. The team's goal is to develop consensus—not obtaining unanimous agreement but **obtaining unanimous commitment** (Wynn & Guditus, 1984). In order to develop unanimous commitment to using an FM system, consider that the involved people can be imagined as three groups: 1) the first group is the student, the parent, and the teacher; 2) the second group is composed of the student's classmates; and 3) the third group is a peer support group.

The next section will describe how to enlist the support of each group and how their support contributes to the overall base of support for the use of an FM system.

At the center of the FM system is, of course, the student. Students with HI in preschool through grades three to four usually do not have strong objections to the device, but as students begin to care more about the opinion of their peers, they are more likely to resist FM use. Strategies to promote FM use include:

- Giving the student ample opportunities to try the system in private and to compare it to a personal hearing aid
- Negotiating a trial period of use and, later, negotiating to limit use to particularly difficult listening situations, identified by the student
- Providing the student with a choice of earmold colors (neon and jewel tone earmolds are available through many earmold labs)
- Discuss coupling options with the student (e.g., snap ring, direct input to personal hearing aids)
- Discuss how to wear the FM (in a pouch, on a belt)

Also part of this first group are parents. Parents are typically in full support of the use of FM, but the educational audiologist should personally discuss this with parents. Parental reservations can undermine the efforts at school. Both students and parents have typically been left out of the decision to use an FM system (Maxon et al., 1991a). If this is the case, the educational audiologist has no reason to wonder why the recommendation for an FM system is not embraced wholeheartedly.

The teachers using the microphones may also have reservations, or feel technophobic and uncomfortable with the responsibility of the technology. It is vital that the educational audiologist obtain full support of the teacher; otherwise the system will be underutilized. Demonstrations, listening with hearing aids and an FM system, and assurance that full follow-up support is always available does much to alleviate potential worries or objections.

The educational audiologist must be confident of the commitment by each member of the first group to using an FM system before bringing the equipment into the classroom.

When the equipment is actually installed in the classroom, the focus of attention becomes the second group, the classmates. The most flexible and interested student, with the enthusiastic support of parents and teachers, may still feel uncomfortable about using an FM system, fearing the reactions from classmates. After the equipment has been adjusted to the individual student, but before it is brought into the classroom, it is **vital** that classmates are enlisted as helpers, supporters, and advocates for using the FM system in their classroom. To enlist classmates, a classroom presentation such as the following is very helpful.

Before the FM is actually put into use, ask the teacher for 30–45 minutes of instruction time with the whole class. Present a unit on Hearing Problems, consisting of the following:

1. Discuss in age-appropriate terms the parts of the ear and potential damage to hearing abilities.
2. Pass out ear plugs. Administer a simple spelling test to the class while they experience this mild conductive loss. Ask the students to describe their difficulties. How many words were spelled incorrectly because they could not hear well? A quicker procedure is to ask students to simply plug their ears with their fingers and listen to a passage while the reader walks around the room. The students are then asked to answer questions about the passage. How did the students feel—frustrated, isolated, inadequate? How much information did they hear, and how much did they have to guess to fill in the blanks?
3. Pass around some demonstration hearing aids. Describe the limitations of hearing aids: too noisy, problems with distance and direction of the speaker.
4. Introduce both components of the FM system. The student's unit looks like a personal headphone radio; the teacher's microphone is like the one used by the principal in the auditorium. Explain the benefits of the FM system in relation to noise, distance, and direction. Involve the student with hearing impairment as much as he or she is willing. For example, while wearing the FM unit, the student can repeat spondees while you move away and out of the room—"He's got his own radio station!"
5. Take time for questions and answers.
6. To conclude, elicit support from the student's classmates by indicating the importance of their help. "Now that you understand a little about hearing problems, we need your cooperation and agreement to help in the following ways: Don't handle the equipment; don't shout into the microphones; practice some ways to improve [the student]'s ability to understand—'Tap me before you talk to me.' " Provide the students with a handout to take home and share with their parents. Also, ask the classmates to teach their parents and siblings what they learned today. The chances are that their parents and siblings also know someone with a hearing impairment.

    This type of classroom presentation promotes the following outcomes that will help to establish support for the FM system: all students are operating with the same shared information, the new technology is de-mystified, tolerance for a new way of doing things is encouraged and expected, and classmates rise to the role of responsible and helpful classroom citizens.

    All this effort to build support for the FM system and the commitment of the student, parents, teachers, and classmates may not be successful in the long term without the third team of a peer support group. With full support from parents, teachers, and classmates, a student using an FM unit may still feel singled out, especially if he or she is the only one in a school in this situation. The educational audiologist is encouraged to develop a support group of students with HI, paricularly if such students are scattered across a school district. Peer support develops relationships among those who share similar experiences and generates strategies that help address difficulties related to those experiences. A peer support group for students who use FM equipment can provide much needed moral support for students who feel isolated in their experiences. Group activities can include field trips, social functions, and pizza parties with information-sharing or an adult with HI as a guest speaker (Leavitt, 1987, 1991).

In summary, these procedures may appear time consuming—and they are! Nevertheless, there are creative ways to minimize the time demands of these activities. For example, if the school district is close to a university with a special education and/or audiology department, graduate students may welcome the opportunity to deliver classroom presentations. Peer support–group activities can be organized or sponsored by a local chapter of Self Help for Hard of Hearing People (SHHH), or by community organizations such as the Rotary or Lions clubs. The important point is to use available resources to develop the support needed for students with and without HI to achieve their potential.

The second issue in using the FM system, monitoring and maintaining equipment, is addressed next. Without consistent monitoring, FM systems will break down or malfunction at a rate similar to that of hearing aids. Bess et al. (1984) found that 50% of randomly checked FM systems (teacher mic, student receiver, or both) were not functioning correctly. Daily inspection is necessary to ensure optimal performance. This check is similar to HA checks, but a check for FM units must also include a listening check of output through both the teacher's mic and the external mics.

It is recommended practice that electroacoustic analysis of the FM system should be conducted at least twice a year (English, 1991). If equipment is available, other performance measurements should include real-ear measurement and sound field testing with warble tones and speech discrimination. The American-Speech-Language-Hearing Association (1993) guidelines are strongly recommended.

Because the FM system is an amplification device, the audiologist is the school professional uniquely qualified to recommend and fit FM units for students with HI (Flexer et al., 1989). School districts have been known to purchase units without audiological consultation and therefore risk overamplification (California Speech-Language-Hearing Association, 1993; Massie, 1993). If there is no written policy for guiding the acquisition of FM technology, the educational audiologist should present the need for such to appropriate administrators, convey a strong concern for their potential liability for damage due to overamplification, and recommend a policy that identifies the audiologist as the appropriate dispenser of FM systems for the district.

Sound Field Amplification   Another technology for amplification growing in popularity is the sound field amplification system. With this system, the teacher wears an FM microphone, but his or her voice is picked up, amplifed by 10 or 15 dB, and transmitted not to an individual student with a receiver but to the whole class by speakers strategically placed around the classroom (the sound field). Sound field amplification ensures that the teacher's voice is louder than background noise and that it is consistently loud to all parts of the classroom. Students with hearing impairment may continue to use an FM receiver or wear their personal hearing aids in the amplified sound field.

The use of sound field amplification was pioneered by the Mainstream Amplified Resource Room Study or the MARRS project (Sarff, 1981). The MARRS project demonstrated significant academic gains among subjects with normal hearing, at a higher level and a faster pace with sound field amplification than without (Sarff, 1981). In addition, teachers have reported experiencing less vocal fatigue and better on-task behavior among their students (Berg, 1987; Finitzo-Hieber & Tillman, 1978; Flexer, 1989; Jones, Berg, & Viehweg, 1989; Leavitt & Flexer, 1991; Mills, 1991).

Sound field amplification has been found to benefit students with fluctuating OM, students with minimal hearing impairment who were not fit with hearing aids, and students with behavior or attention problems resulting from difficulties discriminating speech in noise (Anderson, 1989b; Neuss, Blair, & Viehweg, 1991). Other positive features of sound field amplification are a high acceptance rate among teachers and cost-effectiveness. With less capital outlay, 30 students in one classroom benefit from a sound field system, compared with one student who benefits from an FM receiver.

Because sound field amplification is a relatively new technology, the educational audiologist is encouraged to carefully research the available models and request a trial period before making a recommendation for purchase.

Developing Listening Skills

This chapter has so far addressed the classroom's acoustical environment in terms of reducing noise and increasing the signal-to-noise ratio. These efforts improve the student's ability to hear his or her teacher's instruction. Nevertheless, even when environmental conditions are controlled and the signal-to-noise ratio is optimal, many learners with HI still experience **difficulties in listening**.

We are now ready to address the third strategy to ensure that learners with HI have an optimal listening and learning environment: the development of listening skills. Listening in the classroom implies not just hearing but also **attending to and understanding instruction**. In other words, listening entails not only detecting the presence of a voice, but also discriminating the words, phrases, and sentences of discourse, and understanding their intent. The ability to listen effectively is perhaps the skill most essential to education, because at least 45% of the school day involves listening activities (Berg, 1986). Effort needed to focus on the **perception** of words can detract from the ability to learn what the words **mean** in an instructional context.

Listening skills are dependent on the degree of hearing impairment and the experience a student has in using his or her residual hearing. A hierarchy of listening skills has been identified (Erber, 1982):

- Detection—determining the presence or absence of sound. For example, a student is asked to raise his or her hand when he or she hears a pure tone or spoken word.
- Discrimination—perceiving differences in sound. For example, a student is asked to listen to two stimuli and then describe them as "same" or "different." If different, were there differences in duration, rate, intensity?
- Identification—recognizing a stimulus and identifying it by pointing or repeating. For example, the student is asked to point to the broken chair, or to say the word "ice cream."
- Comprehension—understanding and acting on a stimulus. For example, the student is asked, "Where do you live?" and the student responds, "San Diego."

How can an educational audiologist determine a student's ability to listen? Standard audiometric data will provide only part of the answer. An audiogram gives information about how well a student **detects** pure tones. Speech discrimination scores indicate how well a student can **identify** speech sounds, and careful analysis can inform the audiologist about the student's ability to **discriminate** speech sounds. Nevertheless, additional assessment is needed in order to determine the total picture of all the listening abilities of a student with HI.

Recognizing and Evaluating Listening Difficulties Determining the extent and nature of the listening difficulties that a student with HI experiences can be accomplished with standardized test materials. Typically, the student is evaluated for his or her ability to detect and discriminate stimuli in quiet and noisy environments, and for auditory memory. Materials to assess these listening skills are described in the Resources at the end of this chapter.

In addition to standardized tests, the educational audiologist needs to collect data from the teachers, the student, and from his or her own classroom observation to consider adequately listening demands in the context of a specific instructional area. Edwards (1991a) developed a comprehensive rating scale that identifies teacher concerns regarding student listening skills. The evaluation identifies overall and specific concerns and considers student and teacher interaction strategies.

Intervention: Two Approaches There are two ways to approach intervention with listening skills. The conventional approach to teaching listening skills uses direct instruction that, while necessary, puts the student in a passive role. The second approach teaches strategy skills, which help the student develop strategies in communication repair and encourages him or her to take an active role in problem solving (Elfenbein, 1992). Both approaches will be described here. It is recommended that as maturity and skills advance, the two approaches become integrated to address listening difficulties.

Teaching Listening Skills Erber (1982) described three types of direct instruction for teaching listening skills:

1. Listening instruction can be taught as a highly structured and focused task, with preselected stimulus/response teaching. During a learning task, full attention is directed toward the auditory task at hand through a series of listening exercises.

2. Listening instruction can be taught as a moderately structured task. Here the listening task requirement is part of a more complex learning task, including speech production and comprehension of recent instruction or vocabulary review.

3. Listening instruction can be taught as part of natural conversation. During classroom discussion, the student is guided toward using the context of the conversation to help comprehension. For example, if the discussion is about a field trip, the student learns to guess from the context that a missed word is more likely to be "zoo" than "shoe."

There are curricula available to assist in the development of listening training materials (see Resources). These will provide a framework of instruction as well as a springboard for individualized teaching (Bunch, 1987).

Teaching Strategy Skills Edwards (1991a) described a set of strategy skills that can help learners with HI to repair communication breakdowns and solve communication problems. These strategies include:

- Learning to recognize optimal and difficult listening situations
- Moving closer to the speaker and/or away from noise sources

- Signaling when information is unclear, or when it is difficult to understand teacher or classmates
- Practicing listening to speech in progressively noisier conditions
- Watching a speaker's face
- Asking a speaker to slow down, repeat, or rephrase if necessary

The Role of the Audiologist in Teaching Listening Skills   Depending on the specific job description, the educational audiologist may or may not be actively involved in teaching listening skills to students with HI. As a direct service provider, the audiologist is responsible for assessment and teaching listening skills. However, the audiologist also could be providing only indirect support, by collaborating and consulting with the classroom teacher, the SLP, and other service providers. In any professional level of involvement, however, the educational audiologist is responsible for ensuring: 1) that listening skills are included in a student's IEP if screening indicates a need, and 2) that teachers and other service providers recognize that **listening is an integral part of learning** rather than an isolated training activity that occurs between math and spelling (Flexer et al., 1989). With thought and creativity, listening training can be incorporated into virtually every unit taught in school. Support for developing listening skills all through the day will probably depend on the support that the educational audiologist supplies to the classroom teacher and others.

Psychosocial Issues for Learners with HI

One of the more satisfying aspects of working as an audiologist in a school setting is the opportunity to know students as more than "a pair of ears." The educational audiologist is interested not only in the operational status of the hearing aids and FM system, or the noise level of a classroom. Just as important are the pyschological, social, and emotional adjustments each student makes to learning and interpersonal relationships with respect to hearing impairment. Providing support with counseling in these areas of a student's life is part of a holistic approach to educational audiology services (Edwards, 1991b).

Many audiologists report having very limited training in counseling skills and consequently feel ill-prepared for the task (Flahive & White, 1981; McCarthy, Culpepper, & Lucks, 1986). Despite these concerns, audiologists in schools actually spend considerable time counseling students with HI, most often by providing "informational" or **content counseling**. This type of counseling includes teaching a student how to interpret a personal audiogram, or describing the auditory pathway and explaining a student's hearing impairment, or instructing a student in how to care for and use an amplification system (Von Almen & Blair, 1989).

The **counseling of psychological and social concerns** regarding hearing impairment is also within the purvue of audiology (Clark, 1994). Even if feeling underprepared, the educational audiologist cannot shirk this responsibility when a student's concerns are related to his or her adjustment to HI. Those who feel intimidated by the prospect are encouraged to consider the counseling role as simply a natural part of the dialogue between audiologist and client (Clark, 1994).

Clark (1994) made a sharp distinction between professional pyschotherapy and the role of the "nonprofessional counselor" (p. 5). For example, the audiologist clearly is not to provide long-term support in resolving personal conflicts, which may manifest themselves as guilt or depression. Rather, counseling for the audiologist means helping clients find ways to make practical adjustments in their situations in order to meet specific concerns. Clark advises a "straightforward empathic human response" (p. 6) and sensitivity in the counseling role, as well as awareness of professional limitations (Kricos, 1987).

Psychosocial Aspects With this understanding of the audiologist's role as counselor in mind, let us consider general pyschosocial concerns of all learners, which include:

Self image: personal adjustment, sense of identity, ego strength, dependency, and self care

Social and interpersonal adjustment: peer relationships, family relationships, relationship to authority, risk taking, conformity, social isolation, and ethical behavior

Emotional adjustment: fearfulness, insecurity, anxiousness, negative attitudes, excessive agressiveness, anger, and poor impulse control (California State Department of Education, 1986)

Research has identified many concerns regarding the psychosocial development of children with HI. Various studies have described subjects with HI as less mature and less empathetic and more egocentric, impulsive, rigid, and physically aggressive compared with typical hearing peers (Antia, 1985; Bachara, Raphael, & Phelan, 1980; Davis, Elfenbein, Schum, & Bentler, 1986; Maxon, Brackett, & van den Berg, 1991b; Meadow, 1976; Meadow & Trybus, 1979).

It has been observed that, because of ever-present communication difficulties, children with HI have fewer opportunities to interact with both adults and peers, and so have less experience from which to learn appropriate social behaviors (Antia & Kreimeyer, 1992; Higgenbotham & Baker, 1981). Van Riper and Emerlick (1990) described some reactions of individuals with communication disorders to interactions while experiencing communication difficulties: frustration, feelings of being different, anxiety and fear of failure, guilt, and a sense of inadequacy and embarrassment.

These reactions may be expressed with either hostility or withdrawal. Either reaction could account for the behaviors observed in the studies mentioned earlier. These documented reactions are consistent with data that described a tendency of children with HI to remove themselves from social situtations (Leberberg, Ryan, & Robbins, 1986; Levy-Shiff & Hoffman, 1985).

It is imperative to remember that these and other behaviors are not inevitable, especially if all involved are sensitive to situations and to the learner with HI. After all, it is not difficult to keep in mind that, at a time when a child most wants to be like his or her classmates, a child with a hearing impairment must also receive special instruction that removes him or her from class, experience awkward and embarrassing misunderstandings in learning and social situations, be perhaps the only child in the class or school with HI, and wear a special device to hear (Maxon et al., 1991b).

As mentioned previously, the use of hearing aids and FM systems, because of their visibility, is often a contentious issue for children. Edwards (1991b) reminded us that "it is the wearing of the device which 'amplifies' the difference between the child with hearing impairment and his or her peers" (p. 7). Embarrassment and peer acceptance are powerful variables in the development of a student's self-esteem. Students have been known to sabotage FM equipment when required to use it unwillingly.

Sanders (1993) advised that the audiologist acknowledge the normality of these reactions to hearing impairment. "Perhaps the most helpful way to consider the emotional behaviors of hearing impaired children is to assume that they represent the child's best attempt to deal with an abnormal experience" (p. 374).

The Role of the Audiologist in Counseling Learners with HI   At the very least, the educational audiologist must actively listen and respond to psychosocial concerns expressed by learners with HI, their parents, and teachers. Clark (1994) describes counseling approaches that capitalize on the strong interpersonal relationships that typically develop in school settings.

The audiologist also provides assistance in indirect ways. If a student's inappropriate social behaviors seem attributable to the frustrations of language deficits, collaboration with the SLP can result in focusing on the development of appropriate social skills. Practice with turn-taking and initiation–response behaviors can be integrated into speech and language therapy (Antia & Kreimeyer, 1992; Maxon et al., 1991b; Rasing & Duker, 1992).

Social skills learned in therapy must be practiced in other settings. Classroom teachers may need help from the SLP and/or the audiologist in organizing cooperative learning activities that promote peer familiarity, enhancing the likelihood for acquaintanceship and later friendship (Lee & Antia, 1992). Activities to increase peer interaction should reduce "teacher talk" to a minimum because even verbal praise can interfere with the natural flow of interaction (Rasing & Duker, 1992).

A promising practice described by Meiners (1991) increases peer interaction between students with and without HI. After receiving content counseling about the nature of hearing impairment, students with HI are encouraged to provide a presentation about this material to other students. The information shared with peers may include a description of parts of the ear, types of hearing loss, amplification systems, and communication strategies. A period for questions and answers allows normally hearing students to ask questions they might not ask an adult, such as "How did you lose your hearing?" or "Will you always have a hearing impairment?"

Early observations of the effectiveness of this program find that students with HI seem to grow in their acceptance of their hearing status. Students with HI report that other students seem more relaxed with them, and remember many of the commۇnciation strategies ("Tap me before you talk to me"). The opportunity to interact with classmates and peers as an "expert" may help acquaintanceship-friendship development (Lee & Antia, 1992).

Conclusion   Individuals with HI are a heterogeneous group. There is a large set of variables that can affect the psychosocial development of an individual with HI, including age of onset of hearing impairment, age of identification of HI and first hearing aid fitting, degree of family involvement, and intensity of educational experiences. The individual's personal adjustment to the challenges of hearing impairment is another variable, and, indeed, the adjustment process is not a struggle for all students. For example, a recent study indicated regular-education teachers reported that 88% of their mainstreamed students with HI demonstrated adequate-to-high social skills (Luckner, 1991). As with any other service for students with HI, counseling must meet the individual needs of each learner.

ENSURING THE HEARING ABILITIES OF ALL LEARNERS

The first part of this chapter has described the responsibilities of the educational audiologist in respect to learners with HI. However, as mentioned at the beginning of this chapter, the educational audiologist also has responsibilities to **all** students in the school or district. Again, these responsibilities include developing and supervising effective hearing screening programs, and developing and maintaining aggressive, long-term conservation programs. Both types of programs, for screening and conservation, are described in the following sections.

Screening for Hearing Impairment

Most school districts already have adequate hearing screening programs in place. However, school districts are less likely to provide comprehensive follow-up and management based on these screenings (Roeser & Northern, 1981). Current professional guidelines recommend that the identification of hearing loss is only one part of a comprehensive screening program, which should also include a coordinated referral process, educational management, and counseling for parents and teachers. "It is pointless to identify people with hearing impairment unless there is a concurrent follow-up program to handle their habilitative, educational, and medical needs" (American Speech-Language-Hearing Association, 1985, p. 50).

This section describes the components of a comprehensive hearing screening program, including identification procedures and recommended practices for comprehensive follow-up.

Procedures for the Identification of HI   No one set of guidelines is used in screening programs across the country (Wall, Naples, Buhrer, & Capodanno, 1985). Educational audiologists need to ensure that the schools they serve closely adhere to the guidelines developed by The American-Speech-Language-Hearing Association (ASHA) (1985). The following is a brief summary of procedures for screening for hearing loss:

1. Obtain a hearing history from parents for each child to be screened. Any history of ear infections, recent ear pain, or discharge are important indicators of potential concern.
2. Use individual, not group, screening procedures.
3. Ensure that ambient noise levels do not compromise testing (Harrison, 1971). (See Table 7.3 for acceptable ambient noise levels per testing frequency.)
4. Conduct a visual inspection of the head, neck, and ears, including otoscopy.
5. Screen at 20 dB (ANSI 1969) for 1,000Hz, 2,000 Hz, and 4,000 Hz, both ears.
6. Screen also at 500 Hz (20 dB) if immittance testing is not used.
7. A nonresponse at any frequency for either ear requires an immediate rescreening. Carefully reinstruct and reposition the earphones.
8. A nonresponse at the immediate rescreening, at any frequency for either ear, requires a recheck within 2 weeks.

Table 7.3. Maximum ambient noise levels for screening hearing

Testing frequency	500 Hz	1,000 Hz	2,000 Hz	4,000 Hz
Maximum ambient noise level	41.5 dB	49.5 dB	54.5 dB	62 dB

From American-Speech-Language-Hearing Association. (1985). Guidelines for identification audiometry. *Asha, 27*(5), 40, 49–52; reprinted by permission. Noise levels measured by sound level meter with octave band filter centered on each frequency.

9.   Any failure at the recheck results in a referral for an audiological evaluation.
10. If immittance testing is used, obtain the following five measurements (ASHA, 1990): 1) static admittance, 2) equivalent ear canal volume, 3) tympanic width, 4) tympanic peak pressure, and 5) acoustic reflex.

The combination of a hearing history, otoscopy, pure tone screening, and immitance testing is recommended for a screening program because a complete set of data is needed to provide adequate information regarding fluctuating hearing loss as a result of otitis media.

The guidelines are not intended to be inflexibly applied and should be used with informed clinical judgment. For example, Shaw and Von Almen (1991) pointed out that no recommendation is made regarding pressure equalization (P.E.) tubes. The audiologist may, however, find that a visible P.E. tube appears occluded with wax, or appears to have been rejected by the tympanum before the myringotomy has completely healed. No guidelines are provided, but the audiologist will want to report such findings to the parent, with the advice to consult the child's physician.

ASHA guidelines suggest testing from kindergarten through third grade. However, some states prefer to continue monitoring hearing impairment beyond third grade. For example, in California, students are screened for hearing impairment in kindergarten and grades two, five, eight, and ten or eleven (California Department of Education, 1986). This practice is recommended in light of a recent study by Montgomery and Fujikama (1992), who found that students in second and eighth grades demonstrated a higher prevalence of hearing loss than similar populations did just 10 years ago.

Educational audiologists should ensure that their school districts operate by ASHA guidelines for screening for hearing impairment. As mentioned earlier, the identification of hearing impairment is only the first part of a comprehensive program. We now examine aspects of appropriate follow-up and educational management for a child identified from the screening procedure as having a hearing impairment.

Follow-Up and Educational Management

Referral   If a child does not pass the immediate rescreening, a referral is made for a complete audiological evaluation. The referral process varies somewhat from district to district, but should follow these general guidelines:

> The nature of the referral may depend upon the characteristics of the screening program and the availability of services. For example, the referral may be to a clinic that provides both audiologic and medical services. Alternatively, an audiologic referral may precede the medical referral. If audiologic services are not available, an immediate medical referral should be made upon failure of the screening protocol. (American Speech-Language-Hearing Association, 1990, p. 22)

Many school systems have complete testing facilities that include all audiological services; other districts have none. If a school district has no audiological testing services, community resources should be utilized.

Referrals should not be thought of as a one-way communication, from school to parent with no expectation of response. Rather, a monitoring system must ensure that two-way communication occurs between school and parent and that parents receive the referral notice, understand the test findings, know where to obtain audiological and medical evaluations, know how to obtain copies of test reports in school records, and understand the findings from those tests.

Educational Management   If an audiological evaluation verifies a hearing impairment, it is imperative that the student, the teacher, and the parents know that they can expect support from the educational audiologist. Depending on the needs of the child, this support may include audiological support and/or educational support. Next, we consider each type of support.

If amplification is prescribed for the student, the educational audiologist needs to provide the teacher, SLP, and the student's other team members information for checking and troubleshooting minor hearing aid problems. If the student is a candidate for an FM system or sound field amplification, the audiologist leads the way in providing instruction and follow-up on its use. As emphasized earlier, all systems of amplification, for personal or classroom use, must be checked routinely. The audiologist instructs each student on caring for his or her amplification system and helps the student assume increasing responsibility for its operation.

The educational audiologist also provides support to school personnel so that they are better able to instruct the student with HI. Regular education teachers frequently are not aware of the audiologist's expertise with classroom concerns regarding a child with hearing impairment. In order to establish rapport, it is recommended that an instrument, the Screening Instrument For Targeting Educational Risk (SIFTER) (Anderson, 1989a) be shared with the student's classoom teacher. This user-friendly questionnaire measures the level of a teacher's concerns regarding the student's academic achievement, communication, comprehension, class participation, and school behavior. The teacher rates 15 items, and from the score indicates the student's level of risk in each area. Discussing the results obtained by this or another instrument provides the audiologist an excellent opportunity to address educational issues at length with the teacher, and increase mutual insight and understanding between audiologist and teacher regarding the impact of the student's hearing impairment on work and behavior in the classroom.

Evaluating the Efficacy of a Screening Program   How does the educational audiologist determine if the screening program is actually accomplishing its goals? In order to answer, the audiologist must look at the outcomes of the program and compare them with the goals. While collecting data regarding hearing screening programs, Pelson and Trestik (1987) found significant discrepancies between the specified goals of screening programs and the actual outcomes. For example, 95% of districts surveyed indicated that their hearing screening program included a referral of screening failures to medical and audiological evaluations. However, only about half of all the districts actually made such referrals. In another example, approximately 85% of the districts indicated that their programs required hearing rechecks after a medical referral, but the data indicated that only one third of referred students actually received a recheck.

As a quality check and assessment of efficacy, each hearing screening program should conduct a self-evaluation to ensure that the outcomes of the program meet its goals. Because of a shortage of personnel, hearing screening programs often are not under the supervision of an audiologist (Pelson & Trestik, 1987). However, program evaluation is certainly within the practice of educational audiology. If an educational audiologist is not permitted by the district to supervise the hearing screening program, he or she should, at minimum, offer to evaluate program outcomes. The goal of effective screening programs can then be achieved.

Hearing Conservation Programs

The other responsibility of the educational audiologist in regard to all students is in developing and maintaining aggressive, long-term hearing conservation programs.

The previous section described a program designed to **identify** hearing impairment. These next sections will focus on teaching students how to **prevent** hearing loss.

Students Are at Risk of Noise Trauma   From preschool through high school, many students are not aware that excessive noise levels can be considered a pollutant and a hazard to their hearing health. Our society is a noisy one, and noise is ubiquitous—at home, in the shopping mall, on the road, in the classroom—to the point where we become unaware how noisy it is. Yet the presence and intensity of noise has become so excessive that approximately 10 million persons in our country now have noise induced hearing loss (NIHL). The unfortunate part about this is that **hearing loss from noise exposure**, except in the case of accidental acoustic blasts, **is always preventable**. Education about this preventable hearing impairment must start early, and be reiterated throughout the grades, to help students recognize the presence of high noise levels, understand the consequences of constant exposure to high noise levels, and, most important, learn how to actively prevent NIHL (Anderson, 1991; Frager, 1986; Peppard & Peppard, 1992).

Students may feel that concern for noise levels belongs in the workplace environment (Lankford, Mikrut, & Jackson, 1991). Certainly, students do need to know that careers in the military, agriculture, manufacturing, mining, firefighting, and even aerobics, dentistry, and music expose workers to excessive noise levels that merit the concern of the Occupational Safety and Health Administration (OSHA) (Franks, 1990; Gasaway, 1990; Kryter, 1985; OSHA, 1983; Plakke, 1990; Royster & Royster, 1990b; Williams, 1991).

Awareness of the potential noise exposure in one's future occupation is commendable. However, students must realize that they are not immune to or protected from high noise levels in their daily environments. Table 7.4 lists some of the leisure and work activities and the noise levels they generate that children regularly encounter.

Even the school environment can be excessively loud, especially in gyms, cafeterias, and high school classes for woodshop and vocational technology. Noise levels in these classes range from 85 dB to 115 dB (Lankford & West, 1993; Pindar, 1974). Approximately one-third of schools surveyed do not require the use of ear protection, and, even when it is available, teachers and students often do not make use of this protection (Allonen-Allie & Florentine, 1990; Plakke, 1991; Woodford & Farrell, 1983).

Table 7.4. Noise levels of daily activities

Noise level (dB)	Noise source
140	Firecrackers
130	Live rock music
120	Shotgun
115	Personal stereo headphones, cap pistols
110	Woodworking tools
105	Motorcycle race
100	Snowblower
95	Go-carts
90	Power lawnmower
85	Video arcade
80	Vacuum cleaner
60	Normal conversation
50	Light traffic
40	Buzzing fly
30	Whisper
10	Breathing

Concern about noise exposure must start much earlier than high school, given the data mentioned previously that suggested an increase in hearing loss in school-age children (Montgomery & Fujikama, 1992). Some researchers have recommended that education on prevention of NIHL should be introduced as early as third grade. If postponed until high school, there may be minimal success in changing attitudes regarding the use of hearing protection (Lass, Woodford, Lundeen, & Everly-Myers, 1986; Lewis, 1989).

Of the variety of noises in child environments, perhaps of greatest concern are noise levels generated by personal stereo headphones and live music amplifiers. The output from headphones has been measured at 115 dB (Clark, 1991) (see Figure 7.8). Live rock music has been measured at 112dB at 4 feet from speakers, and at 99 dB at 35 feet from speakers (Catalano & Levin, 1985; Clark, 1990; Danenberg, Loos-Cosgrove, & LoVerde, 1987; Fearn & Hanson, 1989; Royster & Royster, 1990a; Williams, 1991). It was estimated in 1990 that 90% of fourth through sixth graders have and use personal stereo headphones (Clark, 1990). Subjects in research studies have demonstrated significant temporary threshold shifts (TTS) after long-term exposure to high levels of noise, and many subjects do not recover to normal hearing levels within 24 hours. As Newby and Popelka (1992) reminded us, persons highly susceptible to TTS are at serious risk of permanent NIHL.

The effect of loud music on hearing has generated concern among musicians who themselves have experienced NIHL as an occupational hazard. A group called HEAR—Hearing Education Awareness for Rockers—has formed in California to promote education and the use of earplugs at concerts (Kirkwood, 1992).

Other activities that are extremely hazardous to hearing health among school-age children because they involve acoustics blasts are gunfire and firecrackers (Clark, 1991; Cummins, 1990; Kramer, 1990). Children may not be aware that over 50% of recreational handgun and rifle users experience hearing difficulties, compared with 9% of the general U.S. population (Shewan, 1990).

VOLUME CAN REACH 115 dB

- If you can't hold a normal conversation,
- If sounds are muffled or your ears ring after use,
- If you exceed 4 on a volume of 1 to 10,
  IT'S TOO LOUD!

Figure 7.8. It's too loud!

Developing a Program for Hearing Conservation   There are no standard guidelines available to assist the educational audiologist in developing a hearing conservation program (HCP) in a school setting. Programs that have been described in research literature typically include information on these components: 1) basic anatomy of the auditory pathway; 2) the nature of sound, including sound levels of normal conversation and specific activities; 3) the effects of excessive noise levels on the hair cells of the inner ear, as well as the psychological and physiological effects of noise; and 4) procedures to protect one's hearing.

Teaching about sound, noise, and the basic auditory anatomy consists of informational or theoretical text (Frager & Kahn, 1988), which is academic or cognitive information teachers share with learners. After learning about these aspects, learners will know cognitively that their auditory system is vulnerable to injury from high noise levels. In order to be effective, however, a hearing conservation program must also have "mobilizing information." Mobilizing information enables learners to **act on the content** of the curriculum. The educational audiologist provides mobilizing information to learners through teaching them procedures to protect their hearing. They learn to recognize the danger signs presented in Table 7.5, and to take appropriate steps to protect their hearing.

Table 7.5.   Danger signs of noise trauma

1. You find it necessary to shout in order to be heard.
2. You cannot hear what someone is saying 2 feet away.
3. Speech begins to sound muffled, or your ears feel as if they are ringing.

A comprehensive, multimedia, hands-on program in hearing conservation for elementary school students makes use of the following (Chermack & Peters-McCarthy, 1991):

- Pre- and post-program questionnaires
- Lecture with visual aids, including three-dimensional models
- Demonstration of a hearing screening
- Videos
- "Discovery learning," in which students generate strategies to prevent NIHL in their own environments
- Question and answer period
- Distribution of earplugs and a brochure on NIHL to share with family members

Regardless of the format of an HCP, it is recommended that the programs be kept simple, repetitive, interesting, and fun, with relevant role models (Florentine, 1990). Developmentally appropriate programming for third, sixth, ninth, and twelfth grades, ideally presented at the same time students' hearing is being screened, can expand on the core information as needed. Videos by the House Ear Institute (1992) and the Better Hearing Institute (1993) are good supplements to handouts and other instructional materials.

After developing an informative **and** mobilizing HCP, the educational audiologist may likely face the logistical problem of information dissemination: how to reach the wider potential audience? This can be problematic if the district employs one audiologist to work with a student population of several thousand. In such a situation, the educational audiologist will want to collaborate and consult with other professionals working in school settings in the district. Is it possible to essentially "infuse" the program into an existing health curriculum? Are there teachers, health educators, school nurses, SLPs, or student teachers who would be interested in being trained in teaching the material you want students to know? There are a variety of ways to address such a dilemma, all found within the resources (realized and potential) available in your school system.

SUMMARY

The educational audiologist provides a broad spectrum of services for students from preschool through high school. As children with HI get older, they become more conscious of peer approval and so may have difficulties with continued use of hearing aids and FM systems. As children with normal hearing get older, they become more at risk of acquiring noise-induced hearing loss. The educational audiologist has responsibilities to all children in schools to optimize listening environments and to work for the protection of hearing health.

Learning the Language

Review the following concepts from this chapter and discuss with a colleague.

- Signal-to-noise ratio
- Reverberation and reverberation time
- The FM advantage
- Consensus and team building
- Sound field amplification
- Hierarchy of listening skills
- Listening and strategy training
- Content versus pyschosocial counseling
- Screening versus educational management
- Theoretical versus mobilizing instruction

Educational Audiology in Action
Suggested Learning Activities

Project 1. Visit a classroom.

1) Calculate the RT. Consider all surfaces in order to obtain as accurate an estimate as possible. Is this estimate within acceptable levels? If not, what recommendations would you suggest?

2) Examine the room for noise sources. After this examination, ask a teacher what noise sources **he or she** is aware of. Are there discrepancies between the sources you identified and those identified by the teacher?

Project 2. Design a HA monitoring program for elementary school students.

1) Design recordkeeping systems for daily, weekly, monthly, semesterly reports.

2) How would you incorporate into your program the development of self-management of HA care across grades?

3) How do you modify the program for high school students?

4) What self-management skills do you expect a high school student to have regarding his or her hearing impairment and hearing aid needs?

Project 3. Design a hearing conservation program for a target audience of third graders. What goals and objectives do you want to develop into your program? Remember to use a variety of teaching strategies and to incorporate multimedia techniques. If possible, present this program to an actual class. To evaluate the program, ask yourself: Which parts of the program kept student interest? What parts would you revise? Did posttests indicate a change in knowledge and attitudes?

Resources

Materials for Listening Training: Evaluation and Activities

Developmental Approach to Successful Listening (DASL)
American Guidance Services
4201 Woodland Road
Circle Pines, MN 55014

Designed for preschool and elementary-school children with HI. This auditory curriculum consists of activities with daily, weekly, and monthly objectives.

Glendonald Auditory Screening Procedure (GASP). In Erber, N. (1982). *Auditory training* (pp. 48–71). Washington, DC: Alexander Graham Bell Association for the Deaf.

This procedure includes tasks for phoneme detection, word identification, and sentence comprehension, as well as suggestions for adaptive testing procedures.

Minimal Auditory Capabilities Battery (MAC)
Audiotec of St. Louis
330 Selma
St. Louis, MO 63119

This battery uses an audiotape to assess listening abilities. Abilities assessed range from discrimination of intonation of questions and statements to recognition of open-ended sentences that are common in daily life.

Test of Auditory Comprehension (TAC); Auditory Skills Curriculum; Preschool Supplement
Foreworks, Inc.
P.O. Box 82289
Portland, OR 97282

Ten subtests evaluate auditory detection, discrimination, and comprehension abilities. Curricula are designed to teach listening skills, appropriate to age and degree of HI.

A Network for Students with HI

PC Pals Teen Network
Alexander Graham Bell Association
3417 Volta Place NW
Washington, D.C. 20007-2778

This electronic bulletin board for teenagers who are deaf or hard of hearing offers an opportunity to correspond with peers who share similar experiences.

References

Adkins, T. (Ed.). (1993). *Iowa resource manual for the education of students with hearing impairment and educational audiology.* Des Moines: Iowa Department of Education.

Allonen-Allie, N., & Florentine, M. (1990). Survey of noise levels in vocational and technical schools. *Ear and Hearing, 11,* 237–239.

American National Standard Specification for Audiometers. (ANSI S3.6—1969). New York: American National Standards Institute.

American Speech-Language-Hearing Association. (1985). Guidelines for identification audiometry. *Asha, 27*(5), 40, 49–52.

American Speech-Language-Hearing Association. (1990). Guidelines for screening for hearing impairment and middle ear disorders. *Asha, 32* (Suppl. 2), 17–24.

American Speech-Language-Hearing Association. (1993). Guidelines for audiology services in the schools. *Asha, 35* (Suppl. 10), 24–32.

Anderson, K. (1989a). *Screening Instrument for Targeting Educational Risk* (SIFTER). Austin, TX: PRO-ED.

Anderson, K. (1989b). Speech perception and the hard of hearing child. *Educational Audiology Monograph, 1,* 15–29.

Anderson, K. (1991). Hearing conservation in the public schools revisited. *Seminars in Hearing, 12,* 340–358.

Antia, S. (1985). Social integration of hearing impaired children: Fact or fiction. *Volta Review, 87,* 279–289.

Antia, S., & Kreimeyer, K. (1992). Social competence intervention for young children with hearing impairments. In S. Odom, S. McConnell, & M. McEvoy (Eds.), *Social competence of young children with disabilities: Issues and strategies for intervention* (pp. 135–164). Baltimore: Paul H. Brookes Publishing Co.

Bachara, G., Raphael, J., & Phelan, W. (1980). Empathy development in deaf preadolescents. *American Annals of the Deaf, 125,* 38–41.

Berg, F. (1986). Classroom acoustics and signal transmission. In F. Berg, J. Blair, S. Viehweg, & A. Wilson-Vlotman, *Educational audiology for the hard of hearing child* (pp. 157–180) Orlando, FL: Grune & Stratton.

Berg, F. (1987). *Facilitating classroom listening: A handbook for teachers of normal and hard of hearing students.* Austin, TX: PRO-ED.

Bess, F., & McConnell, F. (1981). *Audiology, education, and the hearing impaired child.* St. Louis: C.V. Mosby.

Bess, F., Sinclair, J., & Riggs, D. (1984). Group amplification in schools for the hearing impaired. *Ear and Hearing, 5,* 138–144.

Better Hearing Institute. (1993). *People vs. noise.* (Available from P.O.Box 1840, Washington, DC 20013.)

Bunch, G. (1987). *The curriculum and the hearing impaired child.* Boston: College-Hill Press.

California Speech-Language-Hearing Association. (1993). Position paper on auditory trainers in the schools. *Educational Audiology Association Newsletter, 10*(2), 7–8.

California State Department of Education. (1986). *Program guidelines for hearing impaired students.* Sacramento: Author.

Catalano, P., & Levin, S. (1985). Noise induced hearing loss and portable radios with headphones. *International Journal of Pediatric Otorhinolaryngology, 9,* 59–67.

Chermack, G., & Peters-McCarthy, E. (1991). The effectiveness of a hearing conservation program for elementary school children. *Language, Speech, and Hearing Services in Schools, 22,* 308–312.

Clark, J. (1994). Audiologists' counseling purvue. In J. Clark & F. Martin (Eds.), *Effective counseling in audiology: Perspectives and practice* (pp. 1–17). Engelwood Cliffs, NJ: Prentice Hall.

Clark, W. (1990). Amplified music from stereo headsets and its effect on hearing. *Hearing Instruments, 41*(10), 29–30.

Clark, W. (1991). Noise exposure from leisure activities: A review. *Journal of Acoustical Society of America, 90,* 175–181.

Coleman, R. (1975). Is anyone listening? *Language, Speech, and Hearing Services in Schools, 6,* 102–105.

Crandell, C. (1991). Effects of classroom acoustics on children with normal hearing: Implications for intervention strategies. *Educational Audiology Monograph, 2,* 18–38.

Crum, M., & Matkin, N. (1976). Room acoustics: The forgotten variable. *Language, Speech, and Hearing Services in Schools, 7,* 106–110.

Cummins, R. (1990). Fireworks-related injuries to the ear. *Hearing Journal, 43*(7), 19–24.

Danenberg, M., Loos-Cosgrove, M., & LoVerde, M. (1987). Temporary hearing loss and rock music. *Language, Speech, and Hearing Services in Schools, 18,* 267–274.

Davis, J., Elfenbein, J., Schum, R., & Bentler, R. (1986). Effects of mild and moderate hearing impairments of language, educational, and psychosocial behavior of children. *Journal of Speech and Hearing Disorders, 51,* 53–62.

Dirks, D., Morgan, D., & Dubno, J. (1982). A procedure for quantifying the effects of noise on speech discrimination. *Language, Speech, and Hearing Services in Schools, 47,* 114–123.

Edwards, C. (1991a). Assessment and management of listening skills in school-aged children. *Seminars in Hearing, 12,* 389–401.

Edwards, C. (1991b). The transition from auditory training to holistic auditory management. *Educational Audiology Monograph, 2,* 1–17.

Elfenbein, J. (1992). Coping with communication breakdown: A program of strategy development for children who have hearing losses. *American Journal of Audiology, 1*(3), 25–30.

Elliot, L., Connors, S., Kill, I., Levin, S., Ball, K., & Katz, D. (1979). Children's understanding of monosyllabic nouns in quiet and noise. *Journal of Acoustical Society of America, 66,* 12–21.

English, K. (1991). Best practices in educational audiology. *Language, Speech, and Hearing Services in Schools, 22,* 283–286.

Erber, N. (1982). *Auditory training.* Washington, DC: Alexander Graham Bell Association.

Fearn, R., & Hanson, D. (1989). Hearing levels of young subjects exposed to amplified music. *Journal of Sound Vibration, 128*(3), 509–512.

Finitzo, T. (1988). Classroom acoustics. In R. Roeser & M. Downs (Eds.), *Auditory disorders in school children* (2nd ed., pp. 221–233). New York: Thieme Medical Publishers.

Finitzo-Hieber, T., & Tillman, T. (1978). Room acoustics effects on monsyllabic word discrimination ability for normal and hearing impaired children. *Journal of Speech and Hearing Research, 21,* 440–458.

Flahive, M., & White, S. (1981). Audiologists and counseling. *Journal of the Academy of Rehabilitative Audiology, 14,* 274–283.

Flexer, C. (1989). Turn on sound: An odyessy of sound field amplification. *Educational Audiology Association Newsletter, 5,* 6–7.

Flexer, C., Wray, D., & Ireland, J. (1989). Preferential seating is NOT enough: Issues in classroom management of hearing impaired students. *Language, Speech, and Hearing Services in Schools, 20,* 11–21.

Florentine, M. (1990). Education as a tool to prevent noise induced hearing loss. *Hearing Instruments, 41,* 33–34.

Frager, A. (1986). Toward improved instruction in hearing health at the elementary school level. *Journal of School Health, 56,* 166–169.

Frager, A., & Kahn, A. (1988). How useful are elementary school health text books for teaching about hearing health and protection? *Language, Speech and Hearing Services in Schools, 19,* 175–181.

Franks, J. (1990). Noise in the construction industry and its effect on hearing. *Hearing Instruments, 41*(10), 18–19.

Gaeth, J., & Lounsbury, E. (1966). Hearing aids and children in elementary school. *Language, Speech, and Hearing Disorders, 31,* 283–289.

Gasaway, D. (1990). Noise in the military and its effect on hearing. *Hearing Instruments, 41*(10), 21–22.

Genzel, R. (1971). Acceptable signal-to-noise ratios for aided speech discrimination by the hearing impaired. *Journal of Auditory Research, 11,* 219–222.

Harrison, D. (1971). An investigation into the effect of ambient noise on pure tone screening tests of hearing in schools. *Sound, 5,* 94–96.

Hawkins, D., & Schum, D. (1985). Some effects of FM system coupling on hearing aid characteristics. *Journal of Speech and Hearing Disorders, 50,* 132–141.

Higgenbotham, D., & Baker, B. (1981). Social participation and cognitive play differences in hearing impaired and normally hearing preschoolers. *Volta Review, 83,* 135–149.

House Ear Institute. (1992). *HIP Talk: Hearing is Priceless.* (Available from 2100 W. Third Street, Los Angeles, CA 90057)

Jones, J., Berg, F., & Viehweg, S. (1989). Close, distant, and sound field overhead listening in kindergarten classrooms. *Educational Audiology Monograph, 1,* 56–65.

Kemker, F., McConnell, F., Logan, S., & Green, B. (1979). A field study of children's hearing aids in a school environment. *Language, Speech, and Hearing Services in Schools, 10,* 47–53.

Kirkwood, D. (1992). Washington starts waking up to hazards of recreational noise. *Hearing Journal, 45*(3), 13–23.

Kramer, W. (1990). Gunfire noise and its effect on hearing. *Hearing Instruments, 41*(10), 26–28.

Kricos, P. (1987). Pyschosocial aspects of hearing loss. In J. Alpiner & P. McCarthy (Eds.), *Rehabilitative audiology: Children and adults* (pp. 269–304). Baltimore: Williams & Wilkins.

Kryter, K. (1985). *The effects of noise on man* (2nd ed.). Orlando, FL: Academic Press.

Lankford, J., Mikrut, T., & Jackson, P. (1991). A noise-exposure profile of high school students. *Hearing Instruments, 42*(12), 19–24.

Lankford, J., & West, D. (1993). A study of noise exposure and hearing sensitivity in a high school woodworking class. *Language, Speech, and Hearing Services in Schools, 24,* 167–173.

Lass, N., Woodford, C., Lundeen, D., & Everly-Myers, D. (1986). The prevention of noise-induced hearing loss in the school-age population: A school education hearing conservation program. *Journal of Auditory Research, 26,* 247–254.

Leavitt, R. (1987). Promoting the use of rehabilitative technology. *Asha, 24*(4), 28–31.

Leavitt, R. (1991). Group amplification systems for students with hearing impairment. *Seminars in Hearing, 12,* 380–388.

Leavitt, R., & Flexer, C. (1991). Speech degradation as measured by the Rapid Speech Transmission Index (RASTI). *Ear and Hearing, 12,* 115–118.

Leberberg, A., Ryan, H., & Robbins, B. (1986). Peer interaction in young deaf children: The effect of partner hearing status and familiarity. *Developmental Psychology, 22,* 691–700.

Lee, C., & Antia, S. (1992). A sociological approach to the social integration of hearing impaired and normally hearing students. *Volta Review, 95,* 425–434.

Levy-Shiff, R., & Hoffman, M. (1985). Social behavior of hearing impaired and normally hearing preschoolers. *British Journal of Educational Psychology, 55,* 111–118.

Lewis, D. (1989). A hearing conservation program for high school level students. *Hearing Journal, 3,* 19–24.

Lewis, D. (1994). Assistive devices for classroom listening. *American Journal of Audiology, 3*(1), 58–69.

Lipscomb, M., Von Almen, P., & Blair, J. (1992). Students as active participants in hearing aid maintenance. *Language, Speech, and Hearing Services in Schools, 23,* 208–213.

Luckner, J. (1991). Mainstreaming hearing impaired students: Perceptions of regular educators. *Language, Speech, and Hearing Services in Schools, 22,* 302–307.

Massie, S. (1993). Fitting and monitoring FM auditory trainer units in the schools. *Educational Audiology Association Newsletter, 10*(1), 7–8.

Maxon, A., Brackett, D., & van den Berg, S. (1991a). Classroom amplification use: A national long-term study. *Language, Speech, and Hearing Services in Schools, 22*, 242–253.

Maxon, A., Brackett, D., & van den Berg, S. (1991b). Self perception of socialization: The effects of hearing status, age, and gender. *Volta Review, 93*(1), 7–18.

Maxon, A., & Smaldino, J. (1991). Hearing aid management for children. *Seminars in Hearing, 12*, 365–379.

McCarthy, P., Culpepper, N., & Lucks, L. (1986). Variability in counseling experiences among ESB accredited programs. *Asha, 28*(9), 49–52.

Meadow, K. (1976). Personality and social development of deaf persons. *Journal of Rehabilitation of the Deaf, 9*, 3–16.

Meadow, K., & Trybus, R. (1979). Behavioral and emotional problems of deaf children: An overview. In L. Bradford & W. Hardy (Eds.), *Hearing and hearing impairment* (pp. 395–403). New York: Grune & Stratton.

Meiners, S. (1991). Utilizing students with hearing impairments as resources. *Educational Audiology Monographs, 2*, 53–57.

Mills, M. (1991). A practical look at classroom amplification. *Educational Audiology Monograph, 2*, 39–42.

Montgomery, J., & Fujikama, S. (1992). Hearing thresholds of students in second, eighth and twelfth grades. *Language, Speech, and Hearing Services in Schools, 23*, 61–63.

Neuss, D., Blair, J., & Viehweg, S. (1991). Sound field amplification: Does it improve speech recognition in a background of noise for students with minimal hearing impairments? *Educational Audiology Monograph, 2*, 43–52.

Newby, H., & Popelka, G. (1992). *Audiology* (6th ed.). Englewood Cliffs, NJ: Prentice Hall.

Occupational Safety and Health Administration. (1983). Occupational noise exposure standard, U.S. Department of Labor. *Federal Register, 48*(46), 9776–9785.

Pelson, R., & Trestik, J. (1987). Public school hearing conservation in Oregon. *Language, Speech, and Hearing Services in Schools, 18*, 241–249.

Peppard, A., & Peppard, S. (1992). Noise induced hearing loss: A study of children at risk. *Hearing Journal, 45*(3), 33–35.

Pindar, C. (1974). Noise pollution in the woodworking lab. *Man, Society, and Technology, 34*, 47–50.

Plakke, B. (1990). Noise in agriculture and its effect on hearing. *Hearing Instruments, 41*(10), 22–24.

Plakke, B. (1991). Hearing conservation training of industrial technology teachers. *Language, Speech, and Hearing Services in Schools, 22*, 134–138.

Potts, P., & Greenwood, J. (1983). Hearing aid monitoring: Are looking and listening enough? *Language, Speech, and Hearing Services in Schools, 14*, 157–163.

Rasing, E., & Duker, P. (1992). Effects of a multifaceted training procedure on the acquisition and generalization of social behaviors in learning disabled deaf children. *Journal of Applied Behavioral Analysis, 25*, 723–734.

Reichman, J., & Healey, W. (1989). Amplification monitoring and maintenance in schools. *Asha, 31*(10), 43–45.

Roeser, R., & Northern, J. (1981). Screening for hearing loss and middle ear disorders. In R. Roeser & J. Northern (Eds.), *Auditory disorders in school children* (pp. 120–150). New York: Thieme Medical Publishers.

Ross, M. (1987). Classroom acoustics and speech intelligibility. In J. Katz (Ed.), *Handbook of clinical audiology* (pp. 469–478). Baltimore: Williams & Wilkins.

Ross, M., & Giolas, T. (1971). Three classroom listening conditions of speech intelligibility. *American Annals of the Deaf, 116*, 580–584.

Royster, J., & Royster, L. (1990a). Amplified music and its effect on hearing. *Hearing Instruments, 41*(10), 28–29.

Royster, L., & Royster, J. (1990b). Noise in manufacturing and its effect on hearing. *Hearing Instruments, 41*(10), 17–18.

Sanders, D. (1965). Noise conditions in normal school classrooms. *Exceptional Children, 31*, 344–353.

Sanders, D. (1993). *Management of hearing handicap: Infants to elderly* (3rd ed.). Englewood Cliffs, NJ: Prentice Hall.

Sarff, L. (1981). An innovative use of free field amplification in regular classrooms. In R. Roeser & M. Downs (Eds.), *Auditory disorders in school children* (pp. 263–272). New York: Thieme Medical Publishers.

Shaw, L., & Von Almen, P. (1991). A comparison of ASHA's 1979 and 1990 immittance screening guidelines. *Educational Audiology Monograph, 2,* 58–70.

Shewan, C. (1990). Prevalence of hearing impairment. *Asha, 32*(2), p. 62.

Smedley, T., & Plapinger, D. (1988). The nonfunctioning hearing aid: A case of double jeopardy. *Volta Review, 90*(2), 77–84.

Thibodeau, L., & McCaffrey, H. (1992). The complexities of using direct-input hearing aids with FM systems. *Volta Review, 95,* 189–192.

Van Riper, C., & Emerlick, L. (1990). *Speech correction: An introduction to speech pathology and audiology.* Englewood Cliffs, NJ: Prentice Hall.

Von Almen, P., & Blair, J. (1989). Informational counseling for school-aged hearing impaired students. *Language, Speech, and Hearing Services in Schools, 20,* 31–40.

Wall, L., Naples, G., Buhrer, K., & Capodanno, C. (1985). A survey of audiological services within the school system. *Asha, 27*(1), 31–34.

Watson, T. (1964). The use of hearing aids by hearing impaired pupils in ordinary schools. *Volta Review, 66,* 741–744.

Williams, J. (1991, March 28). Add inner ear to many victims of high impact aerobic exercise. *San Diego Tribune,* E-1.

Wynn, R., & Guditus, C. (1984). *Team management: Leadership by consensus.* Columbus, OH: Charles E. Merrill.

Woodford, C., & Farrell, M. (1983). High frequency hearing loss in secondary school students: An investigation of possible etiologic factors. *Language, Speech, and Hearing Services in Schools, 14,* 22–28.

Yacullo, W., & Hawkins, D. (1987). Speech recognition in noise and reverberation by school age children. *Audiology, 26,* 235–246.

Zink, C. (1972). Hearing aids children wear: A longitudinal study of performance. *Volta Review, 74,* 41–51.

8

Educational Audiology Across the Lifespan

College and Adult Learners

IN 1945, FEWER THAN 500 individuals with hearing impairment were known to be enrolled in college in the U.S. Some 50 years later, almost 350,000 college students report a hearing impairment. This number accounts for 2.7% of the 12.5 million students enrolled in colleges and universities in 1986 (Greene & Zimbler, 1989; Walter & Welsh, 1986).

Enrollment of College Students with HI, Fall 1986:

Hard of Hearing: 2.1% of college population (n = 265,484)
Deaf: 0.6% of college population (n = 80,910)

It is important to remember that this information is provided voluntarily by students; therefore, it is quite likely that the actual number of students with HI is greater than shown here, given the assumption that some persons would choose not to share such information. So we must keep in mind that 2.7% is a conservative operating figure.

Given the increased enrollment, advocates for college students with hearing impairment generally acknowledge that concerns regarding access to higher education are being addressed. However, once in college, students with hearing impairment seem to experience difficulties, resulting in a disturbingly **high dropout or attrition rate**. Approximately 71% of students with hearing impairment leave college before completing a degree (Walter & Welsh, 1986), compared with the attrition rate of students without disabilities, which is 41% (Tinto, 1987).

Educational audiologists typically are not involved in higher education, or the issues faced by college students with hearing impairment (HI). However, given the value placed in our society on a college education, and considering the trend for adults to return to college in order to advance their careers or to develop new ones, as well as the growing recognition of the values of "lifelong learning," educational audiologists have motivation to develop a working understanding of these issues in order to serve their college-bound students.

Also, until recently, forming connections with colleges and universities may not have been considered a priority by educational audiologists. However, because of the new regulations in 1990 of PL 101-476, the Individuals with Disabilities Education Act (IDEA) of 1990, high school special education programs are **required** to "identify transitional service needs for their students, including those for whom postsecondary education is a goal" (West et al., 1993, p. 465). According to IDEA:

> The IEP of each student, beginning no later than age 16 (and at an earlier age, if deemed appropriate), must include a statement of the needed transition services as identified in Section 300.18, including, if appropriate, a statement of each public agency's and each participating agency's responsibilities, or linkages, or both, before the student leaves the school setting. (300.345[b][1])

This mandate gives educational audiologists the responsibility, as appropriate, to serve on transitional planning teams for high school students with hearing impairment and to affect the quality of services the student receives at college (Lincoln, 1993).

To help the educational audiologist provide effective services in this environment, this chapter discusses the following topics. First, the federal legislation that guarantees **access** to a college education for persons with disabilities is reviewed and the implications of this legislation are thoroughly discussed. The next section describes the current challenge of moving **from access to full integration** into both the academic and social systems of college environments. This includes examining the **impact of support services** on the academic and social integration of students with hearing impairment. The final section addresses the imperative need for educational audiologists to help learners develop **self-advocacy skills**, and also looks at issues unique to **adult learners**.

Important Differences!

Students need to know that their basic rights as persons with disabilities do not change when they leave high school and enter college. However, conventional special education support systems do not exist for them in college. Instead of depending on a team of specialists—who perform tests, make recommendations, and ensure that services are provided—students in college must take the initiative in obtaining services. They must identify themselves to the appropriate office on campus, and be specific in requesting the services that they need to succeed in school. Many high-school students indicate that they do not have these self-advocacy skills when they leave high school.

LEGISLATION MANDATING ACCESS TO COLLEGE

Until World War I, postsecondary education for adults with disabilities was relatively rare (Stone, 1983). PL 65-178, the Vocational Rehabilitation Act of 1918, offered vocational services to veterans who had disabilities as a result of that war. This legislation was the first in this century to address the interests of citizens with disabilities, although limiting the support to vocational services.

With the Serviceman's Readjustment Act of 1944 (the so-called "GI Bill," PL 78-346) came the opportunity for college education for all veterans, with and without disabilities. Support for students with disabilities in the area of higher education culminated in PL 93-112, the Rehabilitation Act of 1973, which superseded all previous vocational rehabilitation legislation.

Section 504

PL 93-112, the Rehabilitation Act of 1973, provided legal protection from discrimination for persons with disabilities. (This legislation was reauthorized in 1986 [PL 99-506] and in 1992 [PL 102-569].) Section 504 of PL 93-112 is known as the "civil rights act for the handicapped" (Lewis & Doorlag, 1991, p. 10). In fact, the language of Section 504 is patterned after, and is almost identical to, the anti-discrimination language of Section 601 of the Civil Rights Act of 1964 (Fonosch, 1980; "Legal foundations," 1992; Scotch, 1984).

Section 504, PL 93-112, the Rehabilitation Act of 1973:

No otherwise qualified handicapped individual in the United States, as defined in section 7(6), shall, solely by reason of his handicap, be excluded from the participation in, be denied the benefits of, or be subjected to discrimination under any program or activity receiving Federal financial assistance. (*Federal Register*, 1973, p. 394)

This single sentence has had enormous impact on the lives of citizens with disabilities. In the context of higher education, because virtually all public colleges and universities receive federal assistance, institutions are required to comply with Section 504 of the Rehabilitation Act. It has been estimated that Section 504 protects the rights of 10.5% (1.3 million) of the 12.5 million students enrolled in postsecondary institutions who report having at least one disability (Greene & Zimbler, 1989; Rothstein, 1991).

Section 504 of PL 93-112 originally defined a "handicapped individual" only with respect to employment. However, in 1974, Congress amended PL 93-112 so that the definition considered education as well. The amended act defined disabled persons as "any person who: 1) has a physical or mental impairment which substantially limits one or more major life activities, 2) has a record of such an impairment, or 3) is regarded as having such an impairment" (Sherman & Zirkel, 1980, p. 331). Any student previously identified as having a disability during kindergarten through twelfth grade is considered to be protected by Section 504 (Ballard & Zettel, 1977; Fonosch, 1980; Lynch & Lewis, 1988; White, Karchmer, Armstrong, & Bezozo, 1983).

The Rehabilitation Act also provides a definition of "otherwise qualified handicapped individuals." According to Blackburn and Iovacchini (1982), a qualified handicapped college applicant is one "who meets the academic and technical standards requisite to admission or participation in the program" (p. 210). Note the important differences in these definitions: Academic standards include indicators of academic ability, such as grade-point average, high school rank, and standardized test scores. Technical standards refer to "all nonacademic admissions criteria that are absolutely necessary for a student to successfully complete a program of study" (O'Brien & Ross, 1981, p. 29–30).

Impact of Section 504 on College Students with HI

Section 504 is the civil rights component of rehabilitation legislation that mandates that all programs that receive federal funding must comply with the provisions of the Rehabilitation Act. No age restrictions apply to individuals under section 504, in contrast to the birth–21 age restriction in IDEA. Section 504 also covers individuals who do not meet the educational stipulations of IDEA. For example, if an individual's disability does not directly compromise academic performance (i.e., requiring use of a wheelchair, ramps, and accessible bathrooms), installation of needed accommodations may not be provided under IDEA. Such needed accommodations would, however, be required to be provided under Section 504 (Adams, 1993; Scott, 1991).

Section 504 prohibits discrimination in *six aspects* of higher education: recruitment, testing, admissions, academic adjustments, auxiliary aids, and funding. The following sections discuss each concern with respect to the learner with HI.

Recruitment   Inquiry regarding the existence of a student's disability before admission to a college is prohibited. Only after a student has been admitted can a college make inquiries, and then only for the purposes of accommodating the needs of the student. Students with disabilities often are not aware of this important aspect of their civil rights. While in elementary and secondary schools, students' special needs are protected by IDEA and must be identified and served by the schools. Because institutions of higher learning have no responsibility to identify students with disabilities, **the burden of responsibility shifts to students, who must now actively seek assistance** by making special needs known to the appropriate administrators. Students in high school often are not advised of the differences in the laws affecting colleges while they are in transition from high school to higher education (DuBow, Geer, & Strauss, 1992; Fairweather & Shaver, 1990; Hull, 1979; Office of Civil Rights, 1989; Patterson & Schmidt, 1992; Stone, 1983).

Testing   Admissions testing may not include any test or criteria for admission that disproportionately affects persons with disabilities. In other words, the test must "reflect an applicant's aptitude . . . not the applicant's handicap" (Putnam, 1984, p. 83). Examples of accommodation in standardized admissions testing include revised editions of the Scholastic Aptitude Test (SAT), which are untimed and include services such as sign language interpreters, audio versions of the test, and readers for persons with visual disabilities. Results of tests administered with accommodations are reported as nonstandardized, and colleges and universities are not informed of the nature of the accommodation.

Admissions   Individuals with disabilities cannot be refused admission to a college based on the disability alone. In addition, colleges are prohibited from applying quotas or limitations on the number of students with disabilities to be admitted. There are exceptions to this policy, where public health and safety are considered to take precedence over the rights of a student with disabilities. Admissions policies to professional programs may have such restrictions. For example, the 1979 Supreme Court decision regarding *Southeastern Community College v. Davis* determined that the inability of a nursing student with HI to speechread or understand the muffled speech of supervisors and physicians who wore surgical masks put the safety of patients at risk. Davis was therefore denied admission to a nursing program, the Court concluding that Davis's disability "actually prevents her from safely performing in both her training program and her proposed profession" (DuBow et al., 1992, p. 94). This is an application of a nonacademic or technical standard as an admission criterion mentioned in the previous section in regard to the otherwise qualified handicapped individual, as identified in Section 504.

Academic Adjustments Colleges are not required to make substantial allowances in academic standards for students with disabilities, but colleges must allow equal opportunity for a student with a disability to benefit from the program, without being segregated from other students or limiting participation (DuBow et al., 1992). Adjustments that allow equal opportunity to benefit from the program may include substitution of specific courses, lengthening the time acceptable for completion of courses or degree requirements, and adaptations in the way that specific courses are conducted. For example, learners with HI have substituted an art history class for music to meet a fine arts requirement. In addition, instructors cannot impose rules that would limit the participation of a student with a disability in the class. For example, an instructor could not prohibit use of tape recorders, or refuse to wear an FM microphone. Universities must inform students of their rights to academic adjustments, but it is the student's responsibility to request these adjustments.

Auxiliary Aids Support services such as sign language interpreters, notetakers, taped texts, and readers are to be provided when determined necessary by the student and college. The college is required to inform all students of the availability of support services, as well as the name of the director or coordinator of these services. An exemplary program might provide the following auxiliary aids:

> Help with registration, classroom changes, testing accommodations, notetakers, interpreters, tape recorders and other assistive devices, laboratory assistance, orientation, referrals and follow-up. [It] also assists disabled students in obtaining dormitory modifications, special parking permits, transportation, medical consultation, academic counseling, library assistance, and special financial aid considerations. (Albert & Fairweather, 1990, p. 446)

Funding Costs of aids such as those mentioned in the previous section are not charged to the student or his or her parents or guardians. Often, costs are shared by the state office of vocational rehabilitation or other agencies, but the university has ultimate responsibility for these expenses (DuBow et al., 1992).

Civil Rights of College Students with HI and Other Disabilities

To help individuals with HI and other disabilities understand their rights as college students, the Office of Civil Rights, U.S. Department of Education developed a helpful brochure. Following are some highlights of that document.

> Section 504 applies to all recipients of federal financial assistance from the Department of Education. Recipients include state education agencies, elementary and secondary school systems, colleges and universities, and state vocational rehabilitation agencies. . . .
> Postsecondary institutions receiving federal assistance have specific obligations with regard to handicapped students:

- Handicapped students must be afforded an equal opportunity to participate in and benefit from all postsecondary education programs and activities, including education programs and activities not operated wholly by the recipient.

- Handicapped students must be afforded the opportunity to participate in any course, course of study, or other part of the education program or activity offered by the recipient.
- All programs and activities must be offered in the most integrated setting appropriate.
- Academic requirements must be modified, on a case by case basis, to afford qualified students with disabilities an equal educational opportunity. For example, modifications may include changes in the length of time permitted for completion of degree requirements. However, academic requirements that the recipient [college] can demonstrate are essential will not be regarded as discriminatory.
- A recipient may not impose upon handicapped students rules that have the effect of limiting their participation in the recipient's educational program or activity; for example, prohibiting tape recorders in the classrooms or guide dogs in campus buildings.
- Students with impaired sensory, manual, or speaking skills must be provided auxiliary aids, such as taped texts, interpreters, readers, and classroom equipment adapted for persons with manual impairments.
- Handicapped students must have an equal opportunity to benefit from comparable, convenient, and accessible recipient housing, at the same cost as it is available to others.
- Handicapped students must have an equal opportunity to benefit from financial assistance. A recipient may not, on the basis of handicap, provide less assistance than is provided to nondisabled persons, limit eligibility for assistance, or otherwise discriminate. . . .
- Handicapped students must have an equal opportunity to benefit from programs that provide assistance in making outside employment available to students.
- Students with disabilities must be provided an equal opportunity to participate in intercollegiate, club, and intramural athletics.
- Students with disabilities must be provided counseling and placement services in a nondiscriminatory manner. (U.S. Department of Education, 1987, pp. 5–8)

Although the rights stated above have been protected since 1973, students with HI **still** face difficulties based on a lack of understanding of their abilities by college administrators, faculty, and staff. Consider the following student:

"I am a 27-year-old male undergraduate with a severe hearing impairment. I am majoring in engineering and have worked **hard** for my 3.7 grade point average. For a foreign language requirement, I took French 1 last semester, and just barely pulled off a B in the class. It was just so hard to learn the nuances of the language, even when wearing two powerful hearing aids. I discussed the problem with my advisor, and proposed the following accommodation: to take an anthropology class in place of French 2. My advisor got approval from the foreign language department, and I registered for classes.

Imagine how I felt when the Dean wrote to say he would not approve this request! I made an appointment to discuss this with him, and he said that I was 'hiding behind my handicap' to avoid a hard class that would pull down my grade-point average. I felt like a little kid being reprimanded for something I didn't do. Because I do fairly well in conversation with my hearing aids, he has no idea how hard it is to learn with this hearing loss. He would not even consider changing his mind, and now I have to spend valuable time and energy figuring out how to get legal help. It should never have come to this."
(J.J., August, 1992)

CURRENT CHALLENGE: FROM ACCESS TO FULL INCLUSION

Even with guaranteed rights and support services, the dropout rate among college students with hearing impairment is very high. A model has been developed that examines the longitudinal process of a student's decision to withdraw from college. In the following section, the model of the process by which a student decides to leave college is detailed. Then, the model is applied to college students with HI.

Why Students Leave College: Tinto's Model

In his discussion of student departure from college, Tinto (1987) made several observations. First, 41 of every 100 first-year college students depart the higher education system without earning a college degree. Second, the reasons for departure have until recently been attributed solely to students. Researchers have suggested personality issues, levels of motivation, and degree of maturity to account for student departure. Some characteristics found in past literature have described withdrawing students as aloof, assertive, critical, disagreeable, immature, impulsive, impetuous, nonconforming, with minimal introspective abilities, and with unclear career and educational goals (Cope, 1975; Edwards, Cangemi & Kowalski, 1990; Higgerson, 1985).

These approaches, claimed Tinto (1987), "invariably see student departure as reflecting a weakness or flaw in the individual. Leaving is, in this view, a personal failure on the part of the individual to measure up to the many demands of college life" (p. 87). Tinto contended that, in fact, "there is little evidence to support the notion that there is a unique personality profile" (p. 78) that differentiates the student who leaves from the one who stays.

A third point Tinto made was to caution against indiscriminate use of the term "dropout" for persons who do not complete college. Past research narrowly defined a dropout as a person who failed to obtain a degree at one institution within 4 years (Astin, 1975). Research has not adequately distinguished students who transfer to other institutions (institutional departure), those who leave temporarily (stopouts), and those who leave permanently (system departure). In addition, permanent departure takes several forms. For some students, leaving is a positive action, if they determine that staying no longer serves their best interests. Some students enroll in college with no intention of completing a degree, but enter for personal enrichment or to continue education within their area of employment. Finally, there are students whose goal is to earn a degree but who leave college because of "difficulty meeting the academic requirements and/or establishing membership in the social communities of the institution" (Tinto, 1987, p. 133). Only this last group of students, if they perceive their leaving as failure, should be considered to be dropouts.

A Theoretical Model of Student Departure

Having made these observations, Tinto indicated the need for a theoretical model that might describe the process of student withdrawal from higher education. He considered a study by Durkheim (1951), which closely examined the process of ultimate departure—suicide. One form of suicide Durkheim identified is egotistical suicide and it is described by Tinto as:

that form of suicide that arises when individuals are unable to become integrated and establish membership within the communities of society. Durkheim referred to **two forms of integration—social and intellectual**—through which membership may be brought about. The former refers to that form of integration which results from personal affiliations and from the day-to-day interactions among different members of society. The latter comes from the sharing of values which are held in common by other members of the society. (p. 101, emphasis added)

Tinto saw in this description of egotistical suicide a basis for an analogy for student departure from college. To follow this analogy, student integration within a college community occurs on two levels as well. The extent of the student's academic integration is a function of his or her academic performance and level of intellectual development. The student's social integration is affected primarily by the quality of peer-group interaction and by the quality of the student's interactions with faculty (Pascarella & Terenzini, 1980).

Integration of Students into College Academic and Social Systems

As identified earlier, students may leave college because they are unable to maintain minimum academic requirements; that is, they fail to successfully integrate with the academic system of their college. However, these students account for only 15% of student departures from college. **The remaining 85% of the 41% of students who leave college do so in good academic standing.** In other words, while succeeding academically, the majority of withdrawing students do not perceive themselves as part of the social system of the college. When this need for social integration or community is not met, students are more likely to withdraw from college because "some degree of social *and* intellectual integration must exist as a condition for continued persistence" (Tinto, 1987, p. 119, emphasis added).

Figure 8.1 depicts Tinto's (1987) model of student withdrawal that has been discussed. Student withdrawal is seen as a process that occurs over time. Upon entry to college, the strength of a student's educational intentions, and of his or her commitment to the institution and the goal of obtaining a degree, interact with characteristics of the individual student (pre-entry attributes) to influence the quality of academic and social integration and early goals and commitments (T1). The extent of academic and social integration affects continuing the development of the student's goals and commitments across time (T2). External commitments, such as family and employment responsibilities outside of school, may influence the strength of goal commitments.

Tinto suggested that, as goal commitment increases during this process, there is a corresponding increase in the likelihood of persisting in college. If some degree of personal interaction **in both the academic and social systems** does not occur, a student's commitment to the college and to the goal of a degree weakens, and then he or she is more likely to decide to leave college.

Application of Tinto's Theory of Attrition to Students With HI

Walter and Welsh (1986) pointed out that research has not adequately addressed the high attrition rate of students with disabilities. These researchers considered Tinto's model of persistence and withdrawal and suggested that, "while the intent of the law to provide access is being met, the question still exists whether handi-

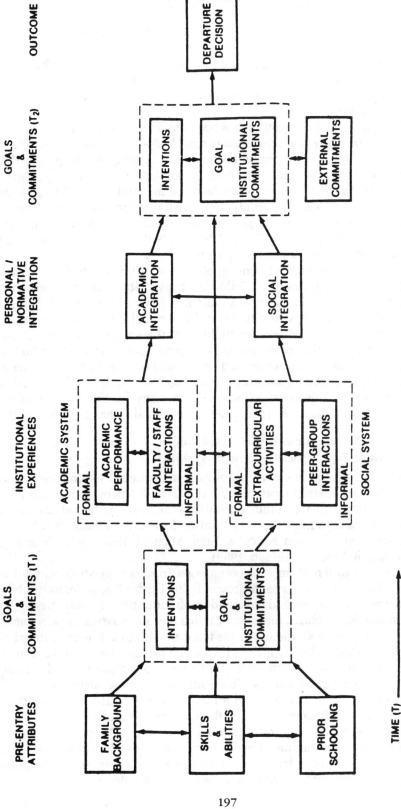

Figure 8.1. A model of institutional departure. (From Tinto, V. [1987]. *Leaving college: Rethinking the causes and cures of student attrition*, p. 114. Chicago: University of Chicago Press; reprinted by permission.) T1, time before institutional experiences; T2, time after institutional experiences.

capped individuals continue to remain isolated both socially and educationally from the mainstream" (p. 6).

Social isolation is a valid concern for students with HI. Research indicates that students with hearing impairment are often lonely in college. Typically, students with HI do not have a supportive and nurturing college community of students and faculty (Nash, 1988).

Incomplete social integration has been observed among deaf and hard of hearing students in many mainstream settings. A deaf adult expressed this circumstance eloquently: "A deaf person is more alone among hearing people than he is when being alone" (Jacobs, 1980, p. 22). The use of sign language interpreters, while facilitating the ability to follow lectured material, can still impede personal communication, as well as participation in group discussion. Deaf students typically report a sense of feeling left out of the college experience without a contingent of other deaf students (Foster & Brown, 1989; Patterson, Sedlacek, & Scales, 1988; Saur, Popp-Stone, & Hurley-Lawrence, 1987).

Persons who are hard of hearing also express this sense of social isolation, stemming from the difficulty of following conversations in many environments, particularly in noisy places and in animated group discussion (Flexer, Wray, & Leavitt, 1990). Consider virtually any college social setting—the cafeteria, hallways, student union—which has highly reverberant listening conditions, with HVAC systems and other noise sources competing with speech. Smaller and more intimate social settings (restaurants, dorm rooms) provide better acoustics but also more speakers to attend to, and conversation moves quickly. Students who are hard of hearing are not likely to participate in discussions that they cannot follow (Berg, Blair, Viehweg, & Wilson-Vlotman, 1986; Flexer et al., 1990; Saur et al., 1987).

The Effects of Academic and Social Isolation on the College Experiences of Students with HI

In many studies of students with disabilities, the issue of isolation does not emerge. Jarrow's (1987) extensive literature review indicated that, overall, student "status as disabled has little impact on their attitudes, adjustment, potential or goals" (p. 45). Other investigators indicated similar findings (Amsel & Fichten, 1990; Kriegsman & Hershonson, 1987; Kroeger & Scalia, 1988; Michael, 1986–1987; Penn & Dudley, 1980; Wiseman, Emry, & Morgan, 1988).

However, a different impression emerges from college students who are deaf and hard of hearing (e.g., Foster & Brown, 1989). Gracer (1989), for example, wrote a paper that recorded her experiences and frustrations through the course of a typical day at college. At the end of the day, she noted how her hearing impairment contributed to the tremendous exhaustion she felt every evening. She considered how her hearing impairment directly affected what she called "the isolation of my experience" (p. 28)—that is, the impression that no one on campus seemed to understand or care about her circumstances. She wondered why the institution had support systems for other groups, but none for her: "I think wistfully of the various people on campus, and professors who share their feelings. Our school even has academic departments devoted to their [other groups'] experiences. On such a socially involved and politically active campus, I feel surprisingly invisible and unique" (p. 28).

The experience of isolation can serve as a starting point for a vicious cycle revolving around student integration. A feeling of isolation can be detrimental to a healthy self-image, which, in turn, can thwart new efforts toward joining peers, which can further increase the sense of isolation (Farrugia & Austin, 1980). Many students with hearing impairment in mainstream settings, while physically integrated, live in virtual isolation because of barriers to communication with others. These students typically demonstrate a less developed self concept than their peers with normal hearing or with their peers with hearing impairment living in segregated settings. The positive variable missing in the mainstream setting appears to be adequate socialization, or "the process by which persons learn the culture of a society and become full participants" (Anderssen, 1988, p. 33).

IMPACT OF SUPPORT SERVICES ON THE
ACADEMIC AND SOCIAL INTEGRATION OF STUDENTS WITH HI

A recent study (English, 1993a) examined the college experiences of students with hearing impairment in relationship to Tinto's model of academic and social integration in college environments. Subjects in the study indicated that they felt highly integrated into the academic systems of their colleges, and that they were making good grades and were satisfied with their academic experiences. They were also strongly committed to the goal of earning a degree, and 93% indicated that earning a degree was important to them. However, they felt significantly less integrated into the social system of their colleges. Many reported a sense of isolation, loneliness, and difficulty making friends. Statistical analysis of these data supported the conclusion that these subjects were at risk of dropping out because of the lack of integration into the social life of their colleges.

Conventional academic support services were widely available, and were being utilized to some degree by virtually all subjects of the study. Support services were found to make a strong contribution to the student's academic integration. For example, notetakers and interpreters contributed to academic success. However, support services had no effect upon the level of social integration among the subjects. The usual array of support services such as notetakers, tutors, and amplification did not help students feel socially connected to the college or help them to develop some sense of community, or overcome the problems of loneliness and isolation. Wiseman et al. (1988) came to a similar conclusion: "If the disabled student feels alienated from the campus, [support services] will not be sufficient to ensure the student's retention in the university" (p. 266). As long as the typical supports provided to students with hearing impairment do not facilitate the development of an inclusive community or a student's sense of belonging, it can be assumed that the **letter** of Section 504 regarding access and nondiscrimination is being met while the **spirit** of inclusion and full participation has yet to be addressed. Typical support services are only a part of helping a student toward the goal of a degree. These academic supports are only part of what a student needs—support services must be provided that help students develop a sense of belonging to the college social system as well.

A New Role for Support Services

These findings clearly indicate that current support services at the college level are in need of revision and expansion. Supports to facilitate social integration are needed that encourage interpersonal relationships. Such support services would develop student support groups, faculty liaisons, and an interdepartmental network of faculty and staff to serve as contacts for students as they complete general education requirements. Important information about the development and effectiveness of support groups on campus for students with hearing impairment is readily available (Berg, 1972; Flexer et al., 1990; West et al., 1993). This is a new area of interest for educational audiologists, who are now becoming members of transition teams for students continuing their education.

The Carnegie Foundation for the Advancement of Teaching (1990) furthered the concept of social integration to the level of community-building. The foundation proposed the establishment of a "caring community" (p. 47) on the college campus, by integrating and engaging students at both the subgroup and institutional level: "As impossible as the goal may seem to be, a modern college or univesity should be a place where every individual feels affirmed and where every activity of the community is humane. Caring is the key" (p. 47).

This need to be part of a community may be particularly important to college students with hearing impairment. Deaf students who interact frequently within their subculture (other deaf peers) have demonstrated a high level of persistence in college (Stinson, Scherer, & Walter, 1987). The value of such a "critical mass" is mentioned by Tinto: "The persistence of minority groups often hinges upon there being a sufficiently large number of similar types of students on campus with whom to form a viable community" (1987, pp. 58–59). The size of the deaf population has been found to be the most important factor for deaf students in choosing a postsecondary program (Innes, 1985). While the value of the critical mass of the Deaf community has been recognized for years, it is unknown how students who are hard of hearing perceive a sense of community as a need. However, we can expect that one student (Flexer et al., 1990) spoke for many others when she said, "Once I understood that I was not alone in the world with a hearing loss, [the support group] was the only thing that helped me through college" (p. 179).

These observations regarding social integration are not meant to minimize the wide range of other difficulties faced by college students with HI. Flexer et al. (1990) reported that students typically enter college with little or no information regarding their legal rights as students (under Section 504), sources of financial assistance, available support services, or even the operation of their personal hearing aids. Because of cumulative language deficits, students with HI are often ill-prepared to meet college reading, writing, and math requirements. The same difficulties that students experienced in high school become all the more challenging with the demands of college.

HOW EDUCATIONAL AUDIOLOGISTS SUPPORT
COLLEGE LEARNERS: STUDENTS AS SELF-ADVOCATES

For students going to college, the ability to advocate for one's education may be as important to success as strong study habits and the commitment to earning a college degree. Most students do not know their legal rights or the range of services that are required to be available for them (Flexer, Wray, Black, & Millin, 1987). As one student with a disability observed, "It took me over a year to find out there were services to help me on this campus" (West et al., 1993, p. 463). A recent study (English, 1993b) indicated that college students with hearing impairment receive services at lower rates than they do at elementary and high school levels. Directors of services for students with disabilities from 28 4-year public universities reported that 158 first- and second-year students identified themselves as having hearing impairment and needing services. Enrollment information collected from *Peterson's Guide to Four-Year Colleges* (1992) indicated that these 28 universities had more than 150,000 first- and second-year students enrolled. Therefore, extrapolated from these data was the conclusion that only **.1%** of the first- and second-year student population sought services to accommodate their hearing impairment. Yet, as we learned at the beginning of the chapter, conservatively 2.7% of the college population are estimated to have hearing impairment. While a large number of college students may not require services, the high attrition rate (71%) of college students with HI strongly suggests that a large number do need services and are not requesting them. However, colleges are not legally underserving their students; given the constraints of Section 504, colleges can serve only students who request assistance. Rather, the conclusion must be that the majority of students are under-serving themselves by not actively seeking out services on their own.

Self-Advocacy Skills

When participating as a member of a transition planning team for college-bound students with HI, the educational audiologist should ensure that skills that enable the student to self-advocate are incorporated in the transition plan. These skills are necessarily selected based on the individual needs of each student (Olmstead, 1990); however, Figure 8.2 outlines the basic focus of a self-advocacy skills curriculum: be informed, be assertive, be persistent.

ADDRESSING THE CONCERNS OF ADULT LEARNERS

Conventional perceptions of college students include the characteristic of youth; that is, the college student from 18 to 24 years of age. However, the reality is being redefined with the increasing numbers of adult learners (i.e., age 25 and older) who are attending college. Demographers predict that by the year 2000, the dominant age group on college campuses will be composed of individuals from 34 to 44 years of age (Burnham, 1982). The growing trend of lifelong learning has been described as an effort to stay current with the knowledge explosion and the needs of an emerging learning society. The term "blended life plan" suggests that work, education, and leisure are more likely to be concurrent, rather than alternating, parts of a life (Cross, 1981).

Educational Audiology and Adult Learners

Educational audiologists are interested in the concerns of adult learners for two reasons: First, it is known that students with disabilities are typically older than the traditional college student. Greene and Zimbler (1989) reported that:

> Postsecondary students who reported disabilities tended to be older than those students who do not report disabilities. For instance, 33% of the handicapped students enrolled in the fall of 1986 were 30 years old or older, but only 24% of the non-handicapped students were in the age group. (p. v)

Are You Ready for College? Is College Ready for You? These skills will help you succeed:

Know your disability. Be able to describe your audiogram and its implications in terms of degree, slope, and severity of impairment in each ear. Know if your hearing impairment has changed over time and, if so, what the likely prognosis is that the impairment will continue to change. Be able to explain the benefits and limitations of your hearing aid; be confident that you can troubleshoot minor problems and find out where to go if you cannot. Be sure you know what kind of batteries you need and where to buy more.

Know your rights. Read and become familiar with the resource books *Legal rights: The guide for deaf and hard of hearing people* (Dubow et al., 1992) and *How the student with hearing loss can succeed in college: A handbook for students, families, and professionals* (Flexer et al., 1990). Learn how Section 504 of PL 93-112, the Rehabilitation Act of 1973 protects and defines your rights.

Decide what you need to succeed in school. Learn about **all** support services, not just the services you have used or the services your college says are available. Try supports you have never had before and find out if they help you.

Determine who is authorized to assist you. Every campus, no matter how large or small, must have a person responsible for providing services for students with disabilities. Typically, this administrator's title includes some variation of "Director of Services for Students with Disabilities." Meet with that person as soon as you arrive and often thereafter.

Seek out social support. Sometimes you may find yourself feeling apart from social activities, or struggling on your own with no one to talk to. The stress of college work, papers, and cramming for exams gets to everybody! The Director of Services for Students with Disabilities may be just the person to turn to for help. If not, try the university or college speech-language pathologist, the department of audiology or of the education of the hearing impaired, and ask for help in developing a support/social group for other students with hearing impairment if one does not exist. Persons with HI who have graduated from college **strongly** advise that you do not try to go it alone.

Persist until you are satisfied! You are the person who must make most things happen in your life. If you do not get help with the problem you are having, try another person, another approach, another suggestion. Look for books in local libraries on how to develop self-assertiveness. This is your education—don't compromise!

Figure 8.2. Self-advocacy skills curriculum.

Second, adult learners, by virtue of their age alone, are more likely to have a hearing impairment (National Center for Health Statistics, 1981; Shewan, 1990). Adult learners may have acquired a hearing impairment relatively recently, and so may not be familiar with the challenge of formal education with a hearing loss. Adult learners with early onset or congenital hearing impairment are likely to have received few or no services in high school (Ross, Brackett, & Maxon, 1982), and so have no experience in seeking out and requesting appropriate services.

Literature addressing the concerns of adult learners has focused on the differences in learning and teaching approaches necessary for these learners. Because the practice of teaching children is termed "pedagogy"—a transmittal of knowledge in the basic skills of reading, writing, and arithmetic—Knowles (1970) developed the concept of **andragogy**, which is the art and science of *helping* an adult, as a colleague, continue to learn. This concept prompted an approach for teaching adults that was different from the directive and controlling approach to teaching children (pedagogy). Adults bring to each learning experience a broad background of experiences, and a particular learning opportunity becomes another thread in the already-rich tapestry of their experiences. Learning for adult learners is typically self-directed and intrinsically motivating (Brookfield, 1986; Knowles, 1970; Werring, 1987). In the following section, more specific characteristics and concerns of adult learners are described.

General Characteristics of Adult Learners

Being older than the typical college student is just the beginning of the differences that distinguish the adult learner. Other qualitative differences include the following. 1) Adult learners have a clear purpose motivating their choice of coursework or degree goals. Even courses taken for self-enrichment are expected to meet specific needs of the adult learner (McWhinney, 1990). 2) Adult learners have an interest in getting their money's worth from their college experience. Adult learners typically pay their own fees and tuition, and view coursework as an investment in order to justify these costs. 3) Adult learners have more demands on their time. Other commitments may take priority over their coursework. Family responsibilities, in particular, take precedence when necessary; in addition, most adult learners are employed full time and must accommodate to those demands as well. In spite of juggling so many responsibilities, adult learners report studying more hours per week than traditional college-age students (Iovacchini, Hall, & Hengstler, 1985; Werring, 1987). Adult learners often experience some stress about attending school, partly because of societal expectations of attention to other commitments, because they have relatively few peers with whom to relate, and because they feel some ambivalence regarding their abilities to meet the demands of college work (Brookfield, 1986; Claus, 1986; Flannery, 1986; Iovacchini, et al., 1985; Richter-Antion, 1986). 4) Adult learners are more actively engaged in the learning process, and are more likely to challenge their instructors rather than assume a passive role. With a background of life experiences, adult learners see the instructor as a peer who can facilitate learning. As actively engaged students, adult learners are more likely to perceive learning as **praxis**, which is the continuous process of activity, reflection upon the activity, and initiation of a new activity. This process engages the adult learner alternately in action and investigation (Brookfield, 1986).

More Research Is Needed

There is a rich body of literature regarding the concerns of adult learners, but virtually no data are yet available to inform us about the experiences of adult learners with HI in college. It is an area open for investigation, and it is likely to receive more attention as the population of adult learners continues to grow.

CONCLUSION

In this chapter, we have examined issues in higher education that have, until very recently, been beyond the scope of services that an educational audiologist provided. However, these concerns are logical extensions when considering the current realities of the continuum of learning experience. Until educational audiology services are directly provided on college campuses, practitioners must capitalize on the opportunity to provide transitional supports to all college-bound high-school students with HI.

An Open Letter to [University of Pittsburgh] Faculty

I am the deaf woman in your class. You know, the one who always has an interpreter in tow. I am the one with the hearing aid that you can't see unless my hair is pulled back, and a useless cochlear implant that you also can't see.

I am the one at whom you look with such skepticism, because I speak, lipread and guess so well that without being told that I am deaf you never would know. I hardly look the part, do I? (Whatever that part is supposed to look like.)

Many of you look at me perplexed, or with annoyance or frustration. Sometimes you say and do things that hurt and bother me, or that indicate disbelief in my "handicap" or the difficulties associated with it. Sometimes you even make me feel that you wonder why I bothered to come to school.

Years ago, when I first went to college, I had much more hearing than I do now. But even then I had problems making people understand what I could do and what I couldn't. Three times I was called in to an administrator's office and told that they didn't want a deaf woman in their department. Needless to say, I got discouraged after three years of this and quit school. I was too young to realize the importance of finishing my education, and I ended up getting shuttled into a field where I couldn't get a job.

When I started losing most of my remaining hearing a couple of years ago, I knew I had to finish college or spend my life doing menial work. I thought that with the passage of time things would be different. People are so much more patient and accepting now, especially the younger generation. But every semester for the past three years, I have encountered at least one teacher who has a major problem with what I am trying to accomplish, and others who just tolerate me, at best.

I didn't choose to get a degree in what would be easiest for me; I chose to go into something I thought was needed, and that would ensure my getting hired despite my "handicap." I chose an area in which I have had to catch up because of what I missed in high school (before the use of interpreters was encouraged and when most deaf students mainstreamed in public schools were ignored). I picked up American Sign Language as a second language two years ago, specifically to have a way to get through school should my hearing fail, as it now is doing. I was even so desperate to finish that I underwent an experimental operation [cochlear implantation], which not only did not work on my congenitally deaf ear but has made me ill as well. Despite this, I have survived three semesters with decent grades.

I really try not to ask for too much. I work hard, stay up late, get up early and drive an hour to and from school daily, in addition to taking care of my family. I make arrangements for my interpreters, for notetakers, and try hard not to ask for special favors from you. All I ask is a little patience, a little respect for something that is very difficult. Don't make light of my signing, or assume that I don't really need it. Go to a class yourself with earplugs in your ears, and try to lipread a teacher who is moving around or facing a blackboard.

Please don't treat me as if I am "deaf and dumb"; that label went out years ago because it's not true. If I ask for help with notes, please don't accuse me of dishonesty or plagiarism. If my interpreter asks if she should be there for a test, don't tell her no, and then give a half-hour lecture on the day of the exam and expect me to hear it. It just doesn't work that way.

If you turn out the lights for a slide presentation, be aware that I won't get a word of what you say, nor will I be able to understand my interpreter in the dark. If I ask you to repeat something or for extra material, please don't sigh and act impatient with me. I am not trying to make you do extra work; I am just trying to understand. I only want the grades that I've earned, not the ones that I don't deserve. If I don't do well, I will do it over, just as everyone else does.

Thank heaven for those rare faculty members who voluntarily offer me their notes, who write the key points on projector transparencies and put them aside so I can catch up later, who bring a flashlight so I won't be in the dark, who don't hesitate to spend some extra time helping me learn, who take me seriously but with a sense of humor, and who view me as an interesting challenge rather than a problem. These teachers realize that the extra time and attention they are giving me does not give me an unfair advantage, but merely a fair chance.

Don't hold my lack of hearing against me. I didn't ask for it, but I also am not apologizing for it. Please let me finish school this time and, more importantly, help me to learn. (Sadler. [1993]. *University Times, 25* [12], p. 2; reprinted by permission.)

Learning the Language

To best serve students in higher education, it is imperative to be able to use the language of the field. Review the following vocabulary and concepts, and discuss with a colleague.

- Access versus inclusion/integration
- Section 504
- Academic adjustments
- Auxiliary aids/support services
- Tinto's model of student departure
- Stopout, dropout, and institutional departure
- Academic and social integration
- Self-advocacy
- Andragogy versus pedagogy

Educational Audiology in Action
Suggested Learning Activities

Project 1. Contact a local college or university and ask for an interview with the Director of Services for Students with Disabilities. Find out the number of students with HI on campus and the types of services provided. Find out if there is a tracking system to determine the dropout, stopout, transfer, and graduation rates of these students. If so, how do these rates compare to statistics found in the literature? Is there a support group on campus, and if so, how does it operate?

Project 2. Ask the director to arrange an interview with a small group of students. Collect information from them regarding their experiences. What advice can they share with incoming students? Do students feel they have a voice in policy development and other decisions that affect them?

Project 3. Contact SHHH: Self-Help for Hard of Hearing People (see Resources for information). Find out the procedure to establish a chapter on a college campus or community. What requirements do they have? What expertise can they share? How many college students belong to SHHH?

Project 4. Develop a questionnaire designed to measure a student's knowledge of rights for students with disabilities, appropriate academic adjustments, and support services that are addressed in Section 504. Pilot your questionnaire with a small group of college-bound high school seniors with HI. How did they respond compared to findings in the literature? Would these students benefit from self-advocacy training?

Resources

SHHH: Self Help for Hard of Hearing People, Inc. (SHHH)
7800 Wisconsin Avenue
Bethesda, MD 20814
(301) 657-2248 (voice)
(301) 657-2249 (text telephone)

This organization publishes a bi-monthly magazine that helps persons who are hard of hearing to develop self-advocacy skills. Members can attend information meetings of local chapters across the country and a national annual conference. Individual membership is $24 per year.

HEATH: Higher Education and the Handicapped Resource Center
American Council on Education
One Dupont Circle
Washington, DC 20036-1193
(800) 544-3284 (voice & text telephone)

This organization provides information on educational support services, adaptations, and opportunities in colleges, universities, vocational and technical schools, and adult education programs through brochures, directories, fact sheets, and newsletters.

Recommended Readings

College Students with Hearing Impairment

DuBow, S., Geer, S., & Strauss, K. (1992). *Legal rights: The guide for deaf and hard of hearing people* (4th ed.). Washington, DC: Gallaudet University Press.

The newest edition of this valuable resource contains vital information for students "leaving the nest" of high school. Chapter 5 specifically covers issues in post-secondary education, describing pertinent court decisions in basic, easy-to-understand terms. Other chapters discuss adult issues in life for high school students, such as health care, social services, employment, and telecommunication accommodations.

Flexer, C., Wray, D., & Leavitt, P. (1990). *How the student with hearing loss can succeed in college: A handbook for students, families and professionals.* Washington, DC: Alexander Graham Bell Association.

This book is recommended as a valuable resource to help educational audiologists support the transition of students from high school to college. The chapters provide comprehensive information for students who do not know how to interpret their audiograms, or to request options available in hearing aids and other assistive technologies, or to assert their legal rights. Readers can learn about the effects of noise in a typical classroom and strategies to address this and other learning problems. Chapter 15, aptly titled "The Real Experts Speak," is written by college students who share their personal experiences, frustrations, and lessons learned. This highly readable and informative book is written for the general reader.

Adult Learners

Brookfield, S. (1986). *Understanding and facilitating adult learning.* San Francisco: Jossey-Bass.

The author defines adult learning as a "transactional drama of interaction." Some principles of facilitating this interaction are developed in this book, which include recognizing that participation in learning for adults is voluntary and most satisfactory when collaborative.

Chapter 4 addresses the self-directed learner and supports the concept of a mix of independent work and group interaction as the most effective way to enhance adult learning. Facilitators of learning should view themselves as resources rather than as didactic instructors.

Cross, K. (1981). *Adults as learners.* San Francisco: Jossey-Bass.

This book well may be considered a classic of adult learning literature. The author discusses the concept of lifelong learning, with the accompanying necessity of restructuring the higher education system to accommodate this phenomenon. Chapter 5 is particularly interesting in its presentation of adult learning capabilities. For example, changes in the speed of learning, and changes in vision and hearing, have only minimal effects on learning abilities in the adult years. Self-perceptions of adults also change throughout their lives, and these changes do affect learning.

Knowles, M. (1970). *Modern practice of education: Andragogy versus pedagogy.* New York: Association Press.

This book is a seminal work in the field of adult education. Knowles describes four principles or assumptions of andragogy (helping adults learn): 1) as a person matures, his or her self-concept evolves from one of a dependent to one of an independent being; 2) he or she accumulates a rich background of experiences; 3) his or her interest in learning becomes more oriented to the development of social roles; and 4) his or her orientation to learning shifts from subject-centered to problem-centered. The author regards adult learning as the mutual responsibility of learner and teacher in the learning/teaching transaction.

References

Adams, R.C. (1993, October 11). Meeting special needs in education. *Advance*, p. 20.

Albert, J., & Fairweather, J. (1990). Effective organization of postsecondary services for students with disabilities. *Journal of College Student Development, 31*, 445–453.

Amsel, R., & Fichten, C. (1990). Interaction between disabled and nondisabled college students and their professors: A comparison. *Journal of Postsecondary Education and Disability, 8*, 125–140.

Anderssen, Y. (1988). Sociocultural implications of mainstream deaf undergraduate students. In K. Jursik (Ed.), *Proceedings of the Third Regional Conference on Postsecondary Education of Hearing Impaired Persons* (pp. 33–37). Knoxville, TN.

Astin, A. (1975). *Preventing students from dropping out*. San Francisco: Jossey-Bass.

Ballard, J., & Zettel, J. (1977). Public Law 94-142 and Section 504: What they say about rights and protections. *Exceptional Children, 44*, 177–184.

Berg, F. (1972). A model for a facilitative program for hearing impaired college students. *Volta Review, 87*, 87–93.

Berg, F., Blair, J., Viehweg, S., & Wilson-Vlotman, A. (1986). *Educational audiology for the hard of hearing child*. Orlando, FL: Grune & Stratton.

Blackburn, C., & Iovacchini, E. (1982). Student service responsibilities of institutions of learning disabled students. *College and University, 57*, 208–217.

Brookfield, S. (1986). *Understanding and facilitating adult learning*. San Francisco: Jossey-Bass.

Burnham, L. (1982). Adults: Not grown-up children. *Community and Junior College Journal, 53*(3), 22–26, 46.

Carnegie Foundation for the Advancement of Teaching. (1990). *Campus life: In search of community*. Lawrenceville, NJ: Princeton University Press.

Claus, J. (1986, April). *Adult students in community college: Learning to manage the learning process*. Paper presented at the American Education Research Association annual meeting, San Francisco.

Cope, R. (1975). *Revolving college doors: The causes and consequences of dropping out, stopping out and transferring*. New York: John Wiley & Sons.

Cross, K. (1981). *Adults as learners*. San Francisco: Jossey-Bass.

DuBow, S., Geer, S., & Strauss, K. (1992). *Legal rights: The guide for deaf and hard of hearing people*. Washington, DC: Gallaudet University Press.

Durkheim, E. (1951). *Suicide*. Translated by J.A. Spaulding & G. Simpson. Glencoe, IL: Free Press. (Originally published as *Le suicide: Etude de sociologie*. Paris: Felix Alcan.)

Edwards, M., Cangemi, J., & Kowalski, C. (1990). The college dropout and institutional responsibility. *Education, 111*(1), 107–116.

English, K. (1993a). *The role of support services in the integration and retention of college students who are hearing impaired*. Unpublished doctoral dissertation, San Diego State University and Claremont Graduate School.

English, K. (1993b). Students with learning impairment in higher education: A follow-up study. *Educational Audiology Association Monograph 3*, 27–31.

Fairweather, J., & Shaver, D. (1990). A troubled future? Participation in postsecondary education by youths with disabilities. *Journal of Higher Education, 61*, 332–347.

Farrugia, D., & Austin, G. (1980). A study of social-emotional adjustment patterns of hearing impaired students in different educational settings. *American Annals of the Deaf, 125*, 535–541.

Federal Register (1973, October 1). Public Law 93-113, Sec 504: Nondiscrimination under federal grants, p. 394.

Flannery, D. (1986, April). *Relationship between multiple adult roles, barriers to learning, and persistence/withdrawal for returning adult students.* Paper presented at the American Educational Research Association annual meeting, San Francisco.

Flexer, C., Wray, D., Black, T., & Millin, J. (1987). Amplification devices: Evaluating effectiveness for moderately hearing-impaired college students. *Volta Review, 89, 347–357.*

Flexer, C., Wray, D., & Leavitt, R. (1990). *How the student with hearing loss can succeed in college: A handbook for students, families and professionals.* Washington, DC: Alexander Graham Bell Association.

Fonosch, G. (1980). Three years later: The impact of Section 504 regulations on higher education. *Rehabilitation Literature, 41*(7–8), 162–168.

Foster, S., & Brown, P. (1989). Factors influencing the academic and social integration of hearing impaired college students. *Journal of Postsecondary Education and Disability, 7*(2), 78–96.

Gracer, B. (1989). WHAT? Chronicles of a college student. *SHHH, 10*(8), 26–28.

Greene, B., & Zimbler, L. (1989). *Profiles of handicapped students in postsecondary education, 1987: Survey Report* (Report No. CS 89-337). National Center for Education Statistics. (Available from Superintendent of Documents, U.S. Government Printing Office, Data series SP-NPSAS-86-87-10 Washington, DC 20402.)

Higgerson, M. (1985). Understanding why students voluntarily withdraw from college. *National Association of Student Personnel Administrators Journal, 23*(3), 15–21.

Hull, K. (1979). *The rights of physically handicapped people: The basic ACLU guide to a handicapped person's rights.* New York: Avon Books.

Innes, C. (1985). The national project on higher education for deaf students: Opinion survey. In J. Gardner (Ed.), *Proceedings of the 1985 Association of Handicapped Student Service Programs in Postsecondary Education Conference* (pp. 56–62). Atlanta, GA.

Iovacchini, E., Hall, L., & Hengstler, D. (1985). Going back to college: Some differences between adult students and traditional students. *College and University, 61*(1), 43–54.

Jacobs, L. (1980). *A deaf adult speaks out.* Washington, DC: Gallaudet College Press.

Jarrow, J. (1987). Integration of individuals with disabilities in higher education: A review of the literature. *Journal of Postsecondary Education and Disability, 5*(2), 38–57.

Knowles, M. (1970). *More practices of adult education: Andragogy versus pedagogy.* New York: Association Press.

Kriegsman, K., & Hershonson, D. (1987). A comparison of able-bodied and disabled college students on Erikson's ego stages and Maslow's needs levels. *Journal of College Student Personnel, 28*(1), 43–53.

Kroeger, S., & Scalia, V. (1988, Winter). Adjustment, performance, and involvement of college students with disabilities. *NASPA Journal* [National Association of School Personnel Administrators], *26*, 137–142.

"Legal foundations." (1992). *TEACHING Exceptional Children, 25*(1), 74–76.

Lewis, R., & Doorlag, D. (1991). *Teaching special students in the mainstream* (3rd ed.). New York: Macmillan.

Lincoln, E. (1993, September). *The new transition requirement: What it means for special education professional practice.* Paper presented at the Tenth Annual Pacific Northwest Institute on Special Education and the Law, Yakima, WA.

Lynch, E., & Lewis, R. (Eds.).(1988). *Exceptional children and adults: An introduction to special education.* Glenview, IL: Scott, Foresman.

McWhinney, W. (1990). Education for the third quarter of life. *Journal of Continuing Higher Education, 38*(2), 14–20.

Michael, R. (1986–1987, Winter). Organizing to meet the needs of handicapped students. *Community College Review, 14,* 36–40.

Nash, K. (1988). Who will be attending postsecondary programs in the next decade? In K. Jursik (Ed.), *Proceedings of Third Regional Conference on Postsecondary Education of Hearing Impaired Persons* (pp. 92–102). Knoxville, TN.

National Center for Health Statistics. (1981). Prevalence of selected impairments, United States 1977. *Vital and Health Statistics, 10*(134), 8–11.

O'Brien, M., & Ross, K. (1981). 504 and admission: Making the law work for the applicant and the college. *College and University, 56,* 26–35.

DC: U.S. Department of Education (ERIC No. ED 292256).

Office of Civil Rights. (1989). *The civil rights of students with hidden disabilities under Section 504 of the Rehabilitation Act*. Washington, DC: U.S. Department of Education. (ERIC No. ED 309595).

Olmstead, G. (1990). Getting ready for college: The where, when and how of succeeding. In C. Flexer, D. Wray, & R. Leavitt (Eds.), *How the student with hearing loss can succeed in college* (pp. 97–111). Washington, DC: Alexander Graham Bell Association.

Pascarella, E., & Terenzini, P. (1980). Predicting freshman persistence and voluntary dropout decisions from a theoretical model. *Journal of Higher Education, 51*(1), 60–75.

Patterson, A., Sedlacek, W., & Scales, W. (1988). The other minority: Disabled student background and attitudes toward their university and its services. *Journal of Postsecondary Education and Disability, 6*(Winter), 86–94.

Patterson, K., & Schmidt, M. (1992). Preparing the college student with hearing loss for success. *Volta Review, 94*(1), 47–57.

Penn, J., & Dudley, D. (1980). The handicapped student: Problems and perceptions. *Journal of College Student Personnel, 21*, 354–357.

Peterson's guide to four-year colleges (22 ed.). (1992). Princeton, NJ: Peterson's Guide.

Putnam, M. (1984). Postsecondary education for learning disabled students: A review of the literature. *Journal of College Student Personnel, 25*, 68–75.

Rehabilitation Act of 1973, PL 93-112. (September 26, 1973). Title 29, U.S.C. 701 et seq: *U.S. Statutes at Large, 87*, 335–394.

Rehabilitation Act Amendments of 1986, PL 99-506. Title 29, U.S.C. 701 et seq: *U.S. Statutes at Large, 100*, 1807–1846.

Rehabilitation Act Amendments of 1992, PL 102-569. (October 29, 1992). Title 29, U.S.C. 701 et seq: *U.S. Statutes at Large, 100*, 4344–4488.

Richter-Antion, D. (1986). Qualitative differences between adult and younger students. *NASPA Journal, 23*(3), 58–62.

Ross, M., Brackett, D., & Maxon, A. (1982). *Hard-of-hearing children in regular schools*. Englewood Cliffs, NJ: Prentice Hall.

Rothstein, A. (1991). Students, staff and faculty with disabilities: Current issues for colleges and universities. *Journal of College and University Law, 17*, 471–482.

Sadler, K. (1993). An open letter to faculty. *University Times, 25*(12), p. 2.

Saur, R., Popp-Stone, M., & Hurley-Lawrence, E. (1987). The classroom participation of mainstreamed hearing-impaired college students. *Volta Review, 89*, 277–286.

Scholastic Aptitude Test (SAT). (Available from College Board SAT Program, PO Box 6200, Princeton, NJ 08541.)

Scotch, K. (1984). *From good will to civil rights: Transforming federal disability policy*. Philadelphia: Temple University Press.

Scott, S. (1991). A change in legal status: An overlooked dimension in the transition to higher education. *Journal of Learning Disabilities, 24*, 459–466.

Sherman, M., & Zirkel, P. (1980). Student discrimination in higher education: A review of the law. *Journal of Law and Education, 9*(3), 301–344.

Shewan, C. (1990). Prevalence of hearing impairment. *Asha, 32*(2), p. 62.

Southeastern Community College v. Davis, 442 U.S. 397 (1979).

Stinson, M., Scherer, M., & Walter, G. (1987). Factors affecting persistence of deaf college students. *Journal in Higher Education, 27*, 244–258.

Stone, B. (1983). Students with invisible handicaps. *College Board Review, 127*, 23–27.

Tinto, V. (1987). *Leaving college: Rethinking the causes and cures of student attrition*. Chicago: University of Chicago Press.

U.S. Department of Education. (1987). *Handicapped persons rights under federal law handbook*. Washington, DC: Office of Civil Rights.

Vocational Rehabilitation Act of 1918, PL 65-178. (June 27, 1918). Title 38, U.S.C. 1401 et seq: *U.S. Statutes at Large, 40*, 617–620.

Walter, G., & Welsh, W. (1986). *Providing for the needs of handicapped students in a postsecondary environment*. Rochester, NY: National Technical Institute for the Deaf.

Werring, C. (1987, Winter). Responding to the older aged full-time student: Preferences for undergraduate education. *College Student Affairs Journal, 7*, 13–20.

West, M., Kregel, J., Getzel, E., Zhu, M., Ipsen, S., & Martin, E. (1993). Beyond Section 504:

Satisfaction and empowerment of students with disabilities in higher education. *Exceptional Children, 59*(5), 456–467.

White, C., Karchmer, M., Armstrong, D., & Bezozo, C. (1983). Current trends in high school graduation and college enrollment of hearing impaired students attending residential schools for deaf persons. *American Annals of the Deaf, 128*(2), 125–131.

Wiseman, R., Emry, R., & Morgan, D. (1988). Predicting academic success for disabled students in higher education. *Research in Higher Education, 28,* 255–269.

9

Future Challenges in Educational Audiology

TWENTY YEARS AGO, DISCUSSION IN the field included the subject of what educational audiology might turn out to be. For example, this suggestion was offered by Alpiner in 1974:

> As we view educational audiology, the term in itself is indicative of **the teaching of content information** to hard of hearing children. Basically, then, we are talking about some kind of audiologist who also is involved in the teaching of content subjects to children, for example, reading, writing, and arithmetic. . . . A basic question that we have to ask ourselves is whether or not we wish to involve ourselves in the content process. (p. 52, emphasis added)

However, as we now know, educational audiologists do not provide direct teaching of content material in the classroom. Instead, the field began to take its present form from the vision and dedication of faculty at Utah State University, led by Fred Berg, Ph.D., professor emeritus, who in 1966 began training audiologists to work in public schools (Blair & Von Almen, 1991). From that work and from seminal texts (Berg, 1976; Berg & Fletcher, 1970), as well as in response to current educational reform, the model for educational audiology services has evolved from the suggestion, cited above, of teaching content material to the model of integral support, which is shown in Figure 9.1.

In this model, educational audiology services are predicated upon the earliest possible identification of HI. Once hearing impairment is identified, educational audiology services provide educational, technical, and psychosocial supports to the learner and family, as well as to **all** involved in the educational system (teachers, related support personnel, classmates, administrators). In the model, these three components—audiologist, learner/family, and educational system—interact and collaborate, focusing on the learner's achievement of academic and social goals.

THE WORK AHEAD

Development of this model does not imply that the field of educational audiology is fully realized. On the contrary, a review of the chapters of this text indicates only some of the areas in which further change and leadership are needed. For example:

- Most states have not defined a set of competencies necessary for audiologists to work in educational settings.

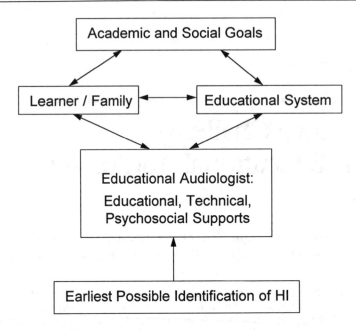

Figure 9.1. Model for educational audiology services.

- Most states do not have established guidelines for providing audiology services in schools.
- Most states have not established a student–educational audiologist ratio.
- Most states have not established procedures to ensure the earliest possible identification of hearing impairment.
- Approximately only 10% of students with hearing impairment receive services in schools.
- Most classrooms have high noise levels and problems with reverberation.
- At least half of personal hearing aids in schools are not functioning if they are not monitored.
- Many students with HI underutilize their listening abilities.
- Many students with HI have psychosocial difficulties and limited access to psychosocial supports.
- Many students do not have the self-advocacy skills needed to succeed in post-secondary and other adult settings.
- Many school professionals do not have basic information regarding the impact of HI on learning, nor are they aware of the contributions and expertise of the educational audiologist.
- Many regular education teachers do not get the technical support they need in order to successfully integrate and teach children with HI in their classrooms.
- Most schools need comprehensive hearing conservation programs.
- Most users of FM systems need both technical and social support.

In addition to these concerns that affect students, administrators, staff, and school environments, newly hired audiologists frequently approach their positions in school settings with initial trepidation, for the following reasons:

- Many audiologists are not aware of the differences between clinical and school settings.
- Many audiologists come to the educational setting with no or limited experience in collaborating with other school professionals.
- Many educational audiologists need to learn about family systems and how to provide services to infants and toddlers within the context of the family.
- Many educational audiologists lack experience in working as part of a transdisciplinary team developing the IFSP and IEP.
- Many educational audiologists do not feel qualified to provide counseling or supervision.
- Many educational audiologists have no experience in public relations.
- Many educational audiologists are not comfortable assuming the role of service coordinator.

Some of the realities cited above are issues of training at the preservice or graduate level, and they must be addressed by accredited audiology programs across the U.S. However, many of these realities can and should be addressed by practicing educational audiologists. "Until educational audiologists become actively involved in the solving of the problems of hearing impaired students in regular schools, there is little likelihood of meaningful change" (Blair, Wilson-Vlotman, & Von Almen, 1989, p. 13). Clearly, although much has been accomplished in and through educational audiology, there is no cause for complacency with so much work still ahead.

To address any one of these concerns means effecting a change in an existing program or system. There is a difference between **responding to change** and **actively seeking change** to improve a program. Responding to change means staying alert to shifts in the learning environment that can affect students with hearing impairment. Environmental shifts can occur from changes in federal or state law, or in changes in pedagogical (teaching) philosophies. Examples of changes in teaching approaches were provided by Edwards (1993), who described two recent changes in teaching styles that have direct implications for students with HI: 1) a move from teacher-directed to child-directed instructional activities, and 2) a move from large-group instruction to small-group learning. Both teaching approaches can produce a subsequent increase in noise levels because of the greater number of voices participating in discussion at any one time. Therefore, it is the responsibility of the educational audiologist to monitor such changes, observe the effects on learners with HI, and advocate appropriate modifications.

Actively seeking change goes beyond monitoring the environment and responding accordingly. To actively seek an improvement in an existing program or system, the educational audiologist will want to develop skills in order to be effective as an agent of change. Strategies that are helpful in promoting proactive change are discussed next.

CHANGE AGENTRY

There is always some change occurring in education. However, not all change in education takes the same form. Four different types of change in education are: 1) changes in knowledge, 2) changes in attitudes, 3) changes in behavior, and 4) changes in group or organizational performance (Hershey & Blanchard, 1982).

The first, change in knowledge, is the easiest to accomplish. However, it is an intellectual change and usually does not change programs. Agents of change have found that as they move down the list, change becomes more difficult to achieve.

How to Actively Change Educational Audiology Services

Following are six suggestions to effect changes in educational audiology services (Blair, 1991). With a small team of individuals who share your interest in improving services:

1. Write a description of the ideal program. What is the team's vision of optimal services for students with HI in this district?
2. Evaluate the current program. What changes need to be made in order to meet the description of the ideal program?
3. Develop both long-range and short-range plans. What can reasonably be accomplished in 1, 2, and 3 years? Select strategies that are superior and effective in obtaining identified goals. Develop a timeline and assign tasks among team members.
4. Obtain support from key decision makers and implement plans with their specific approval and endorsement.
5. Evaluate plans at least annually. Are goals being met? Have the goals changed, and, if so, do plans need to change accordingly?
6. Keep key decision makers up-to-date regarding progress. In other words, advertise! Use public relations strategies recommended in Chapter 7.

Effecting change is typically described as a **process**. The process may begin with a high level of interest, followed by a dip in morale or comfort level as change is implemented. This expected dip is a low point in the process, and it is important to remind participants that it is a **temporary** experience. In time, participants in the change process begin to integrate the new procedure into their routine, see its positive effects, and feel satisified with the change and its consequences (Adams & Spencer, 1988; Lawrie, 1990).

A component vital to the change process is the inclusion of all persons affected by the change. The following is an example that illustrates this point.

A Change that Didn't Happen

In August, a special education director was hired by the school board to develop and implement a curriculum plan that would change special education services. The new director began her work in earnest, only occasionally dropping hints about the plan to some of those who would be affected by the change in curriculum: teachers, resource specialists, and speech-language pathologists. Over the course of the academic year, these professionals began to feel uncomfortable and anxious about the impending change because they had no idea how it would affect them. They began to vocalize their negative concerns about the new plan to parents. The plan was scheduled to be presented in May and voted on by the school board. At that meeting, parents showed up in force to express their lack of support for the plan, and so the board voted it down. The special education director was stunned, completely unprepared for this response to her hard work. It was clear to other professionals, however, what went wrong. One speech-language pathologist shrugged and said simply, "She never shared the ball, so no one wanted to play with her."

What happened here? The special education director thought she was doing what she was hired to do, but in fact, she overlooked one of the key principles in being an agent of change: She did not seek input from individuals who were to be affected by the change. In other words, she worked like a "lone ranger" in a system that is most effective when all team members share opportunities to participate and "play." The reaction to her approach can be described as "group-based" resistance to change in that, over the months, teachers and SLPs as a group felt left out of the process and so were not supportive of it (Berman & McLaughlin, 1978; Guskey, 1986; Lawrie, 1990). The change agent must recognize and prepare for personal and emotional, as well as intellectual, reactions to changes (Weissglass, 1991; Wu, 1988).

To offset negative reactions when working to change entrenched systems, Sexton (1991) recommended building a "power base" of support. Support for innovation or for refinement of an existing procedure or policy can be achieved at several levels: from supervisors, from colleagues, and from parents. At the risk of repetitiveness, it is essential to develop and nurture support from all those persons who will be affected by the changes you seek to implement because the school setting is a culture that thrives on collaboration and shared leadership (Carrow-Moffett, 1993; Edelman, 1991; Fullan, 1993; Lippett, Langseth, & Mossep, 1985; Nelson, 1990; Sarason, 1967).

THE EDUCATIONAL AUDIOLOGIST AS EDUCATIONAL LEADER

The purpose of this entire text has been to provide students and practitioners of educational audiology with information, suggestions, and directions that can lead to improved services for learners with HI. The task may seem daunting, especially when reviewing "The Work Ahead" presented earlier in this chapter. However, this last chapter is meant to encourage and exhort all audiologists in schools to realize that any improvement, no matter how small, is better than none and that employment in school settings includes an obligation to continually seek ways to enhance the educational process. Efforts toward improvements may be considered either as a risk or as an opportunity to provide leadership, even if only in a small way. The educational environment may not totally support the development of "vision, persuasion, or inspiration" (Conger, 1989, p. 14), but needs of students outweigh any concern about risks. In discussing the role of leadership, Gardner (1990) wrote:

> One of the tasks of leadership—**at all levels**—is to revitalize . . . shared beliefs and to draw upon them as sources of motivation for the exertion required of the group. Leaders can help keep the values fresh. Leaders must conceive and articulate goals in ways that lift people out of their petty preoccupations and unite them toward higher ends. (p. 191, emphasis added)

The focal point of this passage is the phrase "at all levels." Regardless of the position of the educational audiologist in the hierarchy of a particular school system, there is always an opportunity to effect change that will improve the learning environment for students with hearing impairment.

Why strive for the best or ideal in services? Why take the chance of rocking the boat? To paraphrase Ross (1991): "This is what we are all about." The field of educational audiology, as with all the support services in special education, is predicated on the search for increasingly effective strategies to support the academic and social success of learners with hearing impairment. To settle for less than the best is to shortchange learners with HI and to leave the challenge of the field unmet.

References

Adams, J., & Spencer, S. (1988). People in transition. *Training and Development, 42*(10), 61–63.

Alpiner, J. (1974). Educational audiology. *Journal of the American Academy of Rehabilitative Audiology, 7,* 50–54.

Berg, F. (1976). *Educational audiology: Hearing and speech management.* New York: Grune & Stratton.

Berg, F., & Fletcher, S. (Eds.). (1970). *The hard of hearing child: Clinical and educational management.* New York: Grune & Stratton.

Berman, P., & McLaughlin, M. (1978). *Federal programs supporting educational change: Implementing and sustaining innovations.* Santa Monica, CA: Rand Corporation.

Blair, J. (1991). Educational audiology and methods for bringing about change in schools. *Seminars in Hearing, 12*(4), 318–328.

Blair, J., & Von Almen, P. (1991). Historical growth of educational audiology and the Educational Audiology Association. *Educational Audiology Monograph, 2,* ii–iii.

Blair, J., Wilson-Vlotman, A., & Von Almen, P. (1989). Educational audiologist: Practices, problems, directions and recommendations. *Educational Audiology Monograph, 1,* 1–14.

Carrow-Moffett, P. (1993). Change agent skills: Creating leadership for school renewal. *NASSP Bulletin, 77*(52), 57–62.

Conger, J. (1989). *The charismatic leader: Behind the mystique of exceptional leadership.* San Francisco: Jossey-Bass.

Edelman, L. (1991). *Developing change-agent skills: Keeping a "people-focus" during organizational change.* Baltimore: Kennedy-Krieger Institute.

Edwards, C. (1993). The changing classroom environment: Implications for auditory management. *Educational Audiology Newsletter, 10*(3), 8–9.

Fullan, M. (1993). Why teachers must become change agents. *Educational Leadership, 50*(6), 12–17.

Gardner, J. (1990). *On leadership.* New York: Free Press.

Guskey, T. (1986). Staff development and the process of teacher change. *Educational Researcher, 15*(5), 5–12.

Hershey, P., & Blanchard, K. (1982). *Management of organizational behavior* (4th ed.). Englewood Cliffs, NJ: Prentice Hall.

Lawrie, J. (1990). The ABCs of change management. *Training and Development, 44*(3), 87–89.

Lippett, G., Langseth, P., & Mossep, J. (1985). *Implementing organizational change: A practical guide to managing change efforts.* San Francisco: Jossey-Bass.

Nelson, N. (1990). Challenges of working in the schools in the twenty-first century. *Practically Speaking, 9*(1), 8.

Ross, M. (1991). A future challenge: Educating the educators and public about hearing loss. *Seminars in Hearing, 12*(4), 402–413.

Sarason, S. (1967). Toward a psychology of change and innovation. *American Psychologist, 22,* 227–233.

Sexton, J. (1991). Team management of the child with hearing loss. *Seminars in Hearing, 12*(4), 329–339.

Weissglass, J. (1991). Teachers have feelings: What can we do about it? *Journal of Staff Development, 12*(1), 28–33.

Wu, P. (1988). Why is change difficult? Lessons for staff development. *Journal of Staff Development, 9*(2), 10–14.

Appendix A

Rights to Due Process in Special Education

I. **GENERAL RIGHTS**

   ALL CHILDREN WITH DISABILITIES HAVE THE RIGHT TO: A free and appropriate public education; privacy and confidentiality of all educational records including the right to see, review and, if necessary, challenge the records in accordance with the Family Educational Rights and Privacy Act of 1974; review and/or obtain a copy of any educational records; placement in the least restrictive environment and the right to enjoy the same variety of programs as are available to nondisabled children in the appropriate school closest to their home (removal from regular classes occurs only when the nature or severity of the handicap is such that education in a regular class with the use of supplementary aids and services cannot be achieved satisfactorily); receive a full explanation of all procedural safeguards and right of appeal (on request, parents will be provided a list of the types and locations of educational records collected, maintained, or used by the district. The district shall inform parents when educational records are no longer needed to provide educational services to the students).

II. **RIGHTS RELATED TO ASSESSMENT**

   YOU HAVE THE RIGHT TO: Initiate a written request for educational assessment; be given a proposed plan for assessment within 15 days from date of referral for assessment; give or withhold consent for the assessment within 15 days from date of receipt of proposed assessment; receive an individual assessment of your child and an explanation of why the assessment was proposed; receive a description and purpose of the procedures and tests and who will be administering them; give written consent for release of any confidential information to be used during the assessment process; seek an independent assessment of your child if you find the school's evaluation inappropriate (this may or may not be at public expense); request any independent assessments and/or assessment information be considered in the evaluation process; obtain, upon request, a copy of the findings of the assessment or assessments conducted.

This document is adapted from a form used by the LaMesa–Spring Valley school district in San Diego County, California. A form like this summarizes information in special education legislation for parents and is often attached to an IEP.

IT IS THE RESPONSIBILITY OF SCHOOL DISTRICTS TO: Evaluate your child with a variety of appropriate tests free of racial, cultural, or sexual discrimination by a multidisciplinary team; evaluate your child in his/her primary language/communication mode; see that information obtained will be used only by appropriate school personnel; determine that tests have been properly validated for the specific purpose for which they are used and are administered by trained personnel; assess the child in all areas of suspected disability; select and administer tests which ensure an accurate reflection of the child's aptitude or achievement level rather than handicapping condition, unless that condition is the factor the test purports to measure; ensure testing is not limited to a single intelligence quotient; prepare a written report of evaluation results; schedule a parent meeting to discuss the assessment, the educational recommendations, and the reasons for these recommendations.

III. **RIGHTS RELATED TO DEVELOPMENT OF INDIVIDUALIZED EDUCATION PROGRAM—IEP**

If special education placement is to be considered, an Individualized Education Program shall be developed within a total time not to exceed 50 days from the date of receipt of the parent's written consent for assessment, unless the parent agrees in writing to the extension.

YOU HAVE THE RIGHT TO: Mutually agree to a time and place for the Individualized Education Program team meeting; be notified prior to and attend/participate and or be represented at the IEP meeting; participate in the development of the IEP; be advised of all alternative programs both public and nonpublic; consent to the whole, or part, of the Individualized Education Program; give, deny, or withdraw consent to placement of your child in a special education program; receive a description of any options the local education agency considered and why they were rejected; appoint a person to act as parent, to be the child's advocate, and to participate in evaluation and individual program meetings with the school; request a list of your child's records and their location; request a copy of the assessment findings.

IT IS THE SCHOOL DISTRICT'S RESPONSIBILITY TO: Notify parents of the meeting early enough that they will have an opportunity to attend; invite the child to participate in the meeting as appropriate; translate proceedings of the meeting into your language/mode of communication; implement the Individualized Education Program as soon as possible following the Individualized Education Program team meeting; conduct an annual review of the Individualized Education Program, or whenever the parent believes the pupil is not making appropriate progress; provide placement outside the local school district in another public school or a private school at public expense if the local schools do not have an appropriate program; provide reassessment of the pupil at least every three years, or more frequently if requested by parent, teacher, or child advocate; describe appropriate alternative placement if attending a local public school is not possible; inform parents when records pertaining to their child are no longer needed and are to be destroyed; provide parents with information on free or low cost legal aid if requested or if a hearing is initiated.

IV. **RIGHTS RELATED TO DUE PROCESS HEARINGS AND COMPLAINTS**

If you wish to appeal a decision regarding identification, assessment, placement, or implementation of your child's IEP, you should contact the local school district administrator and the State Department of Education and request a due process hearing. You may meet informally to resolve any issue(s) relating to the identification, assessment, or education and placement of the child, or the provision of a free, appropriate public education to the child, to the satisfaction of both parties prior to the hearing procedure. You may file civil action if you are dissatisfied with the decision of the hearing officer. If you feel the district has violated Federal and State law regarding regulations governing special education or related services, you may file a complaint with the superintendent of the concerned school district. Parents or guardians may be entitled to have costs of attorneys' fees reimbursed if they prevail in court as a consequence of a due process hearing. The Handicapped Children's Protection Act of 1986, *Public Law 99-372*, states that a court may award reasonable attorneys' fees to parents/guardians of a handicapped pupil who is a prevailing party in any action or proceeding brought under the procedural safeguards' section (section 1415) of PL 94-142.

Appendix B

An Illustrated
Hearing Aid In-Service

3 EASY STEPS—IN LESS THAN 3 MINUTES

1. Battery Check
2. Visual Check
3. Listening Check

Purpose: To maintain compliance with PL 94-142/IDEA, which mandates that "Each public agency will ensure that the hearing aids worn by deaf and hard of hearing children are functioning properly" (*Federal Register*, 1977).

Educational
Audiology
Resource

Battery Check

- Remove battery from hearing aid.
- Place battery on metal contact of battery tester (either " + " or " − " side up). Touch end of flexible wire to top of battery and read the voltage on scale.
- 1.4 to 1.1 Volts is acceptable. 1 V or less indicates a weak battery that needs replacing. (It will die before the school day is over.) No needle movement means a dead battery.
- Replace battery in case with positive (+) side matching " + " on battery door.

Note: A rundown battery may momentarily show acceptable voltage but then recede slowly toward zero. Such a battery is exhausted and should be discarded.

Students can check one battery while you visually and auditorily inspect the other hearing aid.

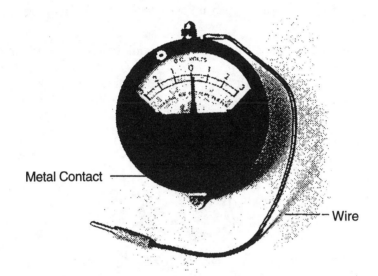

Metal Contact ————   —— Wire

Visual Check

- Casing: Look for cracks, teethmarks, broken battery case. Rotate volume control. It should move without sticking. As volume increases, you should hear feedback. Check switches: **M** stands for microphone (that is, "on"), **T** for telecoil, **O** for off. If switch is labeled **N** and **H** (for Normal and High frequency response), ask parent or hearing aid provider which is correct for the student—it can accidentally be changed.
- The hook: Should be firmly attached to case. Some can be screwed on tighter. Look for cracks.
- Tubing: Should be tightly attached to hook. If it is yellow and/or stiff, it needs to be monitored. It must be free of cracks and splits. Look for wax, dirt, water bubbles.
- Earmold: The canal opening (the bore) must be relatively free of wax. It should be fairly clean, with no cracks or jagged edges. If necessary, remind student to wash earmold in warm soapy water, *after* removing it from the hook.

There is no need to disconnect tubing from the hook in a hearing aid check.

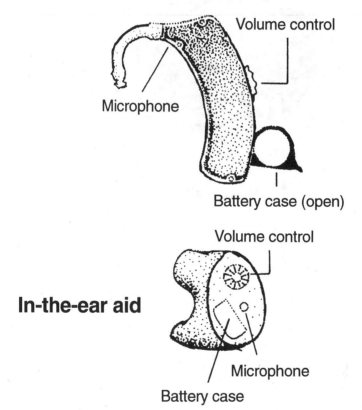

Regarding in the ear (ITE) styles: Since there is no tubing, hook, or earmold for the ITE, only the **case** information applies. You may want to refrain from removing wax that is blocking the canal; the mic is very close to the opening and it is easily damaged. Rather, inform the parent to consult with the audiologist.

Listening Check

- Use stethoscope with rubber tip. Keep earmold on hearing aid.
- Cover the canal of earmold (or ITE aid) with rubber tip.
- While rotating volume control, listen for:
  —linear gain (as volume control is moved up, sounds get louder)
  —static or intermittency (noise through the aid that you don't normally hear or sound cutting on and off)

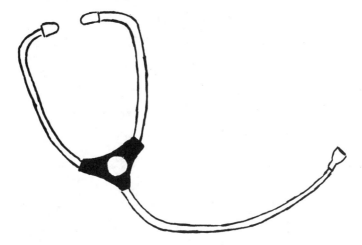

- At a comfortable loudness setting on the volume control, listen for:
  —clarity of sound. Try /s/, /sh/, with mic approximately 12″ away from mouth.
  —clear plosives. Try /ba ba ba/, speaking approximately 18″ from mouth.
  —loose connections. Squeeze case lightly; there should be no intermittency.

When student replaces aid, make sure earmold fits snugly. Volume should be set at approximately ¾ rotation of the volume control. If feedback occurs at ¾, but stops when volume is lowered, the earmold is too small and needs to be replaced.

Finally, check to verify that the student can clearly hear speech input. This can be done with the Ling 5-Sound Test: that is, with the mouth hidden, or with the student looking away, the student is asked to repeat the following sounds in varying order: /oo/, /ee/, /ah/, /s/, and /sh/. These sounds can be combined to form: /soo/, /sah/, /see/ and /shoo/, /shah/, and /shee/.

Index

Page numbers followed by "f" indicate figures; numbers followed by "t" indicate tables.